Social Security Law in Poland

Social Security Law in Poland

Third Edition

Andrzej Marian Świątkowski

This book was originally published as a monograph in the International Encyclopaedia of Laws/Social Security Law.

Founding Editor: Roger Blanpain
General Editor: Frank Hendrickx
Volume Editor: Willy van Eeckhoutte

Wolters Kluwer

Published by:
Kluwer Law International B.V.
PO Box 316
2400 AH Alphen aan den Rijn
The Netherlands
E-mail: international-sales@wolterskluwer.com
Website: lrus.wolterskluwer.com

Sold and distributed in North, Central and South America by:
Wolters Kluwer Legal & Regulatory U.S.
7201 McKinney Circle
Frederick, MD 21704
United States of America
Email: customer.service@wolterskluwer.com

Sold and distributed in all other countries by:
Air Business Subscriptions
Rockwood House
Haywards Heath
West Sussex
RH16 3DH
United Kingdom
Email: international-customerservice@wolterskluwer.com

Printed on acid-free paper

ISBN 978-94-035-0320-2

e-Book: ISBN 978-94-035-0201-4
web-PDF: ISBN 978-94-035-0273-1

Printed in the United Kingdom.

The Author

Professor Dr hab. Andrzej Marian Świątkowski (born on 17 January 1944 in Warsaw) studied law and sociology at the Jagiellonian University in Cracow (1961–1969). He gained a degree in law (1966) and an MA in sociology (1969). After two years clerking at the district court in Cracow, he received a doctorate in labour law from the Institute of Legal Sciences of the Polish Academy of Science in Warsaw (1972).
Dr Świątkowski studied at the Columbia Law School in New York. He gained an LLM degree in labour law from the University of Pennsylvania in Philadelphia (1977). In Poland, he received the habilitation degree from the Jagiellonian University in Cracow in the field of labour law and social policy (1976).
Dr hab. A. Świątkowski spent a year as distinguished research fellow at the National Institute of Public Management in Washington, DC (1977–1978). After returning to his post at the Jagiellonian University, he was appointed to the position of extraordinary professor of law (1984) and ordinary professor of law (1991).
Professor Świątkowski spent one semester as a visiting scholar at New York University School of Law and another semester as a visiting professor at Indiana University. He lectured at various universities in Europe, United States, Argentina, and Australia. He delivered papers at International Industrial Relations Association congresses in Dublin, Helsinki, Oslo, Sydney, Tokyo, Santiago de Chile, and Cape Town.
Professor Świątkowski founded and acted as an editor-in-chief of two legal journals *The Jagiellonian University Yearbook of Labour Law and Social Policy* published in 1989–1999 in English, and *Studies in Labour Law and Social Policy* published since 1994 in Polish. He was also a co-editor of the *East-West Review of Social Policy* published by the Catholic University of Brabant in Tilburg. He also served as a member of the editorial board of *Tilburg Foreign Law Review*.
Since 1989, Professor Świątkowski has acted as the coordinator of the Tempus programme on European social law. Under his academic supervision, more than 500 students received Master of Law degrees at the Faculty of Law and Administration of the Jagiellonian University. Nineteen of the students went on to earn doctorates in

The Author

labour law. He reviewed over thirty doctoral and habilitation monographs in Poland. Three of his former doctoral students employed currently at the Jagiellonian University received a habilitation and were appointed to the position of full professor of labour law at the Jagiellonian University Faculty of Law and Administration. He also served as an external reviewer of three doctoral theses at the Andhra University in India and one in Vilnius (Lithuania). He was asked to submit a professional opinion to support a candidate applying for an honorary doctorate at Harvard University and professorship at Vilnius University in Lithuania. Professor Świątkowski has published more than 700 studies, articles, and reviews and thirty-one books in the field of Polish, international, comparative, and foreign labour law, social security law, and social policy.
In 2002, Professor Świątkowski was elected by the Committee of Ministers of the Council of Europe to serve as an international expert on the European Committee of Social Rights (former Committee of Independent Experts) in Strasbourg. In 2005, he was elected the First Vice-President of that Committee. He served at the European Committee of Social Rights until 31 December 2012. Since 2015 he is employed at the Jesuit University Ignatianum in Cracow.
Professor Świątkowski is a member of the International Employment and Labour Association (former International Industrial Relations Association) and the Society for Labour Law and Social Security. He was awarded an honorary citizenship for the State of Kentucky – 'Kentucky Colonel'.

Table of Contents

List of Abbreviations

ANATU	All National Alliance of Trade Unions (Polish – OPZZ)
ASIF	Agricultural Social Insurance Fund
EFTA	European Free Trade Association
EUR	Euro
FSA	Financial Supervision Authority (Polish – KNF)
ILO	International Labour Organization
IRA	Individual Retirement Account (Polish – IKE)
IRSA	Individual Retirement Security Account (Polish – IKZE)
OPF	Open Pension Funds (Polish – OFE)
PLN	official Polish currency – (EUR 1 equals ca. PLN 4.10)
POASA	Personal Old Age Security Account
SSI	Social Security Institution (Polish – ZUS)
ZOZ	Unit of Integrated Health Services

General Introduction

Chapter 1. General Background

1. Poland is a medium-sized country with over 38 million inhabitants. It is located in central Europe. Poland's territory of more than 120,000 square miles is surrounded by Russia, Lithuania, Belarus, Ukraine, Slovak and Czech Republic, and Germany. Across the Baltic Sea (524 kilometres of coastline), Poland faces Sweden. The modern capital is Warsaw. The ancient capital and the most historic town is Cracow. The country's name comes from Polish Polanie, dwellers of the field (i.e., Poland): 'pole' – field. Most of the country is lowland plain. Arable land accounts for 61% of the entire territory of the country and forest for 28%. Poland is rich in many natural resources such as anthracite, coal, sulphur, copper, iron, zinc, lead, and rock salt.

2. At the time the first edition of this monograph was published (1997), the country was divided into forty-nine provinces (voivodships) with 803 cities and 2,070 rural communes. A two-tiered administrative structure: the commune or the town, and the province (voivodship) existed since 1975. In 1997, there was a disagreement between the two political parties that formed a ruling coalition: the Social Democratic Party and the Peasant National Party in matters concerning the administration of the country. The Peasant National Party preferred a two-tiered administrative structure while the Social Democratic Party favoured a three-tiered administrative structure with a county between communes or town and provinces. The Social Democrats were backed up in this matter by the Democratic Union, an opposition party. Since 1 January 1999, the statutory act of 24 July 1998 (*Journal of Law*, No. 96, item 603) introduced the new administrative structure. At the present time (2013), Poland is divided into sixteen provinces (voivodships). However, still, a disagreement continues to exist between the two leading political parties (the Law and Justice, and the Civic Platform) as to whether or not the seventeenth province in mid-Pomerania should be created. The Civic Platform, which is still ruling the country, was against proliferation of administrative units.

Chapter 2. Historical Background

3. The best summary of Polish political and legal history is presented in an introductory note by Professor W.J. Wagner in the book, *Polish Law Throughout the Ages: 1,000 Years of Legal Thought in Poland* (Hoover Institution Press, Stanford University, 1970). According to Wagner, Poland, which was established as an independent state in 960, celebrated her millennium in 1966: one thousand years of Christianity. Although Polish history spans a much longer period and some of her earliest citizens had been baptized previously, 966, marked a turning point in Poland's political development. It was in 966 when the ruler of the country, Mieszko, first decided to adopt the new faith for himself and for the whole nation and proclaimed Christianity as the official Polish religion. Wedged between powerful enemies – Russia and Prussia – Poland found progress difficult. She was forced repeatedly to defend her independence and territorial integrity against foreign attacks and interference. Poland lost her independence to her neighbours and political enemies (Prussia, Russia, and Austro-Hungarian Empire) for more than 120 years between 1795 and 1918. However, her *baptism* stabilized her status as an independent member of the community of Western nations in Europe.

4. Poland was a pioneer in the development of modern democratic institutions, and in this respect she was more progressive than any other nation. Thus, as early as 1430, the Privilege of Jedlna (*Neminem captivabimus*) guaranteed to the Polish nobility freedom from arbitrary arrest and confiscation of property. The celebrated English Habeas Corpus Act was enacted more 250 years later, in 1689. Thus, in France, until the end of the *ancien regime*, the king could deliver *letters de cachet* – blank arrest warrants – to his favourites for their use against personal enemies.

5. In the fifteenth century, the Polish parliamentary system was developed. While in other nations such as France, Germany, Spain, or Russia the power of the rulers remained absolute for centuries, the authority of the monarchs in Poland had been limited in some ways from the very beginning of her political history. By the Privilege of Koszyce, in 1374, the imposition of taxes by the king without the consent of the nobles was prohibited. The Statute of Nieszawa in 1454 imposed further restrictions on the individual power of the king. The Statute of Piotrków in 1496 established a parliamentary system of government. The constitution *Nihil Novi* of 1505 proclaimed that the king would enact no new laws without the prior consent of the parliament. The constitutional character of Poland's monarchy, in which the power of the king was strictly limited, was further reinforced at the end of the sixteenth century by the *Pacta Conventa*, by virtue of which the kings had to reaffirm all existing laws and privileges and promise to respect them. If a king were to fail to fulfil this obligation, the nation could denounce him and would refuse to recognize his authority.

While most other countries held the belief that a monarch's power was bestowed upon him by God alone, so that a royal title was usually preceded with the words 'By the grace of God', the Poles, always deeply religious, supplemented the phrase with 'and the will of the nation'. Indeed, the principle that the national sovereignty belongs to the whole nation and not to one individual was put into practice at the end of the fourteenth century, when kinship became elective. For two centuries, members of the

Jagiellonian dynasty were always elected to the position, but when the dynasty became extinct, all nobles became eligible. Indeed, a few of the later monarchs were of rather modest descent. The Polish monarchy was called a Republic of the Nobles; it is unique in the history of mankind. The general belief was that this system was the best safeguard for the famous Polish 'golden freedom', and that the highest office in the state should be held by a person who had proven his qualities and capacities. Thus, the position of the king in the constitutional monarchy of Poland was comparable to that of a state president elected for life.

6. Coexistent with political democracy was the deeply embedded tradition of religious tolerance. Poland has been a predominantly Catholic nation during the whole course of her history. But she permitted non-Christians, such as the Muslims and Jews, to settle freely in the country. The great influx of Jews began in the fourteenth century during the reign of Kazimierz Wielki (Casimir the Great), who granted non-Christians special privileges and guaranteed freedom of worship at a time when they were persecuted in other countries. For many years, until the Nazis invaded Poland and exterminated the Polish Jewry, the percentage of Jews in Poland was higher than in any other country in the world.

Another striking result of the Polish spirit of religious freedom was the fact that, while religious disputes and wars raged in all the great European nations from the time of the Reformation and later, such struggles were unknown in Poland. The principle that no one could be prosecuted for his religious beliefs (not articulated in France, for instance, until 1791) has always been recognized in Poland.

7. A further remarkable feature of Polish history is the fact that for centuries she did not wage aggressive wars. She knew how to defend herself and how to deal with aggression; her armies would not only repel invasion but also pursue the enemy deep into its own territory. The Polish army was at times in Moscow, and in Berlin, but her presence was always the consequence of foreign aggression and not of Polish lust for foreign possessions.

For a long time, Poland was the biggest and most powerful country in Europe (especially in the sixteenth century). The kingdom included territories not inhabited by Poles. However, the extension of the state was brought about, curiously enough, by peaceful means, through voluntary unions with other nations. The most famous of these was the union with Lithuania brought by the Union of Krewo in 1387 and reinforced in Horodno in 1413. By the Union of Lublin in 1569, the two nations decided to establish a state in each and maintained a high degree of autonomy while delegating common problems to a central authority. It appears that the Polish-Lithuanian union constituted the first federal state in the world. It existed until Poland was partitioned at the end of the eighteenth century.

8. The Polish Commonwealth fought against aggression and defended freedom and independence not only for herself but also for those who needed her help. For centuries Polish armies struggled with Turks and Tartars throughout central Europe and the Balkans. Probably the most famous of the Polish struggles against the infidels was the defence of Vienna by King Jan III Sobieski in 1683, when the power of Turkey was checked and its army forced to retreat. The role that Poland played in these battles merited her the honourable name of the Bulwark of Christianity.

Poland was one of those rare countries where there were no devastating civil wars and where not a single king was killed by his own nation – a considerable contrast with Italy, for instance, where few princes escaped prison, and Russia, where in the two centuries before the Revolution nearly all the tsars were murdered.

9. It must be observed that during most of her history the Polish 'golden freedom' and democratic institutions could be fully enjoyed only by the minority of the population of nobles. Until very recent times, this was true in all European countries. However, the percentage of nobles in Poland was very high in comparison with that in other nations. It was estimated that the nobility constituted from 10% to 20% of the entire Polish population, while in France, for example, the nobles made up only one-tenth of 1%, and in early nineteenth century England, the electors formed less than 2% of the population.

As for Polish peasants, their situation was generally better than in other European countries. Although their obligations increased over the centuries, such duties were still lighter than those imposed in Germany, and the scope of their liberties was broader than in England. Instances of foreign peasants who took refuge in Poland were not uncommon. Even before the Constitution of 3 May 1791 granted to the peasants freedom and the full protection of the law, a number of landlords had voluntarily emancipated their subjects.

10. The downfall of Poland – the country was partitioned between her powerful neighbours, Russia, Prussia, and Austria at the end of the eighteenth century – occurred during a spectacular renaissance of her moral and intellectual strength. The external causes were evident: she was overpowered by three militaristic, well-organized, and absolutist nations. Historians, however, have in the past asserted that internal factors contributed to the tragedy, for example, that the excesses and abuses of democracy had brought about Poland's weakness and that at the time of crisis it was too late to restore her old might and ability to resist. In particular, it is often said that the constitutional principle of *liberum veto*, which required unanimity for adopting resolutions of the parliament, was a factor in preventing the country from keeping abreast of her neighbours. In practice, the minority did not generally take advantage of its veto power until the middle of the seventeenth century. In the centuries preceding, it was traditional for the minority to yield.

11. A short period of independence between the two world wars was followed by the delivery of Poland to her eastern neighbour, who imposed on her a communist system of government against the desires of the vast majority of the population. The constitutional and legal rules enacted under the communist regime were contrary to Polish tradition and beliefs and were discarded peacefully in 1989. Since June 1989, Poland has enjoyed political freedom and a democratic type of government.

Chapter 3. Origins and Features of the Present System of Social Security

12. In 2017, almost hundred years had passed since the first social security regulation in independent Poland on benefits for sickness was introduced. The roots of the Polish social security system go much deeper than 1919. Since Poland lost its independence and was divided between Austria, Prussia, and Russia, different foreign systems of social security were applied on the Polish territory.

As a result of this political fact, the present social security system is based on similar ideas around which social security schemes were built in Germany and Austria at the end of the nineteenth century. Those ideas include:

(a) solidarity with employees who cannot earn their living due to reasons which are beyond their control: sickness, disability, old age, unemployment, and industrial injury;
(b) complexity of social security schemes; social security covered benefits for sickness and disability, industrial injury, old pension, and unemployment;
(c) mandatory insurance; all blue-collar and white-collar workers were covered, separately, however, by different schemes of social security;
(d) an idea of contribution to the social security fund; social security benefits were paid out of the social security fund based on social security dues paid by employers and employees and contributions made the state treasury. Relationship between dues paid by employers and workers varied depending on the type of social security benefits;
(e) autonomy of the social security fund. The Polish social security system has a foreign origin. The system is based on Prussian legislation: the Statute of 1883 on sickness benefits, the Statute of 1884 on industrial injury, and the Statute of 1889 on retirement pensions.

However, Polish social security law also has its own characteristic national features. One of these features was a systematic drive towards unification of leftovers of separate foreign systems.

The current social security system in Poland, which was reformed in 1999, 2013, and 2017, draws its monetary benefit input from two social security funds, namely from the state-owned Social Security Fund as well as from open retirement funds. Such open retirement funds are privately managed and are known as 'general retirement associations'. The difference between the two systems of funds is based on the monetary input source. Benefits paid out by the Social Security Fund, including retirement, pension, illness, and accident benefits, stem partly from premiums paid by the insured and partly from premiums paid by the insuring employer. Benefits paid out by open retirement funds, on the other hand, are financed from capital raised by the insured. A distinctive feature of the compulsory social security system in Poland is the existence of two concurrent social security funds, the defined, compulsory contribution principle and the capital fund principle based on individual account payments.

13. The reform of the social security system was implemented in 1997 as part of 'Security through variety' social programme. The variety was expressed by introducing a new funded pension scheme (2nd insurance pillar) and sustaining the present then pay-as-you-go scheme (1st insurance pillar). The previous social security system, based on a defined amount of retirement benefit (old-age pension), depended on the amount of remuneration of the insured in the period of covered wages mentioned by the legislature. Within that system persons interested in terminating their employment could become entitled to early retirement or disability pension in a relatively easy way. However, in the newly introduced funded pension scheme, the amount of obligatory *insurance benefits* (2nd pillar) and voluntary insurance benefits (3rd pillar) was based on defined insurance premiums. The authors of the changes in the financial and organizational side of the social insurance system were aware of the fact that the society was aging, which resulted in the necessity of subsidizing 1st pillar. The social insurance and healthcare system's reform of 1999 had a substantial fault in the transitional period, which duration has been calculated until 2060, as it was not based on a coherent strategy with regard to the costs of the change of the system.

14. The lack of financial balance between the two different social security systems with the first based on defined pay-as-you-go scheme (1st pillar) and the second based on the funded scheme (the obligatory funded 2nd pillar and the voluntary 3rd pillar) only enlarged pension privileges for some groups of pensioners. Not until 2008 were some of the reform's original assumptions implemented, that is, limiting the entitlement to early retirement, the increase of retirement age, lowering to 50% (from 7% down to 3.5%) in fees transferred from the Social Insurance Institution to pension funds managing the assets of Open Pension Funds (OFE).

15. On 11 May 2012 an amendment to the act on pensions was adopted (*Journal of Laws 2012*, item 637 with amendments) which increased the retirement age to 67 years and made it equal for men and women. In 2016 the state authorities argued that the social and economic situation of Poland does not justify the increase of the basic retirement age to 67 years. According to the authorities, the labour market and the public healthcare system in Poland was not and is not prepared for the extension of the period of active employment of the insured persons. According to the present state authorities, high unemployment rates among the persons in pre-retirement age and low availability of publicly funded healthcare services do not justify the expectations of the previous government that increasing the retirement age to 67 years will prevent decrease of employment, will maintain a high level of GDP increase and inflow of taxes from undertakings which will not be forced to reduce jobs during the crisis period of limited labour supply. According to the political parties currently governing Poland, the increase of the retirement age to 67 years could not produce the positive effects assumed by the previous governing party since – as shown by the latest statistical data – even if the average period of life of persons at the age of 65 in Poland tends to extend, still it is not accompanied by the extension of the average period of life in good health. According to the current authorities, the life expectancy of Poles is increasing. However, with age, the ability to work is decreasing, not increasing. In this situation the ruling party recognized that a decision on cessation of work, upon reaching the basic retirement age of 60 (women) or 65 (men) should be taken individually by the insured persons. The decision should depend on numerous individual factors, such as: the economic situation of the employer employing workers in pre-retirement age, chances of a dismissed person to find a new job, professional qualifications of the insured, expectations of the insured concerning the living standard upon retirement, and his health condition. Considering the above circumstances, both objective and subjective, in 2015 the state authorities decided to restore the previous basic retirement age of 60 years for women and 65 years for men. This was implemented by the adoption on 16 November 2016 of an act on the amendment of the act on old-age pensions and invalidity benefits paid from the Social Insurance Fund and of several other acts (ustawa o zmianie ustawy o emeryturach i rentach z Funduszu Ubezpieczeń Społecznych oraz o zmianie niektórych innych ustaw) (*Journal of Laws of 2016*, item 38) setting out the conditions for acquisition of pension rights by particular professional groups: judges, public prosecutors, farmers, police officers, and other state security services. The above act amended also other acts governing the social insurance system, the functioning of the pension funds, and funded pensions. The act of 16 November 2016 entered into force on 1 October 2017.

Chapter 4. History of Polish Social Security Between the Great Wars

16. The enormous diversity of the foreign-based social security systems was the most distinctive feature of Polish social security after the First World War. The Western part of the Polish territory – regions called Wielkopolska (Great Poland), Pomorze (Pomerania), and Górny Slask (Upper Silesia) – inherited the Prussian social security schemes listed in Chapter 3. The Southern part of Poland adopted an Austrian system of social security based on three statutes issued in 1887 (industrial injury), 1888 sickness benefits, and 1906 old-age pension benefits for white-collar employees. The Eastern part of Poland liberated from the Russian occupation was *tabula rasa* from the point of view of social security.

To make the picture even more complicated, it is necessary to mention that different parts of Polish territory, which politically belonged to the same foreign system, were influenced by different foreign statutes. Only Upper Silesia, which became part of the Polish territory after the third regional uprising that took place in 1922, was regulated by the German social security legislation due to the bilateral Polish-German Agreement signed in 1922.[1]

Under such conditions, the most urgent task of the young Polish government was the unification of social security laws. Unfortunately, different bills introduced in the years of 1917, 1918, and 1920 were not passed by parliament. Instead of the introduction of Polish social security laws, the state government decided to expand the coverage provided by foreign regulations to parts of the territory that were covered by any social security law. According to this pattern, an Austrian statute of 1887 on industrial injury was extended and applied in 1924 to the eastern part of Polish territory formerly under Russian occupation.

The very first national original statute that regulated benefits for sickness was passed at the beginning of 1919 (Decree of January 1919). It was amended in 1920 (*Journal of Laws*, No. 44, item 272). This statute provided a common coverage to all the working population, farm workers, and domestic servants included. The Act of 19 May 1920 structured administration of sickness benefits around an idea of solidarity of insured people. In effect, administration of sickness benefits was based on the principle of self-management.

Unfortunately, the first attempt to organize a social security scheme upon the principle of self-management failed after nine years. It has never re-emerged since 1929. In 1924, a totally new unemployment benefit was introduced (the Act of 18 July 1924, *Journal of Laws*, No. 76, item 550). In the beginning, it covered only blue-collar workers. After a few months (in 1925) it was extended to white-collar workers (*Journal of Laws*, No. 15, item 97). Unemployment benefits were paid out of the unemployment fund for a period of three months. It reimbursed only a minor part of the lost salary of unemployed people. Because unemployment benefits did not match social security

1. *See* Z. Wyrnikowicz, *Ubezpieczenia społeczne na Řlasku wświetle wykonania Górnośląskiej konwencji Genewskiej* (Social Security in Upper Silesia in the Light of the Geneva Convention), Katowice 1939.

dues paid in order to make a contribution to the unemployment fund, it was necessary for the state to move in and fill the economic gap. Thus, from the very beginning, unemployment benefits lost their legal nature as a benefit paid out of a social security fund and since then they were never considered as payment regulated by social security legislation.

The last statement is supported by an administrative type of argument. Unemployment benefits were never managed by the social security agency. Before the Great Wars and again since 1 January 1990, management was entrusted to local state administrative offices set up to deal with employment and unemployment issues.

The strong drive towards unification of the system of social security did not impede any movement directed towards differentiation of social security schemes. One of the major criteria of that differentiation was the nature of work performed, manual or mental. White-collar workers have been treated differently since the introduction in 1927 of statutory regulations providing benefits in case of disability, retirement pensions, and benefits for death (*Journal of Laws*, No. 106, item 911). Because there was no justifiable relation whatsoever between the above-mentioned various benefits and social security dues, implementation of this statutory regulation was postponed until 1932. On 28 March 1933, the most important piece of social security regulation was introduced – the Unification of Social Security Schemes Act (*Journal of Laws*, No. 51, item 396). This Act introduced regulation concerning old-pension benefits for blue-collar workers. With the exception of agriculture workers who were not covered by the Unification Act and blue-collar workers employed in factories located in Upper Silesia where German social security schemes were effective, the unification act covered the rest of the territory of independent Poland. As in the case of white-collar workers' disparity of input and output, the old-age pension fund has caused first retirement pensions to be paid after five years since implementation of the Unification Act in 1938.

The Unification Act extended coverage of industrial injury schemes. It also increased the amount of benefits paid out of the social security system to injured workers. Finally, it broadened the definition of industrial injury in order to include occupational disease.

Benefits for sickness were also regulated by the Unification Act. The Unification Act did not regulate sickness benefits for farm workers nor for temporary workers. It also shortened from thirty-nine weeks to twenty-nine weeks the period during which benefits for sickness were paid. In addition, the Unification Act lowered the amount of sickness benefits from 60% to 42% of previous wages earned by a beneficiary.

Those changes, unfavourable to insured people, were introduced under pressure from the business community, which wanted to participate in financing social security spending.[2] Outside of the common social security scheme, separate schemes for civil servants, employees employed in state-owned enterprises, such as national railroad, post office, central bank, and liquor and tobacco companies, existed. Those state

2. *See* K. Duch, *Ubezpieczenia społeczne* (Warsaw: Social Security Laws, 1934), 231 et seq.; K. Krzeczkowski, *Idee przewodnie ubezpieczeńspołecznych* (Warsaw: Fundamental Directives of Social Security, 1936); E. Modlinski, *Podstawowe zagadnienia prawne ubezpieczeńspołecznych* (Warsaw: Basic Legal Problems of Social Security, 1968), 257 et seq.; W. Szubert, *Ubezpieczenie społeczne* (Warsaw: Social Insurance, 1987), 129.

companies ran social security schemes that provided more favourable conditions for insured people employed by the state and its enterprises.

In pre-Second World War Poland, even a tiny voluntary social security scheme existed. It covered miners working in the coal mines located in Upper Silesia and the Cracow mining area.

As one can see from this brief description of the development of social security schemes in Poland between the First and the Second World Wars, Polish social security schemes completely emerged after the First World War. For the most part after independence, foreign social security systems (German, and to a lesser extent Austrian) were enforced. A strong foreign influence, mostly German, on national social security legislation was observed during a period in which the Polish government decided to introduce its own social security laws.

The number of insured people in pre-Second World War Poland was lower than the number of people insured in some Western European countries. In 1936, the number of insured people consisted of 14% of the population, while in the United Kingdom it reached 43%, in France 25%, in Spain 22%, and in Italy 17%.

The Polish social security system was adversely affected by the Great Depression. Just before the economic crisis in 1929, 6,284,000 people were covered by unemployment, old-age pension, sickness, and industrial injury schemes. Even ten years later, just before Second World War, 7,782,000 people were insured and the number of people drawing sickness benefits never again reached its highest level, achieved in 1929: 2,662,000 insured. In 1938, 2,254,000 people were covered by insurance granting sickness benefits. The rising number of people covered by social security schemes was made possible due to the extension of industrial injury schemes and the introduction of an old-age pension scheme for blue-collar workers. In 1929, only 932,000 employees were covered by a pension benefits scheme while in 1938, 2,064,000 workers (both blue-collar and white-collar) were eligible for retirement pension benefits.

The distinctive character of Polish social security was expressed by the lack of any direct relationship between particular social security benefits and individual social security dues. The Polish system of social security was based on the disposition of average risk regardless of age, health, and type and conditions of work performed. Comparison of contributions to and expenses paid from the social security funds show, with some exceptions concerning unemployment benefits for blue-collar and white-collar workers in 1933 (a deficit of PLN 3,000,000 – złoty;[3] at the current exchange rate = EUR 714,285), in 1934 (a deficit of PLN 200,000 = EUR 47,619), and sickness benefits (a deficit of PLN 19,400,000 = EUR 4,619,047 in 1933 and PLN 7,800,000 = EUR 1,857,141 in 1934), that since introduction of the unification social security law, the Polish system of social security proved to be financially sound.

3. The currency rate for the Euro against the zloty is as at July 2013 rates.

Chapter 5. The History of the Social Security System on Polish Soil During the Second World War

17. There is no information concerning social security regulations on the former Eastern Polish territory, which fell under Soviet occupation in September 1939. After the German invasion of the Soviet Union in June 1941, part of the eastern Polish territory was incorporated into occupied Polish territory under German administration (*Generalgouvernement* – GG). The other part of the formerly Polish independent state was incorporated into the *Third Reich*. In the former Polish territory incorporated in Germany, the Nazi government took over Polish social security institutions. It was done by appointing Germans as heads of those institutions. Soon the Germans took steps to extend the coverage of German social security regulations upon former Polish territory incorporated into the German state. In Upper Silesia, that process was done at the beginning of 1940.

It is important to note that German social security laws were applied to both native Germans born and naturalized citizens. Poles were discriminated against and forced into a second-class citizen status. Poles were not eligible for certain kinds of social security benefits. Also, they were deprived of the right to social security benefits. Those benefits were dependent upon the discretion of the German administration. Therefore, in former Polish territory incorporated into Germany, social security regulations ceased to exist as far as Poles were concerned.

By an ordinance issued in October 1939 by Dr Hans Frank, the German governor of occupied Poland, the former Polish social security administration and social security schemes were restarted under German control. The purpose of this act was to keep Poles alive as a cheap labour force. Soon enough, in March 1940, the right to social security benefits was abolished. Instead of benefits, relief grants were introduced and issued at the discretion of the German-controlled social security administration. Shortly thereafter, social security regulations ceased to exist within the boundaries of the formerly independent Polish state.

Chapter 6. The History of Polish Social Security after the Second World War

§1. During the Period of the Socialist Regime (1945–1989)

18. After Second World War, the Polish social security system was influenced by the Beveridge Plan. As in other European countries, the Polish government was convinced that modern social policy must help people to cope with incidents arising out of certain types of risks, enabling them to earn money and support the insured persons and members of his/her family. The socialist regime that took over political power in post-Second World War Poland eagerly accepted the second directive included in the Beveridge Plan: to help people to cope with family problems. In order to carry out this plan family allowance was introduced in 1948 (Decree of 28 October 1947, *Journal of Laws*, No. 60, item 414). Thus, a family was considered one of the social risks in Poland. Promptly, social security dues to cover this unusual risk were introduced. Before looking into details of the socialist social security system, it must be mentioned that the first five years after the Second World War were devoted to the process of rebuilding of an independent national social security system, a system that was influenced by ideas coming from the Soviet Union regardless of the fact that the unification of social security law passed in different political environments was reintroduced.

In a country officially governed by the representatives of the working class, it was not possible to maintain an old-fashioned idea according to which both parties to employment contract: employees and employers must make at least equal contributions to social security dues to social security fund(s). Since 29 September 1945, only employers were made to pay into social security funds the social security dues on behalf of their employees. The state itself felt relieved from a legal obligation to contribute to social security funds.

The other important ideological change was unification of social security benefits paid to white-collar and blue-collar workers. After all, blue-collar workers constituted the core of the working class. Therefore, the Decree of 13 December 1946 introduced a right to sickness benefits as high as 70% of the previous salary to workers regardless of the type of work they performed (mental or manual) from the first day of absence from work. Before the decree, white-collar workers were entitled to draw a full salary for the first three months of sickness.

On 13 June 1946, an ordinance issued by the Minister of Labour and Social Help stopped the process of previous differentiation of disability benefits, which before the Second World War was based on the type of work performed and introduced one disability benefit for all categories of workers. The amount of this benefit was differentiated on the grounds of the length of employment (seniority principle).

The new political regime brought important changes into the organization of social security. Regretfully, the Act of 20 July 1950 (*Journal of Laws*, No. 36, item

333) abolished the pre-Second World War tradition of self-management of social security schemes and created the State Social Security Agency. The Ministry of Labour and Social Help controlled this agency.

Five years later, on 2 February 1955, the state agency administering social security schemes was dismantled (*Journal of Laws*, No. 6, item 31). According to the ideological belief that the state was about to collapse and its functions were to be taken over by various organizations of 'working people', the state decided to voluntarily transfer its function in the field of social security to trade unions. This change was not accomplished completely. Trade unions took over only tasks related to the administration of short-time benefits paid out of social security funds. Long-term benefits such as old-age pensions and disability benefits were kept under direct control of the local state administrative office.

Again, after five more years, on 13 April 1960, the State Social Security Agency was re-created (*Journal of Laws*, No. 20, item 119; No. 23, item 134). Since then, the state bureaucratic organ has been in charge of administration of all social security benefits paid both on long- and short-term bases except unemployment (administered by local employment offices), old-age pension, disability benefits paid to: miners (administrated by the Ministry of Mines), railroad workers (administered by the Ministry of Transport), military personnel (administered by the Ministry of Defence), police officers (administered by the Ministry of Internal Affairs), and members of the judiciary (administered by the Ministry of Justice).

The socialist state expressed its imperial attitude in financial matters. At the end of the 1940s, independent social security funds were cancelled (The Act of 1 March 1949, *Journal of Laws*, No. 18, item 109 and ordinance of the Council of Ministers, 8 March 1949, *Journal of Laws*, No. 18, item 121). All income collected from social security dues and expenditure paid out to beneficiaries of different social security schemes were incorporated *in toto* into the central state budget. At that time, it was difficult to make any legal distinction between social security dues and taxes. This peculiar system of financing social security benefits survived twenty years regardless of the different administrative changes that took place in the meantime in the field of social security (e.g., transferring matters of administration of social security benefits to trade union organizations).

In 1968, limited financial reform in the area of social security was introduced (the Act of 23 January 1968, *Journal of Laws*, No. 3, item 7). The old-age pension fund was reintroduced together with an obligation placed upon employees to contribute by paying social security dues to that fund. The old-age pension fund did not enjoy full autonomy from the central state budget. The Minister of Finance was a main dispatcher of that fund financed in half by contributions paid by employers in social security dues.

Partial separation of the old-age pension fund from the central state budget was made possible because in the mid-1960s two separate social security schemes, one for artisans (Ordinance of the Council of Ministers of 19 June 1965, *Journal of Laws*, No. 26, item 173) and the second for non-employed under contract of employment group of working population (Ordinance of 28 December 1966, *Journal of Laws*, No. 1, item 2), were introduced. Since in semi-private business social security benefits depended on contributions in social security dues paid by beneficiaries on their own behalf, it was necessary to create two funds within the state central budget. Therefore, in the second half of the third decade of the socialist regime, a small step was made towards financial autonomy of various social security funds.

The first unification of social security benefits in socialist Poland was made on 25 June 1954 by the Act on Common Retirement Pensions (*Journal of Laws*, No. 30, item 116). The title of this act was misleading, because this particular statute also dealt with disability benefits. The Act of 25 June 1954 unified regulations concerning old-age pension and disability benefits to all group of workers regardless of their legal source of employment relationship (contract of employment, or an administrative decision – nomination).

This act started a negative legislative practice of extending its coverage only to groups of beneficiaries who earned their respective titles to social security benefits at a given date. In the case of the Act of 25 June 1954, the date was set up on 1 July 1954. Thus two groups of beneficiaries were created: those who were drawing social security benefits paid from the 'old' system (the system in existence prior to 1 July 1954) and those who drew social security benefits from the 'new' system (the system created after 1 July 1954). Since that day, in the Polish legal language used by social security experts, new terms were introduced – an 'old portfolio' and a 'new portfolio'. Those terms made a carrier within years of economic depression in which inflation started to consume the better part of social security benefits paid out of the state central budget.

The socialist regime was not prepared to deal with inflation. After all, inflation did not fit into the ideology preached by the state at that time. In the first half of the 1970s, the state tried to cope with inflation by adopting ad hoc measures. In 1974 (the Act of 25 May 1974, *Journal of Laws*, No. 21, item 116), 1977 (the Act of 31 March 1977, *Journal of Laws*, No. 11, item 43), 1982 (the Act of 14 December 1982, *Journal of Laws*, No. 40, item 267 on old-age pensions and disability benefits), and 1983 (the Act of 1 February 1983, *Journal of Laws*, No. 5, item 32 on old-age pensions and disability benefits for mine workers; the Act of 28 April 1983, *Journal of Laws*, No. 23, item 99 on old-age pensions and disability benefits for railroad workers), one time measures were adopted. The state government was always surprised that it found it necessary to duplicate and eventually triplicate the measures necessary to restore the previous value of social security benefits. The automatic mechanism of value protection of social security benefits (valorization) was introduced as late as 1 March 1986, thirty-two years after inflation became a problem for social security laws.

As a positive feature of social security in socialist Poland, one must mention a considerable expansion of social security benefits. Slowly but gradually, almost all segments of the Polish population were covered by different social security schemes. This process of expansion of social security schemes addressed at the beginning towards employees who performed work under a contract of employment started in the 1970s. In 1971, members of agriculture cooperatives were included into a system of state social security (the Act of 26 October 1971, *Journal of Laws*, No. 27, item 255). The following year, artisans followed suit (the Act of 8 June 1972, *Journal of Laws*, No. 23, item 165). Writers and artists were covered in 1973 (the Act of 27 September 1973, *Journal of Laws* – 1983, No. 31, item 145). In 1975, people performing work under different types of civil law contracts were enlisted (the Act of 19 December 1975, *Journal of Laws* – 1983, No. 31, item 156). Individual farmers were insured in 1977 (the Act of 27 October 1977, *Journal of Laws*, No. 32, item 140). However, individual farmers had already enjoyed free medical care since 1972. In 1989, members of the clergy were included as the last group of insured people into the state social security system (The Act of 17 May 1989, *Journal of Laws*, No. 29, item 156).

Critics of the previous social security system often say that it did not guarantee a high level of benefits. They do forget, though, that the socialist idea was to move forward the whole society *en masse* and at the same time. In the field of social policy, this idea was transposed into the state's ambition to fulfil the needs of all members of the socialist society and to provide them with social security benefits. Due to economic shortage, it was not possible to carry out this overly ambitious plan. However, at a minimum level, all citizens were provided with some kind of social security benefits.

The socialist government not only provided people with benefits but it also demanded certain behaviour from them. A comparison of state contributions and demands would make an interesting story taking into account the fact that employers deducted from employee payrolls social security benefits that the state called 'state's contributions', and these were de facto contributions of insured to needed, channelled through the state central budget and later through various social security funds.

The state government also demanded performance from workers. The workers, however, were eager to take advantage of social privileges and social rights brought by a new political system. The main battlefield between the state administration and employees reluctant to work at any cost were short-term social security benefits: sickness benefits first and family benefits later on.

The Decree of 6 May 1954 introduced an employee's right to sickness benefits on the very first day of illness (*Journal of Laws*, No. 22, item 78). Naturally, after that more workers wanted to take advantage of this favourable regulation. The state administration struck back in order to prevent workers from going on sick leave. Those workers who abused their right to sickness benefits were deprived of benefits for an entire period of illness. If they were caught for the second time during the same year continuing abusive practices, they were additionally deprived of sickness benefit for the first three days during any legitimate sickness leave within the next year. State-owned enterprises were obliged to check whether or not their employees used sickness leave and accepted sickness benefits accordingly with social security regulations. Despite those regulations, the number of working hours lost due to excessive (according to the government's estimates) sickness leave was rising. Therefore, the Statute of 23 January 1968 (*Journal of Laws*, No. 3, item 12) decided to remove workers' rights to sickness benefit for the first three days during any sickness in case the absence from work was caused by abuse of alcohol. Later, in 1975, by the act mentioned in the next item, a disciplinary sanction (25% deduction of sickness benefit within the next year) was adopted in order to deprive 100% of sickness benefit from those workers who were unable to work because of taking part in a street fight, who took even one day of unauthorized leave of absence from work, were discharged without notice (summary dismissal), or decided to walk out of work on their employer (The Act of 24 October 1975, *Journal of Laws*, No. 34, item 185).

In order to make state enterprises sensitive to the issue of authorized use of sickness benefits, the ordinance issued by the Council of Ministers on 24 October 1975 transferred the duty to pay sickness benefits from the State Social Security Agency to employers. Thus, sickness benefit was paid out of the budget of the state-owned enterprises.

The other interesting change made by the socialist government in regulations concerning sickness benefits was the introduction of a direct relationship between social security benefits and length of service. It was done in the Act of 23 October 1975, which amended the previous act on sickness benefits issued on 17 December 1974 (*Journal of Laws*, No. 47, item 280). Only employees with at least eight years of service were entitled to 100% of sickness benefits.

The direct relationship between long-term social security benefits and seniority was also adopted by the Act of 14 December 1982 on pension benefits and disability benefit (*Journal of Laws*, No. 40, item 280). Therefore, the state opted for an indirect relationship between social security benefits, both paid on short- and long-term basis and social security dues.

The direct relationship was introduced by an ordinance issued by the Minister of Labour, Wages, and Social Affairs on 31 May 1974 (*Journal of Laws*, No. 21, item 127) between family benefits and the amount of income earned by working member(s) in poor families. A gesture to increase family benefit for poor families was followed by a decision to deny the right to family benefit to those employees who without the authorization of their employer decided to take at least one day off from work. This restrictive measure was abolished by the ordinance issued on 22 December 1981 by the Minister of Labour, Wages, and Social Affairs (*Journal of Laws*, No. 32, item 191).

As far as industrial injuries are concerned, the Act of 1954 introduced a special type of benefit to victims of industrial accidents and occupational diseases (*Journal of Laws*, No. 25, item 116). This benefit paid by the State Social Security Agency was not higher than the disability benefit paid out of common disability insurance. However, victims of industrial injuries were in a position to claim an additional allowance out of funds managed by employers. Because state employers were obliged to insure their businesses in the State Insurance Agency, any additional payment to victims of industrial accidents and occupational diseases was paid out of the funds managed by the insurance agency.

The Act of 23 January 1968 made an important change to this system (*Journal of Laws*, No. 3, item 8). The act made it impossible for state-owned enterprises to buy insurance against industrial injuries and occupational diseases occurring during the course of employment. Thus, the Law of 1968 shifted legal responsibility for industrial injuries from the state insurance agency to state-owned enterprises. Even industrial injury benefit was paid by the State Social Security Agency to state-owned enterprises in whose premises accidents had happened and whose workers were injured during accidents, and the state-owned enterprises were obliged to reimburse this payment out of its fund to the State Social Security Agency. Therefore, the sole risk for industrial injuries was imposed by the Law of 1968 upon employers. The Act of 12 June 1975 followed suit (*Journal of Laws*, No. 30, item 144).

The distinctive character of social security laws issued by the socialist regime in Poland after the Second World War is shown only in one matter: a considerable extension of personal coverage that included practically all members of society. Apart from this feature, it is rather difficult to present a sound conclusion that would appropriately reflect the various stages of the four-and-a-half decades of the socialist system in Poland.

During those years, three major reforms of long-term social security schemes were conducted. Taking into account that short-term benefit was also regulated several times, one can conclude that under the socialist regime, the Polish social security system was hectic. Even the state government, which by the definition adopted by the socialist system should always be eager to control each single social and economic matter, gave up the process of managing social security benefits and transferred partially administrative matters in the field of social security to trade unions.

As expected, in a state that was run in the name of blue-collar workers, social security benefits were closely connected with the length of employment. As far as social security regulations were concerned, preferences were given to workers with the highest seniority and lowest wages. It was apparent that there was also a close link between the right to certain types of social security benefit (mostly paid on a short-term basis) and work discipline.

Taking all of this into consideration, a picture of the social security system under socialism is quite grim. Hard work and low benefits were the most obvious features of the system. People did not comply for a long time since they were treated equally badly by the system that made them believe they were getting those benefits for free.

§2. Separate Social Security Schemes for Self-Employed People

19. The Act of 18 December 1976 concerning the social security scheme for people who were engaged in any type of business activity (organized at their own risk, producing goods, and providing services to unknown customers) provides coverage to all individuals (legal entities excluded) bearing Polish citizenship, registered according to legal regulations concerning business activity. In the case of two individuals running a common business in a legal form of partnership that was not formed as a legal entity, each of the aforementioned individuals was subject to separate social security coverage. There was also a possibility of the same individual running two or more separate types of business ventures. In such a case, only one social security relationship was formed between an individual and the State Social Security Agency.

The social security scheme for self-employed people was based on the principle of individuality: one self-employed person, regardless of his/her legal relations with any other individual or his/her various business activities, could establish only one social security relationship, provided he/she did not work on a part-time basis as an employee hired under an individual contract of employment. Individuals engaged in business activity were subject to the separate scheme for self-employed people only if they were not covered by the general social security scheme as wage earners employed at least on a part-time basis. Any employment that kept an employee busy at work for at least 50% of regular working time counted on a daily and weekly basis (four hours per day and twenty-three hours per week) was considered part-time work.

Those individuals who were not covered by the general social security scheme at all, for example, students entitled only to certain social security benefits (e.g., invalidity benefits), were subject to the provisions of the Act of 18 December 1976.

A similar principle applied to those individuals who decided to start a business activity on their own upon retirement. People who drew long-term pension or invalidity benefits from the general social security scheme were not entitled – in principle – to additional coverage provided by the Act of 18 December 1976.

The key word in the last paragraph is 'in principle'. The Act of 18 December 1976 provided in conjunction with the Statute of 14 December 1982 for an opportunity of separate social security coverage of any beneficiary who upon earning his/her social security benefit had decided to suspend (partially or totally) his/her claim to social security benefit due to resuming employment, or engaging himself, or herself into business activity that entitled them to earn an additional right to a different social security benefit under a separate social security scheme.

On the other hand, there was a particular category of self-employed person (advocate) that was covered by the general social security regulations regardless of the specific legal status of this category of self-employed person. Some advocates were considered to be employed as counsellors at the legal departments of state-owned enterprises, instructors, or professors of law engaged in teaching activities at least on a part-time basis. The legal arrangement concerning the legal rights of advocates to social security benefits was rather exceptional.

It even provided for an obligation on the part of already retired advocates upon reaching the age of 70 years to maintain a contribution in the form of social security dues to the social security fund if an already retired advocate decided to carry on his/her legal duties. According to the principle of automatic coverage, of any person who fell within the legal requirement of any social security scheme, a social security relationship starts *ex lege* on the very day a self-employed person decides to start a business activity. The Act of 18 December 1976 assured coverage within six months after the day a business activity was stopped by an insured self-employed person.

The law concerning social insurance of self-employed people also provided a coverage for their 'helpers'. According to the legal definition, any person was considered a 'helper' if such an individual who is helping to run a business was either a member of the immediate family or maintained a common household with a self-employed person. The Act of 18 December 1976 required that a 'helper' should provide a self-employed person with professional help at least on a part-time basis. Again, part-time help meant that such person had to be busy for at least half of the working day (four hours) and half of the working week (twenty-three hours) helping a self-employed person with his/her professional activity.

The Act of 18 December 1976 was quite strict on the matter of which category of people fell within the category of a member of family of the self-employed person. The definition of a family member included: spouse, both natural and adopted children, children who were placed with foster parents if one member of such a family was considered self-employed, parents who adopted children, stepfather, stepmother, parents-in-law, grandparents, grandchildren, sons-in-law, daughters-in-law, and brothers and sisters-in-law.

All the above-mentioned people enjoyed the legal status of 'helper' and were covered by the Act of 18 December 1976, which provided a social security scheme for a self-employed person. The 'helper' was insured under the condition that he/she was at least 16 years old and continued his/her activity in helping to run the business conducted by a self-employed person for a period of at least six months. Naturally, the same legal requirements that concerned a self-employed person, including his/her lack of coverage by any additional social security scheme as wage earner or his/her already established right to an old-age pension or invalidity benefit, which were being taken advantage of, did apply to a 'helper'. A 'helper' was covered by social insurance from the first day of the month in which he/she started to help a self-employed person to his/her business. The legal duty to report a 'helper' to the State Social Security Agency and to pay on behalf of such person social security dues was the duty of the self-employed person (the duty to insure). However, a 'helper' could take advantage of legal regulations written in Article 3, section 2 of the Act of 18 December 1976 and resumed contribution for a social security scheme of self-employed for an additional six months after ceasing his/her activities as a helper. If the 'helper' decided to do so, he/she had to take care of social security dues on his/her own.

Contrary to regulations concerning self-employed people a social security relationship did not start automatically from the day a 'helper' was hired to help a self-employed person to run his/her private business. As stated earlier, the conclusion of a social security relationship with a 'helper' depended upon the decision of the self-employed person to report to the State Social Security Agency that he/she decided to employ someone who was close to him/her to run a private business. Thus, a social security relationship was not initiated by the helper. As a result of this exceptional regulation, the Act of 18 December 1976 clearly provided that a period of employment performed by any person who was de facto helping the self-employed person before such a person was reported to the social security agency as de jure helper could not be taken into account while computing the period covered by a special social security scheme for self-employed people. In the case of a 'helper', a three-month waiting period was introduced as a legal condition to acquire the right to sickness and maternity benefits. It applied to any case of illness except illness caused by an industrial injury.

Far more restrictive requirements concerning the waiting period necessary to earn invalidity benefits were introduced in the case when a member of a family or household of self-employed person decided to help him/her to run a private business at a late stage of someone's professional activity. The Act of 18 December 1976 considered anyone who decided to enter into a new professional career upon reaching the age of 45 as a late starter. In order to prevent any misuse of the social security fund, the law stated that a 'helper' who decided to start his/her professional career by helping his/her relative or another person with whom he/she shared a household after reaching an age of 45 years in order to earn his/her right to an invalidity benefit had to be insured at least for ten years during a period of twenty years before the disability started, or before the day on which an application for an invalidity benefit was submitted to the State Social Security Agency.

20. The social security scheme for self-employed people was financed by the beneficiary himself. His/her contribution amounts to 38% of his/her declared income and could not be lower than 60% of the average national monthly wage. A self-employed person deposited his/her contribution from his/her declared income with the social security fund. Contributions were placed in a bank. Therefore earned interest was one of the means of financing different social security schemes run by the social security agency. The differences between income from contributions of self-employed people and expenditure were covered by state subsidies. Thus, the state was vitally interested in how the monies paid out of the fund are spent. One of the major problems with the social security scheme of self-employed people was that some of those schemes declared an enormous monthly income, paid social security dues for a short period of time, and tried to take advantage of the scheme by claiming high short-term benefits (sickness benefits). In order to curtail this abusive practice and to protect the social security fund, the state government issued in July 1991 regulations according to which any person employed by a private employer or a self-employed person could declare an increase in his/her monthly income by only 50%.

21. Under the social insurance scheme for self-employed people, both benefits in kind and cash were paid according to the concept of risks against which all people (employed, semi-self-employed, and self-employed) were covered under the National Social Security Law. Therefore, self-employed people were entitled to old-age pensions, benefits provided in the case of death, incapacity for work, unemployment, and family allowances. They were covered by the medical care provided by the national health service:

(a) an old-age pension:

A retirement pension was payable to an insured self-employed person who had attained a certain age: 60 years for self-employed females and 65 years for self-employed males. There were no special requirements concerning the right to an old-age pension for self-employed people provided by the Act of 18 December 1976. However, the law states that a contribution to the social security scheme for self-employed in the form of social security dues should be submitted for at least five years during a certain period before an effective application ought to be submitted to the social security agency (Article 9, section 3). Thus, a self-employed male who was applying for an old-age pension was obliged to prove that he contributed to the social security fund for at least five years during twenty-five years. The rest of this period, which was twenty years, ought to be evidenced as a period in which work under an employment contract was performed by a beneficiary *in spe*, or the prospective beneficiary was serving in the army, spent sufficient time in school, or was engaged in the fight for freedom and liberty.

A female applicant was obliged to prove she contributed to the social security fund in dues for at least a five-year period during twenty years.

The other condition – a proper relationship between the age factor and both the employment and contributory period to the social security fund – was applied on the similar basis to self-employed people as it was applied to wage earners. Thus retirement age should be reached within the period of contributions in social security dues by a self-employed person, or in the next five consecutive years.

The old-age pension was calculated in the same fashion for self-employed people as it was calculated for employees. The same calculation is used because all retirement pensions regardless of the scheme were calculated according to the formula specified in the Act of 17 October 1991. The old-age pension for self-employed people was calculated on the basis of a one-year contribution at a time since 1992 up to a maximum of ten years contribution in social security dues in 1999.

In order to figure the exact amount of any social security benefit for self-employed people, the State Social Security Agency had to establish the yearly income for a given applicant. It was based on an applicant's declaration and contribution to the fund in social security dues. Then the State Social Security Agency had to establish a relationship between the individual's yearly income and the average income in the given year. Next, it was necessary to calculate the median of yearly percentage income. As a last step in the process of calculation of a social security benefit, the State Social Security Agency multiplied the median and the average monthly income of the applicant. As a result of those calculations, the State Social Security Agency established an individual base platform for each beneficiary.

An old-age pension was counted in the following way: 24% of a basic platform plus 1.3% of a base platform for each year a self-employed person contributed to a social security fund by way of paying social security dues out of his/her monthly declared income plus 0.7% of a basic platform for each year regarded as being countable by the State Social Security Agency for the purpose of establishing legal rights to social security benefits.

(b) survivor's pension:

The spouse, children, and parents of a deceased self-employed person were entitled to a survival pension (Article 5, item 4 of the Act of 18 December 1976). Survivor's benefits were counted as other family benefits on a basis of the amount of benefit to which a deceased member of a family was entitled. In the case of the only person surviving being a family breadwinner, the survivor was entitled to a family pension which was equal to 85% of the benefit to which the deceased person was entitled. In the case of a deceased person being survived by two members of his/her family, they were entitled to 90% of the benefit to which the deceased person was entitled. In the case of three survivors, they were entitled to 95% of the social security benefit to which the deceased person was entitled.

If a self-employed person was a victim of an injury caused by the type of professional activity he/she was conducting, surviving members of his/her family were entitled to a survivor's pension provided by the Act of 12 June 1975 on industrial injuries and occupational diseases.

(c) sickness allowances and invalidity benefits:

The sickness and invalidity insurance scheme for self-employed people guaranteed benefits to those self-employed people who were incapable of performing any type of work due to illness, maternity, or disability of the first or the second category who had not yet reached pensionable age. The sickness benefit was subject to the condition that self-employed people ceased all professional activities for a period of illness which took at least thirty consecutive days. Sickness benefits did not depend on the degree of the self-employed person's incapacity for work. In opposition to this, invalidity benefits were awarded only if a self-employed person fell within one of two out of the three categories of disability, either group one or two. The formula used for calculation of a disability benefit was the same as the one used to calculate an old-age pension.

Maternity benefit was awarded to a self-employed female who delivered a child either during a period in which she was covered by the social security scheme for self-employed people or within a period in which sickness benefit was paid after the conclusion of the social security relationship. The self-employed female was entitled to maternity benefit provided by the general social security scheme for female employees.

(d) unemployment benefits:
There was no distinction between a jobless person who was formerly employed, semi-self-employed, or self-employed as far as the right to unemployment benefit was concerned. Anyone who was willing and able to work was entitled to unemployment benefit. Naturally, unemployment benefit could not be provided for someone who was already self-employed. Such a person did not suit the legal definition of an unemployed person. According to Article 2, section 1, item 9 of the Act of 16 October 1991 on Employment and Unemployment, an unemployed person was a person ready and willing to accept employment under contract of employment, provided that such person was not self-employed in the non-agricultural sector of the national economy.

(e) family allowances:
Family allowance was payable to self-employed people on the same legal conditions as to workers covered by the general social security scheme designed to suit family bearing needs of the employed person. Family allowance was payable in order to support the claimant's own children, children of the claimant's spouse, adopted children, and children placed by family courts into the claimant's custody. Family allowance also was paid in order to support the claimant's grandchildren and his/her brothers and sisters that the claimant began to take care of before their majority.

22. The Act of 18 December 1976 did not contain any special provisions concerning both administration and finances of the social security scheme for the self-employed. It meant that the general rules concerning all social security schemes applied to administration and finances of this particular scheme. All social security schemes, with the exception of the separate occupational schemes for miners, railroad workers, professional soldiers, police officers, and prison guards, were administered by the State Social Security Agency. This agency was a public institution established by the state government. The social security agency administered all social security matters of self-employed people together with the risks caused by sickness, industrial injuries, and occupational diseases. It also administered alimony allowances for all employed, semi-self-employed and self-employed mothers taking care of children who were not supported by their fathers.

23. The legal protection of beneficiaries covered by the social security scheme for self-employed people was carried out along the same lines of protection for people covered by the general social security scheme.

24. There were few differences between the general social security scheme and the scheme developed for social security protection of self-employed people. Since both schemes were constructed along the same or similar lines as far as territorial scope of application, administration, finances, and legal protection of insured people and beneficiaries was concerned, the only differences were in legal requirements that were prescribed by the social security scheme for self-employed people. Those requirements differed from the requirements stated in the general social security scheme by the following points:

(a) there was a lack of automatism in application of the social security scheme for self-employed people as far as the coverage of a 'collaborator' is concerned;
(b) the State Social Security Agency maintained total control over administration of all benefits paid out of the social security fund. This applied particularly to the short-term benefits which under the general social security scheme were being administered by state-owned enterprises;
(c) social security dues were paid to the fund exclusively by insured people;
(d) certain benefits, such as sickness benefit were paid in the case of prolonged inability to engage in professional activity;
(e) minor invalidity which qualified an insured employee for a benefit prescribed for a third category of invalidity did not entitle a self-employed person to any benefit at all.

Apart from the above, there was no difference in the amount of benefit and allowances paid to various categories of insured people covered by various social security schemes. As an effect of the described legal arrangements, 1,113,153 self-employed people were insured in 1992 in Poland, and 1,001,067 contributed to the social security fund by paying social security dues. There were 39,600 formerly self-employed persons who drew old-age pensions, and there were 55,700 people who drew invalidity benefit out of the social security fund for self-employed people. There were 29,100 people who drew family benefits from the above-mentioned fund.

The average old-age pension drawn by self-employed people was as high as Polish zloty (PLN) 1,584.401 (after denomination PLN 158 = EUR 40) per month while the average retirement benefit paid to a retired employee amounts to PLN 2,127.438 (after denomination PLN 212 = EUR 55). The monthly difference of PLN 542,947 (after denomination PLN 54 = EUR 14) between the old-age pension of employed and self-employed people reflects the 7% difference in social security dues contributed by self-employed (38%) and 45% paid by employers on behalf of their employees. It also resulted in a tendency among self-employed people to insure themselves on a minimum level by declaring a lower income and therefore paying less in social security dues.

§3. Changes in Social Security That Took Place with the End of the Socialist Period in Poland

25. Nothing changed in the social security laws in Poland between the years 1989 and 1991. On 17 October 1991, the Polish Parliament introduced an act that officially dealt with a valorization of social security benefits (*Journal of Laws*, No. 104, item 450). In fact, this act changed the legal structure of long-term social security benefits in democratic Poland. The above-mentioned act amended thirteen social security statutes issued between 1973 and 1990.

The Act of 17 October 1991 introduced a major change in the state social security system. This act dropped the former distinction between working periods and periods that were treated on an equal footing with working periods regardless of whether or not work was performed. Currently, a distinction is made between periods for which insured people have contributed to the social security fund and periods for which social security dues have not been paid. The periods for which an employer contributed to the social security fund on behalf of his employees are listed in Article 2, section 2 of the Act of 17 October 1991.

The above-mentioned statute puts on overall ceiling on the number of years that may be included by the State Social Security Agency for the purpose of establishing legal rights to social security benefits. This ceiling may not exceed one-third of the period counted for social security benefits for which social security dues were paid.

The new regulation has changed the basis on which social security benefits are counted. The statute extends to ten years the period of time for which social security dues are paid with a purpose of computing the amount of social security benefits. The new system of counting social security benefits is not an easy one. In order to figure out the exact amount of any social security benefit, the State Social Security Agency must establish the applicant's yearly income. Then the State Social Security Agency has to establish the relationship between yearly income and average income in a given year. Next it is necessary to calculate a median of yearly income. This median serves as an indicator of the basis for any social security benefit. As a last step, the State Social Security Agency multiplies the median and the average monthly income of the applicant. As a result of those calculations, the State Social Security Agency establishes an individual platform for each beneficiary.

Old-pension benefit and disability benefit of people who were declared as included at least into a second class of disability are counted in the following way: 24% of the basis platform plus 1.3% of the basis platform for each year an employed person or his/her employer contributed in the social security fund in social security dues plus 0.7% of a basis platform for each year treated by the Act of 17 October 1991 as accountable by the State Social Security Agency for a purpose of establishing the legal right to social security benefits.

Disability benefit for any person declared an invalid of a third category is equal to 75% of a disability benefit to which an invalid of a second category is entitled.

Family benefit is counted on the basis of the amount of benefit to which a deceased member of a family was entitled. If the deceased person was survived by one, two, or three members of his/her family, remaining members of family are entitled to (respectively) 85%, 90%, or 95% of the benefit to which deceased person was entitled.

With the exception that a victim of an industrial injury and members of deceased worker during such accident may sue his/her employer for damages, some changes have been made in the law that regulates legal claims that came out of industrial injuries. Still, the same Statute of 12 June 1975 as amended in 1983 is enforced. However, Article 40 of this act, which limited the right to claim a compensation for industrial injuries, was struck out by the Act of 24 May 1990 (*Journal of Laws*, No. 36, item 206).

Some changes were introduced in sickness and family benefits. The same regulations issued on 17 December 1974 and later amended are still enforced. Those regulations are supported by the Act of 1 December 1994 of family and nursing benefits (*Journal of Laws*, No. 4, item 17).

A completely new benefit called an unemployment benefit was introduced by the Statute of 28 December 1989 (*Journal of Laws*, No. 75, item 446). This act was changed by the Law issued on 16 October 1991 (*Journal of Laws*, No. 106, item 457) and later by the Act of 14 December 1994 on Employment and Unemployment (*Journal of Laws of 1996*, No. 47, item 211 as amended by the Act of 6 December 1996, *Journal of Laws*, No. 147, item 687). As one may see, the legal, administrative, and financial framework of the present social security system in a democratic Poland has been subject to very little change. Very little change has been made in financing social security schemes. No changes have been made in organization of the system. A few changes, mostly related to long-term benefits, have been introduced since the first democratic government was elected in June 1989. The democratic Polish social security system is still heavily reliant on the non-socialist state, both in financing social security fund (input) and guaranteeing payment of social security benefits (output).

§4. Polish Social Security During the Twenty-Seven Years of Democratic Poland (1989–2017)

I. Social Security Regulations

26. Polish Social Security Laws during the twenty-seven years of Democratic Poland contained several sets of legal regulations. Majority of them were issued under the previous regime, in the 1970s and the 1980s.

The first set of legal regulations dealt with an organization and financing of the national social security system. The Statute of 25 November 1986 as amended provided that the state guaranteed the payment of social security benefits in case of maternity leave, together with family benefit, old-pension benefit, survivors benefit, and disabled benefit. The state also guaranteed payments of social security benefit in case of illness or industrial injury.

The state implemented its obligations towards insured people by way of its agency: Social Security Administration. This agency was the part of the state government. It was controlled by the minister of Labour and Social Policy. Financial control over the Social Security Administration, however, was executed by the Minister of Finance. This was done so, even the Act of 25 November 1986 provided that the State Social Security Administration handles the financial matters of the Social Security Fund established for the purpose of self-financing activities of the social security system.

The Act on Organization and Financing of the National Social Security System obliged employers to contribute to the social security fund social security dues on behalf of their employees. Social security dues were the main revenue of the Social Security Fund. At least they were listed by the act as the number one revenue. However, the number two revenue was listed as contributions from the state budget to the social security fund.

Therefore, the major change between the previous system and the present system of financing social security benefits, both of them established by the past socialist government, was a minor diversion in raising the revenues. Prior to the day on which the Act of 25 November 1986 was enforced, employers were obliged to contribute in social security dues directly to the state budget. Then the state financial authorities assigned some financial resources to support expenditure for social security purposes. Therefore, formerly, social security dues clearly played the role of taxes. During the first seven years of the Democratic Poland, this role was more camouflaged since employers were acting under direct obligation to pay the social security dues to a separate fund. This fund, however, was not totally separated from the state budget. The state not only controlled the Social Security budget but also made a substantial contribution to support it. The last statement clearly indicates the most important issue of the social security system during the transition period. The social security system during the first seven years of Democratic Poland largely depended on the state finances. Since the state was in economic disarray, the shape of the social security system during the first seven years of Democratic Poland did not vary from the appearance of its master, the state.

The second set of social security laws contained legal provisions passed by Parliament on 17 October 1991. This was an act that dealt with valorization of social security benefit and changes to former (issued in 1982) regulations according to which old-age (retirement) pension benefits and disability benefits were established. This particular statute ceased to serve its purpose after 31 December 1993.

27. This particular act specifically amended:

(a) The Act of 14 December 1982 on old-pension, family and disability benefits.
(b) Articles 86 and 88–91 of the Act of 26 January 1982 concerning teachers' legal rights to social security benefits.
(c) Articles 112–114 of the Act of 12 September 1990 concerning legal rights to social security benefits of university professors.
(d) Article 27 of the Civil Service Act of 16 September 1982 concerning legal rights of civil servants to social security benefits.
(e) Article 23 of the Act of 22 March 1990 concerning the legal rights to social security benefits of municipal employees.
(f) The Act of 27 September 1973 concerning the legal rights to social security benefits of writers and members of their families.
(g) The Act of 19 December 1975 concerning the legal right to social security benefits of self-employed people and members of their families.
(h) The Decree of 4 March 1976 concerning the legal rights to social security benefits of members of agriculture cooperatives.
(i) The Act of 18 December 1976 concerning the legal rights to social security benefits of an individual conducting independent industrious ventures.
(j) The Act of 28 April 1983 concerning the legal rights to social security benefits of railroad workers and members of their families.
(k) The Act of 1 February 1983 concerning the legal rights to social security benefits of miners and members of their families.

(l) The Act of 17 May 1989 concerning the legal rights of clergymen person to social security benefits.
(m) The Act of 12 June 1976 concerning the legal rights of workers who suffers from industrial injuries.

The Act of 17 October 1991 amended virtually all legal regulations concerning long-term social security benefits, such as old-age pensions, family, survivors, and disability benefits as well as industrial injuries to which insured persons were entitled regardless of their professional associations.

The Act of 17 October 1991 introduced major changes in the national security system. The new legal regulations abandoned the former distinction between working periods and periods that were treated equally with a working period, even de facto work that was not performed. Currently, a distinction is made between periods for which insured people or his/her employer contribute to the social security fund in social security dues and periods for which social security dues are not paid.

The periods for which an employer contributed to the social security fund on behalf of his employees were listed in Article 2, section 2 of the Act of 17 October 1991. The full list contained twenty-nine items. Those items fell into one of the ten below-listed categories:

(a) work performed under a contract of employment;
(b) service regulated by a civil service act, such as military duty, police work, prison guard duty, and border patrol;
(c) work performed for a foreign employer outside Polish territory;
(d) involuntary employment done on behalf of Nazi Germany during Second World War and the Soviet Union between the days of 17 September 1939 and 31 December 1956 as well as or on behalf of allied military forces till 31 December 1945;
(e) periods of a young person's apprenticeship before 1 January 1975;
(f) periods of involuntary unemployment;
(g) periods in which public functions in parliament were performed;
(h) any period covered by a social security scheme in which any type of professional or business activity was conducted;
(i) any period of employment performed independently on behalf of any state-owned enterprise which was covered by a social security scheme; one important requirement, though, was that an individual who was engaged in this type of activity was earning at least as much as 50% of the minimum monthly income defined by the provisions of the Labour Code;
(j) periods in which an individual older than fifteen years of age was drawing so-called sportive stipend paid out of the state-sponsored fund.

Among periods which were regarded as being countable by the social security agency for a purpose of establishing legal rights to social security benefits the following periods were listed:

(a) years in which a person applying for social security benefits was forced to go into the underground during the Second World War and post-Second World War years with a purpose of fighting for freedom;
(b) years spent in interment after martial law was introduced on 13 December 1981;
(c) years in which a waiver from contributions to social security dues was granted (periods in which an individual was collecting sickness benefits);
(d) years devoted to a care shown towards a minor child, or a dependent member of the family of an insured person;
(e) years in which an unpaid leave of absence was granted for a reason listed in the Act of 17 October 1991;
(f) years in which education was completed according to a programme issued by an institution of higher education;
(g) a period not exceeding one year in which voluntary unpaid work at hospitals or clinics was performed for a purpose of getting professional medical experience.

The Act of 17 October 1991 put an overall ceiling on the number of years that may be included by the State Social Security Agency for the purpose of establishing the legal right to social security benefits. This ceiling may not exceed one-third of the period counted for social security benefits for which social security dues were paid.

The law also provided that periods covered by an individual farmers' social security scheme together with years in which a person who was claiming social security benefit was working on his/her private farm were taken into consideration as equal to periods for which social security dues were contributed.

The Act of 17 October 1991 drastically changed the basis on which the amount of social security benefits was counted. The statutory law exceeded – on the basis of one year at a time up to a maximum of ten years in 1999 – the length of time for which social security dues were paid for the purpose of computing the amount of social security benefits. For those who claimed social security benefits for before 31 December 1992, the social security agency was obliged to take into consideration the income from three consecutive years out of the last twelve years (1981–1992). On the other spectrum, the law provided that for those who claimed benefits out of the social security fund between 1 January and 31 December 1999, the social security agency had to take into consideration their earnings achieved in ten consecutive years out of the last twenty years (1980–1999). Income from one job only was taken into consideration by the social security agency computed the basis for any social security benefit regardless of the number of jobs performed at the same time by the same applicant.

That system of computing of the level of any social security benefit was rather complicated. In order to figure the exact amount of any social security benefit, the State Social Security Agency had to establish the yearly income of the applicant. Then it had to establish – using percentages – a relationship between the former mentioned figure and average income in a given year. Next it was necessary to calculate a median of yearly percentage income. A median served as an indicator of the basis for any social security benefit. As a last step in the process of calculation of social security benefit, the State Social Security Agency multiplied the median and the average monthly income of the applicant. As a result of the above-mentioned calculations, the State Social Security Agency established an individual basis platform for each beneficiary.

An old-age pension, and disability benefit of a disabled person who fell into the first or second disability category, was counted the following way: 24% of a basis platform plus 1.3% of the basis platform for each year an employed person or his/her employer contributed into a social security fund by way of paying social security dues plus 0.7% of basis platform for each year regarded as being countable by the State Social Security Agency for the purpose of establishing the legal rights to social security benefits.

The disability benefit for any person defined as an invalid of the third category was equal to 75% of the disability benefit to which an invalid of the second category was entitled.

Family benefits were counted on the basis of the amount of benefit to which a deceased member of a family was entitled. In the case of the only person surviving being a family breadwinner, the survivor was entitled to family benefit equal to 85% of the benefit to which the deceased person was entitled. In the case that the deceased person was survived by two members of his/her family, they were entitled to 90% of the benefit to which the deceased person was entitled. In the case of three survivors, they were entitled to 95% of the social security benefit computed in the way described earlier.

The third set of legal regulations dealt with rights to social security benefits to which employees were entitled in the case of industrial injury. The Act of 12 June 1975 concerning social security benefit for a person who suffered an industrial accident or an occupational disease as well as benefits for members of family who survived after the death of a family breadwinner had been amended several times since its enactment. However, the only major change introduced into this law by the new parliament was done by the Act of 17 October 1991. In Article 11, section 4 of this act provided that social security benefit to which the victim of industrial accident was entitled to should not be lower than 80% of a basis platform of an old-age pension benefit (a second category of disability caused by an industrial injury) or 60% of the former in the case of a third disability category.

The fourth set of legal regulations dealt with unemployment benefit. The Act of 16 October 1991 on employment and unemployment changed the previous legal regulation concerning unemployment benefits issued on 28 December 1989.

The new legal regulation defined an unemployed person (Article 2, section 1, item 9) as 'a person who is able and willing to take a full-time job, who is actually jobless and does not study in a night school or does not attend a school which conducts education on an extramural bases'. An important indicator of willingness to work was an act of registration as an unemployed person with the state employment agency. On average, an employment agency refused to register any person who is under 18 or over 60 (female) or 65 (male). An employment agency also turned down applications to be registered as unemployed by a person who:

(a) earned his/her old-pension benefit;
(b) owns an individual farm;
(c) is self-employed;
(d) is disabled and as effect of this defect cannot be employed even on a part-time basis.

An unemployed person was entitled to unemployment benefit only if the state employment agency could not provide a jobless person with the offer of a suitable job or was unable to furnish him/her with an offer to start a vocational training, or was unable to get him/her engaged in a public works project.

Taking into consideration the previous experience, the Act of 16 October 1991 introduced a new requirement as a precondition for getting unemployment benefit. According to the regulation stated in Article 23, section 1, item 2 of the statute on employment and unemployment, only an individual who was employed or covered by a social security scheme for at least 365 days during the past eighteen months was eligible for unemployment benefit. This regulation was introduced to cut off unemployment benefit for people who were never employed and decided to take advantage of the newly introduced social security payment, the unemployment benefit. The above-mentioned legal condition did not apply to five categories of people listed in section 2 of Article 23 of the employment and unemployment Act of 1991. Among those categories were:

(a) redundant workers and employees;
(b) graduates;
(c) soldiers discharged from the army who decided to register at an employment agency, employed within three months from the day of ceasing to perform military services;
(d) women out of parental leave of absence who registered within six months starting from the last day of their respective leave of absence;
(e) workers who run out of coverage of the services provided by the state social security, such as a maternity, sick leave, or temporary disability benefits who registered within six months as unemployed at the state employment agency;
(f) ex-convicts released from a correction centre who decide to register as jobless within three months of their release under the condition that they were eligible for unemployment benefit during the last twelve months before conviction;
(g) workers who – after vocational training set up by the state employment agency – were not employed due to a reason caused by the state-owned enterprise or other employer for a required period of 180 days were eligible for unemployment benefit under the condition that they registered at the state employment agency within the next seven days starting from the day of their dismissal.

The amount of unemployment benefit used to be directly related to the amount of personal monthly income of the unemployed person and to the length of joblessness of the former person. An unemployed person was entitled to 70% of his/her average income for the period of the first three months as the unemployed. For the next six months, an unemployed person was entitled to draw 50% of his/her previous monthly income. After nine months of unemployment, he/she drew 40% of the previous income.

The law on employment and unemployment set up both maximum and minimum standards for unemployment benefit. Unemployment benefit could not exceed the level of nationally set up average monthly income regardless of the previous individual income of an unemployed person. It could not be lower, though, than 33% of a person's income.

A jobless person lost his/her right to unemployment benefit under one of the circumstances listed below:

(a) when such a person disregarded a legal obligation to report to the state employment agency after being called upon;
(b) when such a person remained outside the Polish territory or put himself/ herself into a position which made him/her unable to accept a job offer;
(c) when such a person walked out on his/her last employer or was summarily discharged;
(d) when such a person turned down the proposition of a physical check-up as a prerequisite to accepting an employment offer;
(e) when such a person received credit which enabled him/her to start an independent business activity;
(f) was temporarily detained by the police;
(g) his/her income from part-time employment exceeded 50% of the national minimum monthly income;
(h) was called for military duty;
(i) was drawing social security benefits;
(j) was getting benefit for the purpose of taking care of her/his minor child (a paid leave of parental absence);
(k) was a member of a family in which either a spouse was earning more than twice the national monthly average wage or an average income of a single family member exceeded 33% of the average national monthly salary.

Unemployment benefits were paid out of an unemployment fund. The Minister of Labour and Social Policy administered a payment out of that fund. Similarly to the social security fund, the unemployment fund collected social security dues paid by employers on a compulsory basis regardless of their mandatory contribution to the social security fund. Like the social security fund, the unemployment fund was not entirely independent from the state budget. The state contributed a great deal to the unemployment fund by creating public works for the unemployed, encouraging them to accept a job training in those areas of industry and in services that the state, acting through its employment agency, is trying to support. Out of the unemployment fund, vocational benefit was being paid to those jobless workers who were willing to start a new professional career.

Since 1 January 1995 new regulations concerning unemployment benefits had been introduced. According to Article 23 of the Act of 14 December 1994, the right to unemployment benefit was granted to an unemployed person who during the twelve months prior to the registration date at an unemployment agency was employed or covered by the social security scheme for at least 180 days.

Within those above-mentioned 180 days, periods in which military service was performed or parental leave of absence granted are covered.

Unemployment benefit was paid on a lump sum basis. Only people in a certain age bracket (female over 55, males over 60) who lost their jobs due to being made redundant were entitled to 75% of their previous wages as unemployment benefit. Unemployment benefit was paid for a maximum period of twelve months.

The right to draw unemployment benefit ceased to exist in the following situations:

(a) an unemployed individual failed to report to the state employment agency;
(b) an unemployed individual turned down without good cause an offer for employment or a proposal submitted by the state employment agency for retraining;
(c) an unemployed individual terminated his/her contract of employment with notice or was dismissed by an employer due to his/her fault.

Those conditions for drawing unemployed benefits were severed by the Act of 6 December 1996 (*Journal of Laws*, No. 147, item 687). On the first day of the seven months since this act was published (1 July 1997), only people employed for at least 365 days within the last eighteen months prior to the date of registration as unemployed were entitled to draw unemployment benefit.

Since 1 January 1997, unemployed people with a length of service of less than five years were entitled to 80% of unemployment benefit. Those with service of twenty years or longer were entitled to 120% of the standard unemployment benefit announced by the minister of labour and social policy (a lump sum principle).

Again since 1 July 1997 the right to unemployment benefit was lost by those people who terminated with notice or by agreement with their employer their employment contract within six months prior to the date of registration with the state employment agency.

Those changes made during the first seven years of Democratic Poland had been introduced with the idea of making it more difficult to become eligible to receive unemployment benefits.

The Act of 6 December 1996 introduced a new type of unemployment benefit: pre-retirement benefits (zasilki przedemerytalne). This benefit was paid to unemployed people:

(a) with thirty years (female), or thirty-five years (male) employment service, regardless of the age of the unemployed individual;
(b) within a certain age bracket 58 (female) and 63 (male) and with a length of service qualifying them for an old-age pension;
(c) laid off workers and employees age 55 (female) and 60 (male) with a length of service required by statutory regulations on old-age pensions;
(d) redundant people with 35 years (female), or 40 years (male) length of service.

Pre-retirement benefits were as high as 120% of standard unemployment benefits. The Act of 6 December 1996 set up the maximum amount for those benefits. They could not exceed 90% of the average monthly wage earned by people entitled to those benefits.

The fifth set of legal regulations dealt with social security benefit paid in case of illness and maternity. The Act of 17 December 1974 on sickness and maternity benefits paid in cash was amended on 5 May 1983. It had not been changed significantly since then. New regulations concerning family and nursing benefits were introduced by the Statutory Act of 1 December 1994 (*Journal of Laws*, No. 4, item 17).

The sixth set of legal regulations that has been recently introduced dealt with healthcare insurance – the Act of 6 February 1997 (*Journal of Laws*, No. 28, item 153). This act was enforced on 1 January 1999. It is one of the first statutory regulations in the area of social security that is designed to reshape the old national social security scheme, which was rooted in the previous political system.

28. Significant changes in the Polish social insurance system were introduced during the last five years. The retirement age of 67 was established under the act of 11 May 2012 on the amendment of the act on old-age pensions and invalidity benefits paid from the Social Insurance Fund (ustawa o zmianie ustawy o emeryturach i rentach z Funduszu Ubezpieczeń Społecznych). Under the said act, starting from 1 January 2013 the retirement age which was previously 60 for women and 65 for men was gradually increased and equalized to finally reach 67 years for both sexes. The process covered women born after 31 December 1952 and men born after 31 December 1947. According to the introduced changes, the retirement age of women born in each subsequent quarter falling after 31 December 1952 and the age of men born after each subsequent quarter falling after 31 December 1947 was increased by one month in comparison with the retirement age of persons born during the previous quarter. The target retirement age of 67 years for women was planned to be reached on 1 October 2040, and for men on 1 October 2020. The equalization of the retirement age at 67 years was to cover women born after 30 September 1973 and men born after 30 September 1953. The process of increasing and equalization of the retirement age was planned for a period of 28 years in relation to women (age increase by 7 years, from 60 to 67 years) and 8 years for men (age increase by 2 years, from 65 to 67). Identical changes were introduced in the pension schemes covering farmers, judges, and public prosecutors.

29. Apart from the increase and equalization of the retirement age of the insured, the act of 11 May 2012 introduced several other changes, connected directly or indirectly with the increase of the retirement age to 67 years. The changes concerned:

(a) introduction of a new type of pension benefit – a partial pension payable to the insured before reaching the basic pensionable age of 67 years. The partial pension was intended to mitigate the increase of the retirement age. It was available to women who were at least 62 years old and who had at least 35 years of insurance period, either contributory (in connection with performance of work) or non-contributory (in connection with taking care of children during employment). It was available also to men who were at least 65 years old and who had at least forty years of social insurance period. The partial pension amounted to a half of the full pension paid from the Social Insurance Fund. A precondition for the entitlement to such pension was termination of an employment relationship. The amount of the partial pension was adjusted to the amount of the lowest full pension. After having reached the basic retirement age, the partial pension was converted – upon request of the interested party – into a full pension. However, the basis for the calculation of the full pension was reduced by the amount of the partial pension already paid to the insured person. Almost identical legal mechanism was implemented in the social insurance system of farmers; however, in this case when a person covered by the farmers' social security system reached the retirement age, the partial farmer's pension was ex officio converted into the full pension. The basis of such pension was not reduced by the amount of the partial farmer's pension already paid out to the insured;

(b) restrictions on the application of provisions enabling early retirement by farmers, judges, and public prosecutors. By the date of entry into force of the act of 11 May 2012, farmers were entitled to an old-age pension after they have reached the age of 55 (women) and 60 years (men), if they were subject to insurance for a period of at least 30 years and they ceased their agricultural activity. The public prosecutors and judges were becoming entitled to receive pension after they have reached the age of 55 (women who have worked in the judiciary for at least 25 years) or 60 years (men who worked as judges or public prosecutors for at least 30 years);

(c) payment of periodic funded pensions from OPE until reaching the age corresponding to the retirement age for men. Because of the increase of the retirement age to 67 years, the right to funded pensions was gradually extended in 2014–2020 for women born after 31 December 1948 until they have reached the age of 67;

(d) unification of the insurance period which gives entitlement to the lowest pension of men and women. Equalization of the retirement age of men and women was accompanied by equalization of the required contributory and non-contributory periods which were decisive for increase of the pension to the minimum amount for men and women born after 31 December 1948. Since 1 January 2014 the period for women has been extended by one year every two years until reaching the target twenty-five years' insurance period after 31 December 2021. The period of payment of contributions for a person receiving care benefits was extended to twenty-five years;

(e) adjustment to the increased retirement age of the rules on which a so-called hypothetical period of service is included in the amount of the invalidity benefit, at the rate of 0.7% of the basis for calculation of the pension per each year which the worker lacks to reach the full twenty-five years of contributory and non-contributory periods, starting from the date of submission of an application for the invalidity benefit until the date on which the pensioner would reach the retirement age specified for women – the target age of 67 years;

(f) reduction of the pension calculation basis by the amount equal to the gross amount of the previously collected pensions granted before a worker has reached the extended retirement age;

(g) waiver of the requirement to terminate employment upon establishment of the entitlement to pension for work in specific conditions or in specific nature;

(h) allowing voluntary payment of pension insurance contributions by all persons who do not meet the conditions for the mandatory insurance coverage.

The increase of the retirement age was justified by the process of ageing of the population, lower fertility rates, and at the same time an extended life expectancy of Poles. These processes were expected to deteriorate in the future the proportion between the social insurance contributors and persons in post-working age receiving pension benefits.

Following the change of the state authorities after the parliamentary and presidential elections in 2015, the new authorities found that the economic mechanisms which encourage the insured to remain longer in their employment, based on the formula of a defined, individual insurance contribution, applied for the calculation of pension, allow the insured who have reached the retirement age applicable before the date of entry into force of the act of 11 May 2012 (i.e., 1 January 2013) – it is 60 years for women and 65 years for men – to take an independent decision on cessation of their professional activity and on retirement. Considering the above, the current Polish authorities adopted an act of 16 November 2016 on the amendment of the act on old-age pensions and invalidity benefits paid from the Social Insurance Fund. The act fulfilled the promise made during the election campaign to restore the previous earlier retirement age – 60 years for women and 65 years for men.

30. During the first twenty-seven years of the Democratic period, the Polish social security system was in a peculiar state. Old regulations were being enforced in a new political, economic, and social environment. As far as social security regulations were concerned, Poland was committed to changing its social security laws drastically. An office responsible for reshaping Poland's social security regulations was created. There were signs that this office was working on the re-creation of the country's social security scheme based on three pillars: common (compulsory), group (voluntary), and individual (voluntary) insurance. Since the debate on changes in the country's social security system is a highly political issue, it was difficult to imagine that the new social security system could be introduced in this century. The impossible became possible and the system which was previously subject to minor amendments was now significantly changed. This brought forward the assumptions presented in the previous edition of the book that regardless of prospective changes, the current system will be effective for a period as long as the next twenty-five or thirty years. This is because the proposed changes will not affect people over 50 years of age. The changed pension scheme became applicable to persons above the age of 50 years as from 1 October 2017. The observation of the Polish political scene suggests that the opposition parties declare that after their victory in the next parliamentary election, the previous extended retirement age applicable in 2013–2017 will be restored in two and a half years. During the first twenty-seven years of Democratic Poland, the legal framework of the present social security system had been subject to minor changes. The social security system still relied heavily on the state, both in the way of financing the social security fund (input) and guaranteeing payment of social security benefit (output). This financial reliance on the state is the most significant headline of a major deficiency of the previous Polish social security system. Major changes of the system concerning increase as from 1 January 2013 of the retirement age up to 67 years and subsequent lowering of the age to 60 years for women and 65 years for men in 2016 were made during the last several years, following publication of the previous, second edition of the book. The present, third edition, presents not only the changes made in the acts amended by the act of 11 May 2012, in force from 1 January 2013, to the extent relating directly to the retirement age, but also the related amendments to the transitional provisions governing the factual situations which occurred in connection with the increase and equalization of the retirement age to 67 years for men and women and subsequent lowering of the retirement age to the previous level, that is 60 years for women and 65 years for men.

Following the publication of the second edition, certain changes were introduced in the Polish social insurance system as regards regulation of child benefits paid within the social insurance scheme under the act of 11 February 2016 on the state support in raising children (*Journal of Laws of 2016*, item 195) provided to families raising the second and each subsequent minor child at a fixed amount of PLN 500 (ca. EUR 120)[4] per child. The act entered into force on 1 March 2016. The first period for which the entitlement to the child benefit was fixed started upon entry into force of the above-mentioned act and ends on 30 September 2017. According to the commentators of the Polish internal policy, the announcement of introduction of the said benefit, fulfilled within a short period after the elections, significantly contributed to the change of authorities in Poland.

The current edition will also present changes restricting the functioning of OFE which were introduced in 2017 in the act of 28 August 1997 on the organization and functioning of pension funds (*Journal of Laws of 2017*, consolidated text, item 870) and in 2014 in the act of 21 November 2008 on funded pensions (*Journal of Laws of 2014*, item 1097), as well as in the act of 6 December 2013 on the amendment of certain acts in connection with setting out the rules for payment of pensions from the OFE (*Journal of Laws of 2013*, item 1717)).

II. Personal Scope of Application

31. As in other countries, the division in professional social security schemes was based upon the differences between the prospective beneficiaries.

Employees, within the meaning of the employee insurance scheme governed by the Law of 14 December 1982, are those who were bound to their employers by an individual contract of employment. This act also covered individuals not working, such as advocates in private practice, people working at home, people employed by state-owned enterprises under the civil type of contract, students of various types of schools (high schools, undergraduate, graduate, and postgraduate students of universities and other institutions of higher learning, for example, academies), and semi-professional sportsmen drawing so-called sportive stipends. Members of the families of the above-mentioned categories of beneficiaries were entitled to certain types of social security benefit.

In principle, benefits were awarded to those who perform work within the boundary of the Polish territory (Article 1). The social security legislation enacted on 29 December 1989 on employment altered this old-fashioned requirement. According to Chapter 6 of that act, any type of employment performed by a Polish citizen abroad under both international and individual agreements was considered as employment within Polish territory if the Polish enterprise responsible for carrying on contract paid social security dues and contributed to the Labour Fund on behalf of Poles employed outside Poland.

4. The currency rate for the Euro against the zloty is as at June 2017 rates.

The law provided that contribution to both the social security fund and the labour fund should equal the amounts of dues and contributions made by Polish employing employed Polish citizens within the boundary of Poland earning the average monthly salary. Only contributions to the Labour Fund on behalf of people working abroad were six times higher than dues paid on behalf of employed people in Poland (12% compared to 2%).

Those workers who decided to take employment abroad on their own were only entitled to employee insurance on the condition that they notified the local employment office in Poland of their employment and contributed to both the Labour Fund (12%) and the social security fund (order of the Minister of Labour and Social Policy of 1 March 1990). Again, the average monthly income in Poland served as a basis for setting up the level of dues and contributions.

A contract of employment was considered as a contract under which an employee performs work personally under the authority of an employer at the employer's risk in return for a wage.

Some other above-mentioned groups of people entitled to social insurance benefits were only submitted to a limited number of employee schemes. Semi-professional sportsmen and students were entitled to healthcare, disability, and unemployment benefits. Some people were excluded from unemployment benefits, such as those who refused to report to local employment offices, those who had within thirty-day periods turned down two consecutive job offers, and those who earned the right to other social security benefits.

As already mentioned, certain specific group of employees were completely excluded from the common employee insurance scheme. They were submitted to their own professional social security systems. It is necessary to point out that the common employee insurance system based on the Act of 14 December 1982 and separate professional insurance systems were related to that extent that in case a separate insurance system did not cover certain areas legal rules established by the common insurance system were applicable.

Under the sickness and maternity scheme for employees, the scope of insured people was extended to the immediate members of family of self-employed people employed by them on a contract basis, but only if the contract-employed immediate members of self-employed people lived in the same household with the self-employed family members employing them and only if their employment was reported to a social security agency before sickness or pregnancy occurred.

Employees who were employed on a full-time basis who were covered by insurance schemes provided by the sickness and maternity scheme drew family allowances, with the exception of women and disabled people working at least 50% of the regular working time, which was – according to the Labour Code – a time up to the maximum eight hours a day and forty-two hours per week. If labour regulations did not provide for a certain number of working hours, work was considered full-time employment if workers' salary equalled at least the minimum monthly salary earned in Poland. Individual farmers and members of their family covered by a farmers' insurance scheme were entitled to family allowances governed by the Decree of the Council of Ministers of 9 May 1986 amended on 19 June 1990 if they were not entitled to family benefits out of a different social security scheme (e.g., an employee scheme).

The second vital requirement was low income per capita in a farmer's family. Strangely enough, 'low income' was considered any amount of monies lower than 100% of the average yearly income of a private farmer.

Those who were unemployed within the period of twelve months after graduation from vocational school, high school, or any institution of higher learning (university, polytechnic, etc.) at one time had been eligible for unemployment benefits as young graduates regardless of their age and family status. The level of unemployment benefit depended on the level of education and length of unemployment. A university graduate, for example, was entitled to 200% of minimum wage for the first three months of joblessness; 150% for an additional six months, and 100% after ninth months of unemployment. Graduates of vocational school earned 150% for the first three months and after that period was entitled only to benefit equal to 100% of minimum wages.

Unemployed people drawing old-age pensions, as well as those who owned farms or were engaged in any type of business activity, were not allowed to accumulate unemployment benefit: In order to fight unemployment, employment training was provided by local employment offices. Those unemployed people who decided to participate in such ventures were entitled to vocational benefit equal to 80% of their previous earnings for a period of six months. This period was extended to twelve months. People unemployed because of work injury or occupational disease were entitled to vocational benefit equal to 100% of their former salary. Unemployed graduates could get vocational benefit equal to 125% of the minimum wage. The law provided that vocational benefit could not be lower than 40% of the minimum monthly salary. Benefit was indexed to average national monthly wage and raised with wage increases. Unemployed people drawing vocational benefit were entitled to (as employed people were entitled to) a family allowance.

The Act of 14 December 1994 has changed the policy towards unemployed graduates. They had been treated in the same way as other unemployed people unless they were directed for special training designed to help unemployed people to find employment. During that training period, they were entitled to 1/40 unemployment benefit for each day of such training.

Every natural person who carried out an industrious activity in Poland at his/her own risk and was not bound by an individual contract of employment was considered self-employed. Such people were covered by the social insurance scheme developed by the Law of 18 December 1976 as amended on 15 July 1989. This piece of law covered heterogeneous groups of people. The scope of this group was defined by the meaning of 'industrious activity' (działalnosç gospodarcza). It covered people engaged in construction, small industry, and commerce. This insurance scheme also covered people who collaborated on a professional basis with self-employed people if they were family members of an insured self-employed person or were members of his/her household. According to the law, both self-employed and collaborators were covered by the insurance scheme if they were employed on the basis of a contract of employment on a full-time basis or were working part-time spending on the job more than 50% of scheduled working time. Those who were covered by separate social security schemes were not entitled to sign up for an additional self-employed insurance scheme even if they were self-employed full-time. Those who qualified for social benefits under the separate social security scheme could be covered by insurance scheme for self-employed only on request.

The following categories of self-employed, taking into account the nature of their activity, were excluded from the insurance scheme for self-employed:

- artisans;
- writers;
- advocates;
- clergy.

The sickness and invalidity insurance schemes provided benefits in money and kind (Medicare, drugs, etc.) for the beneficiary himself/herself and members of his/her family who were dependent on the beneficiary. The category of dependent persons consisted of spouses and minor children. Childcare leave benefit served its purpose by enabling working women (or men with the previous consent of the child's mother) to take personal care of a small child (up to four years). It extended leave of absence from work up to three years. A short leave of absence could be taken by one parent in case of emergency (unexpected, temporary close down of kindergarten) or in case of sickness of a child not older than 14 years of age.

It should be mentioned that in the case of sickness of a member of the beneficiary's family, a short leave of absence (up to fourteen days per year) could be taken. The Law of 17 December 1974 did not specify the relationship between the next of kin. So, short-term leave benefit could be taken in the case of illness of ascendants (parents or other older family members) of the beneficiary.

Income maintenance was payable to employees who were transferred to another type of work due to their difficulties in adjusting to working conditions that could, according to the best knowledge of a medical examiner, cause occupational disease. The beneficiary was then entitled to benefit, which compensated for a decline in wages for a period of at least three months. This benefit could be extended to six months. Income maintenance was also paid to formerly unemployed workers who after a period of vocational training accepted a new assignment and whose earning capacity was therefore reduced. The maximum period of eligibility for such benefits extended to three months. This benefit equalled the difference in wages between the new and old assignment. Every Pole entitled to old-age pension or disability benefit who resided in Poland had a legal guarantee of minimum social benefits that equalled: 35% of average monthly salary (for the beneficiary drawing old-pension benefit or disability benefit classified in group I or II). The beneficiary of III group was entitled to benefit equal to 35% monthly salary only when they reached a certain age: 55 years of age for women, 60 years of age for men. The minimum social benefit was equal to 27% of the average monthly salary that was guaranteed to disabled people classified as the group III of disability younger than age 55 (women) and age 60 (men).

Anyone in need could apply for the social assistance that the public centres of social help provided under the law of social help.

III. Risks and Benefits

32. The level of social security benefit in Poland was linked to the index of average monthly wages on the national scale. The social security law set up an entire system of valorization of social benefits. The primary task of this measure was to catch up with growing wages. It was done by raising the economic base for social benefits and multiplying it by an indicator of valorization. The valorization indicator was reached by dividing foreseen quarterly income and income that in the past served as the base for the last valorization.

A. Old-Age

33. Under the social insurance schemes for employees and self-employed persons, old-age benefit (retirement pension) was payable to insured people who had attained a certain age. The pensionable age was 60 years of age for female employees and self-employed women and 65 years of age for male employees and self-employed males. The second important condition for retirement benefit was the length of employment. It is necessary that the male employee was employed for twenty-five years; women employees for twenty years. To the period of employment could be added: a specific period of time spent by an employee at schools, raising children, serving in the army during Second World War, and serving sentences in prison as a retaliation for the fight for freedoms and liberties. The third condition was the relationship between those above-mentioned factors. The retirement age should be reached within the period of employment or the following consecutive years.

Under certain conditions, for example, due to redundancy, it was possible to take early retirement after thirty-five years (women) or forty years (men) following the period of employment. A reduced retirement pension could be drawn by an employee who took early retirement after twenty years (women) and twenty-five years (men) of service under the condition that within five years after the decision concerning early retirement was made, a beneficiary reached the necessary retirement age. The retirement pension was cut by 3.5% of its base for each year of the remaining five years.

The retirement pension of an employee and self-employed person was counted according to the formula specified in the Law of 14 December 1982. It contained 100% of the first 3,000 (after denomination 300) PLN = EUR 71.43 and 55% of the remaining amount of wages earned during the last working quarter of a year or the consecutive three years chosen by the beneficiary out of the last twelve years of employment.

B. Death

34. The spouse, children, and parents of a deceased employee or injured and deceased self-employed person were entitled to a widow(er)'s pension. The formula for accounting the level of this benefit was exactly the same as the formula for calculating retirement pension benefit. The spouse was entitled to benefit, subject that she (widow) is over 50 years of age (women) or 65 years of age (men) or was disabled or was bringing up at least one child, grandchild, or brother or sister of the deceased employee not older than 16 years of age (if one of the previously mentioned people was continuing education, the age limit is higher – 18 years of age). There was no age limit in case of taking care of a disabled child entitled to disability benefit placed in the I or II group of disabled persons. If the conditions for a widow's pension were not satisfied, the pension continued to be paid for one year from the day of the death of her husband. If she decided to take up vocational training necessary for acquiring new qualifications, she was entitled to draw pension for two years. A so-called pseudo widow was entitled to pension benefits if she was eligible for benefits on regular grants and was entitled to alimony decided by the family court.

The natural and adopted children of a deceased employee were entitled to pension until 16 years of age or, if they continued education, until 25 years of age. Disabled children qualified as invalids of the I or II group and were entitled to a pension as long as they lived. Grandchildren, brothers, and sisters, and other children had a right to pension benefits if they were generally qualified and were supported by the deceased employee for at least a period of one year before his/her death, did not earn the rights to pension from another source (e.g., after their parents) or their parents were not able to support them, or if the deceased person was established as a child's guardian.

Parents were entitled to a pension if the deceased employee had supported them directly (the Law of 14 December 1982 did not state for how long) and if they met the requirement set up by the law for widow(er)s and were at least 65 years of age.

On the death of an employee due to industrial injury or occupational disease, higher benefits were provided. Benefits were calculated as a percentage of the base for counting social security benefits. The amount depended on the number of people entitled to pension benefits: one person was entitled to 70%; two people were entitled to 75%; and three people were entitled to 85%.

C. Incapacity for Work

35. The sickness and invalidity insurance scheme guarantees benefits to employees who were incapable to work and who had not reached the pensionable age on the condition that he/she had ceased all professional activities due to disease or an injury that was recognized as such by a specially appointed medical committee. Sickness benefit did not depend on the degree of the employee's incapacity for work. Its length directly related to the kind of disease. Regardless of the benefit amount, this benefit could not be prolonged more than twelve months. If beneficiary's state of health gradually improved, he/she was entitled to rehabilitation benefit for another twelve months. After that period, an employee was entitled to a disability pension. There are three different categories of invalid. The amount of disability benefit paid depended on a decrease in the earning capacity of the beneficiary and his/her health. The formula for counting disability benefit was the same as that used to estimate old-age pension.

The sickness and invalidity insurance scheme for self-employed people was nearly the same as that for employees. It differed only in the number of categories, instead of three there were only two categories (I and II). An invalid of the III group who was self-employed was not entitled to any benefit at all.

If the incapacity for work of an employee was due to industrial injury or occupational disease, he/she received more favourable benefit than his/her counterpart who was unable to work due to health conditions. Industrial injury benefit equalled

100% of the base on which any benefit was counted in the case of disability qualified as group I or II. A person described as an industrial invalid of the III group was entitled to 75% of previous monthly wages (assuming that all his salary was qualified as a base for benefit).

D. Unemployment

36. Unemployment benefit was only provided for a previously employed person willing to continue employment and for unemployed graduates. In order to be entitled to unemployment benefit, the employee had to have difficulties in finding a job, be willing to take a professional assignment on the basis of an individual contract of employment, and registered himself/herself in a local employment office. As already mentioned, the eligibility for unemployment benefit of recent graduates was also recognized by the Law of 28 December 1989. This law provided vocational and unemployment benefits for those employees who lost their jobs for any reason. Vocational benefit was paid to all unemployed individuals who were willing to take vocational training up to six (or twelve months) organized by the state employment agency. The amount of monthly vocational benefit was related to the event that caused the unemployment. The law set up a minimum level of vocational benefit. It flatly stated that such benefit cannot be lower than 40% of the average monthly salary. The Act of 14 December 1994 continued to regulate vocational benefit for unemployed people. Vocational benefit was as high as 115% of unemployment benefit.

Vocational and unemployment benefits were paid out of the Labour Fund. An unemployed person was entitled to draw unemployment benefit from the Labour Fund seven days after he/she is declared as unemployed and registered at a local employment office. Before the state employment agency decided to put such a person on the Labour Fund payroll, it was obliged to check first of all for the opportunities to schedule vocational training or to work out opportunities to arrange for an unemployed person some kind of government-subsidized type of employment. Unemployment benefit was paid only if the above-mentioned arrangements did not work out. As already mentioned, the level of unemployment benefit depended on the length of joblessness. Unemployment benefit was either matched to the worker's previous monthly wages or – in the case of a recent graduate – to a national minimum salary.

Where a person drawing unemployment benefit was partially employed or engaged in any professional activity that enabled him/her to draw a monthly wage not higher than the established national minimum salary, the unemployment benefit was cut by 50%. Needless to say, a partially employed or self-employed person earning more than a minimum wage was not entitled to draw unemployment benefit from the Labour Fund.

According to the Polish social law, a worker's rights and privileges were based on their length of service. For that reason, the law on unemployment benefits provided that the time in which an unemployed person drew unemployment benefit, for a period of up to twenty-four months, was included in the period of employment time for the sake of continuity of the total length of service. This practice held true based on the condition that the unemployed person took a job within one month from the day he/

she finished a vocational training or on the condition that they accepted a job offer within twelve months from the day that the unemployment benefit was granted.

E. Medical Care

37. Medical services were free of charge for insured employees, self-employed people, and people dependent upon them (members of their families). However, these groups of people were obliged to pay for drugs and other medicinal therapies at a reduced cost.

F. Family

38. Family allowance was payable in respect of the claimant's own children, children of their spouse, adopted children, or children placed by family courts into the claimant's custody. Family allowance was also payable in respect of the claimant's grandchildren and his/her brothers and sisters whom claimant' started to take care of before their maturity. An important condition was the legal and social status of the last category of persons. They should be considered orphans or people in need.

Normally, family allowance was payable up to 16 years of age of a minor child studying in school, with this period extended to 25 years of age in the case of a student. If a beneficiary was 25 years old and graduated within a year, he/she was entitled to family allowance for another year. Handicapped children or children incapable of work who were awarded the I or II group of disability were entitled to child allowance indefinitely.

Family allowances included only a normal and special child allowance. There was a flat rate for every able person for whom family allowance was paid. Children of a less able-bodied claimant, as well as spouses who were over 75 years of age, were entitled to special family allowance.

Maternity benefits were covered by the Law of 17 December 1974 on maternity and sickness benefits. The professional family allowance schemes for self-employed people were identical to the scheme set up for employees. As a matter of fact, the law on the social security system of self-employed people of 18 December 1976 clearly provided that the ordinance issued by the Minister of Labour and Social Policy of 10 April 1989 concerning child allowance for employees and members of their families should be directly applied to self-employed people.

G. Need

39. Those employees, as well as other people covered by the social security scheme set up for an employee's purposes, were entitled if they were not eligible for benefits provided under the Law of 14 December 1982 to apply to the President of Social Security Agency for appropriate benefits provided by the employee's social security scheme.

The Law of 14 December 1982 set up certain conditions on which an application was made. They were as follows: if an applicant could not, due to his/her age or state of health, accept an employment offer, or he/she did not have any financial means to support himself/herself.

On the grounds of the social help law, every person had the right to the social assistance necessary for him/her to lead a life according to basic human needs. The administrative bodies were free to decide who qualifies for a social grant; however, its judgment was subject to control by an administrative court on the grounds of its legality.

IV. Adjudication

40. Disputes between insured employees or self-employed people and the state security agency were in the first instance referred to the boards of overseers of local security agencies. Despite the constitutional declaration according to which justice should be served in the courts of law only in Poland, social security cases were tried still in contradiction to the Roman law principle *nemo iudex in sua causa*. At the higher level, appeals against an administrative decision made by boards of overseers were referred to the district social security courts.

Some cases were brought up by appeal of the Minister of Justice, Minister of Labour and Social Policy, First President of the Supreme Court, Ombudsman, Central Office of the nationally recognized labour union, such as, for example, Solidarnosc or All National Alliance of Trade Unions (ANATU) – OPZZ to the Administrative, Labour, Social Security, and Public Affairs Chamber of the Supreme Court.

The social security courts were fully autonomous legal institutions integrated within the judiciary. They did not deal with any other type of case other than social security cases defined in Article 476, section 2 of the Code of Civil Procedure of 17 November 1964 as amended. They were composed of one professional judge who was appointed until he/she reached retirement age and of two lay judges.

The application of law by the social security courts was similar to that of civil courts, although less formal, and the principles of the civil procedure were applied. Like the civil court, the social security court was entitled to hear the opinion of any type of expert witness. Since most of the social security cases involve some arguments related to the state of health of the beneficiary, the social security courts have a list of medical experts.

The decision made by the social security court was final and binding to the parties since the district social security court was acting in the capacity of an appellate court. Extraordinary measures were taken when the central organs mentioned above decided that the case must be tried by the Supreme Court. Only a few legal matters dealing with social security fell outside the jurisdiction of the social security courts. The Constitutional Tribunal was empowered to examine all social security laws and decided upon a request submitted by the proper authority whether or not certain acts complied with the principles declared in the constitution. The civil courts were competent to solve legal disputes concerning the damages of the insured person caused by employers neglecting his/her duties defined by the Law of 14 December 1982 as well as claims brought by social security against beneficiaries who refused to pay back improperly delivered social benefits. The litigation cost in the social security court was borne by the state.

V. Labour Agreements

41. Despite the fact that in Poland social security law was treated as, and, in fact, still is treated as a branch of labour law, the Polish social security law was never regulated by collective agreements. Collective bargaining served as an important indicator of the freedom of social partners to create their legal obligations free from the interference of the state. There were no legal obstacles whatsoever to regulate social security matters by negotiating collective agreements. The statutory regulation on collective agreement, the Act of 29 September 1994, which amended Chapter XI of the Labour Code, did not list social security matters along with other matters that could not be regulated by social partners during collective bargaining. Article 240 §3 of the Labour Code listed five items that cannot be regulated by collective agreements. Those items included legal protection against termination of an employment contract by the employer, legal claims in case of unjustified or illegal dismissal, disciplinary proceedings, maternity and parental leaves of absence, and legal protection of wages. Of note is that those items did not include questions regulated by the law of social security. Therefore, social partners were free to negotiate social security matters, or at least that was the theory. In practice, none of the recently concluded collective agreements dealt with social security issues. The social security area was an exclusive domain of the state.

Chapter 7. Sources of Contemporary Social Security Law

§1. General

42. The structure of contemporary social security legal sources has been undergoing important changes at the end of the twentieth century and the beginning of the twenty-first century. Demographic factors such as increasing longevity of individuals covered by social security schemes and decreasing fertility rate were the major reasons for changes made in organization and financing of the national social security schemes. The Polish national social security scheme only partially depends on the solidarity principle among various generations of beneficiaries. Under the previous system, completely based on the principle of 'pay-as-you-go', a generation of active insured individuals contributed to the system out of which social security benefits were paid to those insured who were no longer able to carry on with their professional activities. The new open social security system, which came into force on the 28 August 1997 by the Organization and Functioning of Retirement Funds Act (*Journal of Laws of 1997*, No. 159, item 667 as amended), differentiated between those who are entitled to retirement benefits. The elderly insured – that is, those who were born before 1 January 1949 and who were 50 years old or older on the day the retirement amendments were made – are entitled to retirement benefits based on the existing retirement regulations. Those who were born after 31 December 1948 and who did not turn 50 on the day the above-mentioned amendments were made would have their level of retirement benefits determined upon the amount of funds collected within their individual Social Security Office (ZUS) accounts in conjunction with the open social security fund account opened by the insured. The contemporary Polish social security system is based on the division of contributory and non-contributory social benefits. Only the contributory ones are covered by the national social security scheme. The second important feature of the current social security system in Poland is the division between social security benefits paid in cash and social services delivered in kind. As a result of that distinction, healthcare services are treated separately by the national legislator. The third important change that was introduced into the national system of social security is the financial and organizational distinction between three types social security: in case of retirement, invalidity, and industrial injury. Various funds out of which social security benefits are paid are based on the strict relationship between social security dues and prospective benefits. The national system of social security is divided between three categories of benefits paid in case of incapacity to work due to old-age and invalidity: one time; short-term; long-term. At the present time, three different systems of an old-age benefit exist: the previous one based on the Act of 14 December 1982 as amended. That system is applied to those insured who were born before 1 January 1949. Those insured individuals who were born after 31 December 1948 and before 1 January 1969 may choose between old and new insurance systems: the new one based on the Act of 17 December 1998 and the old one which is to be enforced for at least fifteen to twenty years. Those who were born after 31

December 1968 are completely covered by the new social security scheme. Therefore, it is necessary to provide information on two systems of social security (old and new) that are enforced at the same time in Poland. Those two different social security systems have one thing in common: an obligatory coverage within the limits of the first pillar. An important distinction between the compulsory and mandatory system of coverage available with the various social security schemes also should be mentioned. Those insured individuals covered by the new system of social security scheme paid in case of retirement must take part in the so-called second pillar of social security. Other members of the society may participate in that part of the social security scheme on a voluntary basis. All of them are free to decide whether or not they participate in the various legal forms of other social security activities, such as employee programmes established by their employers or individual insurance. These additional methods of social security coverage are listed under the common title: third pillar social security schemes.

§2. Legislation

43. The Polish system of social security is based on statutory acts. The basic statutory act is the Law of 13 October 1998 on the social security scheme. In Article 1, the act defines the notion of the 'social security scheme'. It embraces old-age pensions, invalidity benefits, sickness and maternity allowances, industrial accidents, and occupational diseases. Old-age pensions are based on three pillars that are regulated by the following statutory acts: the Act of 22 August 1997 on employees retirement programmes (*Journal of Laws of 1997*, No. 139, item 932 as amended); the Act of 28 August 1997 on organization and functions of retirement funds (*Journal of Laws of 1997*, No. 139, item 934 as amended); and section II of the Act of 17 December 1998 on pensions and invalidity benefits (*Journal of Laws of 1998*, No. 162, item 1118 as amended). The Act of 25 March 2011 on the amendments to certain acts connected with functioning of the social security system regulated the relations between two mandatory pillars of retirement insurance (pay-as-you-go and funded schemes). It allowed to transfer liabilities and contributions from one pillar to another without causing threat to the balance of the diversified insurance scheme. Another major amendment in the social security system gradually introducing uniform retirement age of 67 for both men and women was introduced by the Act of 11 May 2012 on the amendment to the act on retirement and disability pensions from the Social Insurance Fund and certain other acts (*Journal of Laws of 2012*, item 637 – the internet system of legislation) section III of the Act of 17 December 1998 on pensions and invalidity benefits covers invalidity benefits. Sickness and maternity allowance are regulated by the Act of 25 June 1999 on the cash benefits in case of illness and maternity – the unified version is published in *Journal of Laws of 2005*, No. 31, item 267. Family allowances are regulated by the Act of 28 November 2003 (*Journal of Laws of 2003*, No. 228, item 2255 as amended). Maternity leaves (full-time, additional or parental) were unified for working men and women irrespective of the legal basis of employment or the legal nature of employment (contractual obligation or service relationship) by the Act of 28 May 2013 on the amendment to the act – Labour Code and the amendment to certain acts (*Journal of Laws of 2013*, item 675).

Industrial accidents and occupational injuries were regulated by two statutory acts issued on the same day – 30 October 2002: the Act on Social Security in Case of Industrial Injury and Occupational Diseases (*Journal of Laws of 2002*, No. 199, item 1673 as amended) and the Act on Social Protection in Case of Injuries and Occupational Diseases (*Journal of Laws of 2002*, No. 19, item 1674 as amended). The Act of 17 December 1998 covers neither health nor unemployment insurance. It also does not cover social assistance. Technically, healthcare and unemployment covered by the first edition of the volume on social security in Poland (Kluwer 1997) should not contain any remarks on legal foundations of the contemporary Polish system of health and unemployment insurance. For the reason that all volumes related to the national social security systems must be written along the same lines in order to enable readers to compare different legal systems, in the current edition basic remarks on health and unemployment insurance are included.

The main statutory regulation concerning healthcare is the Act of 23 January 2003 on Common Insurance in the National Health Fund (*Journal of Laws of 2003*, No. 137, item 887). An unemployment insurance is regulated by the Act on Promotion of Employment and Institutions of Labour Market of 20 April 2004 (*Journal of Laws of 2004*, No. 99, item 1001).

The most important feature of the present national system of social security in Poland is a broad coverage of insured members of the population. In Article 6, section 1 of the Act of 13 October 1998, there is a list that contains twenty-one social groups covered by the national social security scheme. Among those categories are both employees, wage earners, self-employed workers, civil servants, military and paramilitary personnel, clergymen, professional politicians, convicts, and recipients of social assistance. At present, the national social security system is no longer based on the relationship regulated by the individual labour law. Social security law, which was and to a great extent still is related to labour law, becomes associated with other branches of insurance regulations: personal and commercial. Owing to five habilitations in 2012 in the field of legal science based on monographs on social security law from the universities of Białystok, Gdańsk, Poznań, and Wrocław, social security law is taught in almost half of the public law faculties in Poland.

§3. Adjudication

44. Social security cases are being adjudicated by the social security agencies according to the legal procedure regulated by the Code of Administrative Procedures. Those agencies issue administrative decisions. Those decisions may be challenged by insured people in the labour and social security courts. The lowest labour and social security courts – the district labour and social security courts – adjudicate cases concerning the following benefits: sickness, maternity, family, and death, as well as compensation for industrial injuries and occupational diseases. The other cases related to matters of social security are adjudicated by the district courts. The district courts act in capacity of appellate courts for social security cases adjudicated by district courts. Appeal in social security cases tried in the first instance by the regional courts are treated by the appellate courts. Extraordinary control of the appellate court order is performed by the Supreme Court. Cassation (skarga kasacyjna) may be brought in social security matters only in cases in which the value exceeds PLN 10,000 = EUR 2,380. An important exception from this rigid rule is applied in cases related to old-age pensions and invalidity benefits and social security coverage (Article 398^2, paragraph 1 of the Code of Civil Procedure).

§4. Labour Agreements

45. The Labour Code does not allow social partners to conclude agreements concerning social security matters in those areas that are regulated by state acts (Article 240, paragraph 2). Argumentation *a contrario* helps to reach conclusion that under the above-mentioned provision of the Labour Code, there is no obstacle to conclude collective agreement, which contains stipulations concerning mandatory and complementary social security benefits. Social partners, though, do not take advantage of the above-mentioned provision.

Part I. The Institutions

Chapter 1. Public Institutions

§1. Ministerial Departments

46. The Minister of Labour and Social Policy takes responsibility for organization and functions performed by the State Social Security Agency. The sole responsibility for the health insurance is subject to the competence of the Ministry of Health. Under the supervision of that minister, the National Fund for Protection of Health is managed. The Minister of Labour and Social Policy is responsible for the unemployment insurance. This insurance is run by the Fund of Labour (Fundusz Pracy). The Act of 13 October 1998 states that the state departments responsible for the administration of social security benefits are: (a) the social security agency (ZUS); (b) the Old-age pensions' society; (c) the Old-Age pension society. The ZUS undertakes decisions concerning retirement premiums and benefits associated with open retirement funds, known as 'capital fund retirements'.

Due to the idea of unification of various social security schemes, the Act of 13 October 1998 was passed on the legal and administration status of the State Social Security Agency (ZUS). This state-owned institution manages the obligatory social security schemes. It contains a headquarters office situated in Warsaw and branch offices around Poland. It is controlled by the Minister of Labour and Social Policy. That Minister decides on the matter of organizational structure of State Social Security Agency, its scope of power, and its working methods. According to the regulation on the social security agency, the State Social Security Agency must be an independent administrative body within the government. It must enjoy legal entity. Thus, the social security agency participates in legal disputes as an independent governmental institution. Having been awarded independence from the central government, the State Social Security Agency could act as an owner towards any property that so far is under its administration only.

§2. Public Institutions

47. All branches of the Polish social security system are under the administrative supervision of the State Social Security Agency (Zakład Ubezpieczeń Społecznych

– ZUS). The State Social Security Agency is the public institution that performs the task to collect social security dues and to allocate the funds between various social security funds. Its branch offices are responsible for issuing decisions concerning old-age pension and invalidity benefits. The State Social Security Agency is run by a board. It is composed of two to four members. They are elected by the Boards of Overseers. That board is composed of fifteen members. Five of its members should represent insured people. Five members must represent employers, and five of the board members will act as representatives of the state government. Members of the board are elected by trade union organizations (members representing the interests of insured people) and employers confederations (those who sit on the board as employers representatives), and are appointed by the prime minister (members representing the government) to a five-year term.

The state security agency is run on a day-to-day basis by its director general. Within the director's scope of power are laid down the following prerogatives: hiring and firing his deputies, head of the medical examiners, branch directors, as well as director of the foreign branch of social security benefits. The director general is appointed to his position by the prime minister. Only the minister of social policy is entitled to submit a motion for the above-mentioned nomination.

Chapter 2. Position and Competence of the Public Institutions

48. The State Social Security Agency is responsible for the administration of social security benefits coming out of different schemes. In particular, the State Social Security Agency will be empowered to:

(a) declare the duty to insure;
(b) make a judgment whether or not insured individuals are able to keep working or whether they are eligible for disability benefits;
(c) collect social security dues and run different social security funds;
(d) oversee any other institutions, both state-owned or private in any matter related to the above-mentioned activity connected with the social security benefit.

The social security agency will be responsible as an exclusive agent to run the state's social security schemes. According to the provision of Article 2, section 4 of the law on the State Social Security Agency, the agency is also empowered to manage any additional social security scheme. It is interpreted as an indicator that in the supplementary, private social insurance schemes introduced by any private parties (e.g., social partners) are trusted to run as their agent by the state social security administration.

The most important purpose of activity of the State Social Security Agency is management of the general social security fund. The fund is raised from the contributions from social security dues, grant-in-aid from the governmental treasury office, and income from any industrious activity of the State Social Security Agency. Out of the social security fund, social security benefits are paid together with the other expenditure of the social security agency. Within the social security fund, five separate funds are created from which separate social insurance schemes are covered. These five funds are:

(1) retirement fund;
(2) disability pension fund;
(3) sickness, birth, and death benefits fund;
(4) industrial injury and occupational accidents benefit fund;
(5) reserve demographic fund.

Acting as an independent governmental agency, the social security agency is overseen by the minister of labour and social policy. The minister is allowed to control the social security agency and conduct a survey as to whether or not its activity is being handled properly, both from the point of view of social security laws and social policy directives. Any administrative decision taken by the social security agency contrary to the rules of the social security law is declared by the law to be null and void. The statement of the minister of labour and social policy taken within thirty days from the day the decision is published declares voidance of such decision. Within the next thirty days, the latter decision taken by the minister of labour and social policy could be appealed by an interested party (the beneficiary on behalf of which a decision was taken is not allowed to take legal action because the Superior Administrative Court does not review individual cases in social security matters) to the Administrative Court. Either the board or the general director of the social security agency is empowered to take similar legal action on behalf of the agency.

Chapter 3. Private Institutions

49. Social security ceased to be an exclusive domain of the state. Private institutions play a bigger role in managing social security. There are mutual funds run by private insurance companies active in social insurance. The legal basis for the retirement societies (Towarzystwa Emerytalne) and private retirement institutions (zakłady emerytalne) is the Act of 28 August 1997 on organization and functioning of retirement funds (*Journal of Laws of 1997*, No. 139, item 934 as amended). The retirement societies are organized in the legal form of stock companies. Their only and exclusive activity is to collect and allocate cash for payment to the members of the fund of their pension after they have reached the retirement age. The pension funds are liable to the members of the fund for damage caused as a result of non-performance or improper performance of the obligations relating to the management and representation of the fund. They set up retirement funds, administer them, and represent those funds in any relations with the third parties. Private retirement institutions are also organized as stock companies with the legal duty to provide services to those individuals who are willing to contribute in additional social security dues to the voluntary system of old-age pension. Private social security institutions are controlled by the State Commission established in 2002 with the exclusive duty to protect legal and economic interests of insured individuals taking part in the second and third pillars of the national retirement scheme. This Commission also controls the process of managing the private social security funds by the private insurance companies. Since those funds are deposited in the banks, one of the major duties of the Commission is to cooperate with the National Central Bank, which exercises the state control over other banks (public and private).

50. The funded retirement system has been systematically modified since its beginning. The legislature made some changes in the organization and functioning of the OFE (the act of 26 June 2009, *Journal of Laws No. 127*, item 1048); it restricted the entitlement of the pension funds to operate an acquisition activity, it reduced the amount of social insurance contributions transferred to the OFE, it transferred a part of the pension entitlements of the insured from OFE to ZUS (the act of 25 March 2011, *Journal of Laws* No. 75, item 398), in order to finally, under an act of 6 December 2013 (which entered into force on 1 February 2014) on the amendment of certain acts in connection with setting out the rules for payment of pensions from the OFE (*Journal of Laws*, item 1717): (1) transfer to ZUS the bond assets of OFE; (2) introduce a voluntary participation in OFE; (3) reduce an insurance contribution in OFE to 2.92%; (4) introduce a ban on investment by OFE into Treasury bonds, other Treasury securities and financial instruments guaranteed by the Treasury; (5) activate OFE to implement less conservative investments policy; (6) reduce the maximum amount of a contribution fee to 1.75%; (7) lay down the rules for payment of pension benefits from the resources deposited in the OFE accounts. The act of 6 December 2013 introduced a minimum level of OFE investments in shares. It amounted to 75% by the end of 2014, 55% by the end of 2015, 35% by the end of 2016, and 15% by the end of 2017. In accordance with the procedure laid down in that act and in a regulation of the Council of Ministers of 21 January 2014 on the transfer of assets by the OFE to the Social Insurance

Institution (ZUS) (*Journal of Laws*, item 117) on 3 February 2014 the assets exceeding in total PLN 153.15 billion (EUR 36.64 billion) were transferred from OFEs to ZUS. The treasury bonds with a value of PLN 134.08 billion (EUR 32 billion) were offered for acquisition to the Ministry of Finance of the Republic of Poland in exchange for the guarantees of payment from the Social Insurance Fund of pension benefits corresponding to the value of the assets recorded in the ZUS sub-accounts. ZUS recorded on the sub-accounts the value of the funds corresponding to the value of the accounting units redeemed by OFE on 31 December 2015. Another regulation of the Council of Ministers of the same date laid down the information obligations of the OFE towards the insured and state institutions (*Journal of Laws of 2014*, item 142). Members of OFE again may decide whether their contributions transferred to OFE through ZUS should still be used to finance the funded pensions. They could decide for the first time in a period from 1 April until 31 July 2014 during a so-called transfer window. Since 2016 the possibility of an insured to decide whether to stay in OFE or transfer to ZUS will be open every four years. The contributions which have so far been collected in OFE, except for those redeemed on 3 February 2014 at 51.5%, will remain in OFE until an insured reaches the age of 10 years below the (normal) retirement age. From that moment ZUS will start a gradual withdrawal of contributions from OFE. The act of 6 December 2012 introduced the concept of a so-called security zipper mechanism. In order to guarantee safety and protection of funds accumulated in OFE, a mechanism was introduced which consists in gradual, starting ten years before the retirement age, withdrawal of capital accumulated in the accounts of pension funds members. New contributions are not transferred to the OFE fund but are registered on individual accounts of persons insured with ZUS. The first 'security zipper' started its operation on 31 October 2014. The dates, methods, and procedure for the transfer of funds accumulated in an account of an OFE member to the Social Insurance Pension Fund operated by ZUS are laid down in a regulation of the Council of Ministers of 1 October 2014 (*Journal of Laws*, item 1418). According to this regulation, by the 10th calendar day of each month ZUS should inform OFE of its members who reached or will reach during the month concerned the age of 10 years below of the retirement age. On the fifth working day of the successive month OFE will redeem the accounting units which are subject to transfer to ZUS. Within two working days from the date of redemption, OFE will transfer to a bank account indicated by ZUS the resources accumulated in the account of OFE member, corresponding to the value of redeemed accounting units.

51. The amendments made by the act of 6 December 2013 also apply to fees borne by the OFE members and a rate of return of insurance contributions. OFEs may collect fees in a form of deduction of not more than 1.75% of the amount of contributions paid by the insured. OFEs lost their entitlement to collect the minimum required rate of return and – in a period from 1 July 2014 until 30 June 2016 the Polish Financial Supervision Authority (KNF) was obligated to fix a periodic rate of return on each day of assessment of the value of the accounting units and is obliged to inform both the KNF and the general public.

52. Apart from the private social security institutions, there are also other private insurance companies that provide an additional guarantee to insured groups of individuals benefits in case of sudden accidents (nieszczesliwych wypadków – NW). Because employers use those funds to cover risks that might occur among workers and members of their immediate families, their personal insurance became a supplementary type of insurance to the compulsory social security schemes.

Private insurance institutions such as Warta, Commercial Union, Nationale Nederlanden, Poland, and others run their businesses on behalf of the statutory regulation, an Act of 28 July 1990 on insurance activities. This act does not distinguish between commercial and personal insurance. Polish employers are under legal obligation to enter into insurance contracts in case of industrial injuries while employing foreign employees in Poland, and posting Polish employees abroad. Employers are free to enter into insurance contracts on behalf of individuals performing work under the civil type of contracts other than a contract of employment. Decree of the Council of Ministers of 18 August 1976 (*Journal of Laws*, No. 29, item 172) regulates all legal details of additional insurance coverage mentioned above.

Open Retirement Funds gather and manage funds accumulated from insurance premiums. The above funds are managed by the General Retirement Associations, legally formed as joint stock companies. The rights to create such open retirement funds are granted by the Polish Financial Supervision Authority. The task of these funds is to manage individual retirement accounts of the insured persons as well as to pass on to the Social Security Office (ZUS) funds for retirement payments.

The ZUS is solely authorized to hand down decisions in such matters of premiums and benefits stemming from social insurance sources. Open Retirement Funds have a legal entity the moment they are entered into the retirement funds register and are then bound by the social security insurance laws. The National Depository for Securities monitors the money transfer of benefits between open retirement funds.

53. From the perspective of 2013, it should be stated that the reform of the social security system of the 1990s was only partially successful. The most spectacular example for the aging of the society is the relation between the number of contribution payers and the number of pensioners. Demographical aspects caused the change where two payers who contributed for one retirement benefit before 1999 had to be replaced by four payers from then on. All the above made the Polish government support the new funded pension scheme very actively. As I have already mentioned, in the pay-as-you-go scheme, which is based on the idea of solidarity between working population and the pensioners, the amount of benefits for persons entitled to them was dependent on the social insurance contribution defrayed by labour force. That scheme functioned in Poland exclusively until 1998 and was widely criticized as costly and discriminating. Still the most crucial aspect of it was that public authorities concluded it might result in financial collapse within the next twenty years. Due to the aging of society, the number of contribution payers decreased drastically with simultaneous increase in the number of established pension entitlements. What made that possible was not only the easiness with establishing the entitlement to pensions but also the unwillingness to continue employment on the part of active payers. It should be remembered that in the pay-as-you-go pension scheme the amount of pension benefit was not correlated with the amount of pension contribution. Moreover, high unemployment rate among working population that wanted to work and pay contributions dramatically worsened the already difficult financial situation of the state. In order to guarantee pension entitlements for persons who decided to retire, the state was forced to subsidize pension benefits. Demographical aspects, unemployment, and willingness to retire early caused a difficult situation creating a real threat to the stability of the Polish social insurance system as well as economic growth. Towards the end of the twentieth century, public authorities came to a conclusion that a radical social security system reform needed to be performed.

It was assumed that the change in the pension scheme would be possible through incentives offered to increase work activity, increasing retirement age up to 67, limiting black economy by encouraging employees to enter social security systems, both obligatory and voluntary ones. The authors of the social security reform anticipated that all of the ideas above were conceivable only if a *funded pension scheme* was established. That is how the II pillar emerged, which embraced younger contribution payers. The authors of the reform claimed that sustaining the existing subsidized pay-as-you-go scheme as guaranteed by the provisions in force together with introducing the new funded pension scheme for younger payers would grant the security of benefit payments for both groups in the following years. The introduction of two completely different funding sources of pension benefits was to guarantee social safety in Poland.

Therefore, two public and mandatory pillars of pension insurance were created. The first, larger one, covering over three-fifth of the older part of the society (pay-as-you-go scheme) and the latter, smaller one, designed for two-fifth of the younger generations (funded pension scheme). Pay-as-you-go scheme incorporated insurance institutions presented in the historical background of the monograph and Chapter 2 part one: The institutions – position and competence of the public institutions. Nowadays in Poland exists two concurrent pension schemes, that is to say the previously existing public mandatory defined pension scheme (pay-as-you-go scheme) and the newly created in 1998 public mandatory funded pension scheme (known as the second pillar) managed by the open retirement funds. The second pillar stems from the direct dependency between the premiums invested on the financial markets by private companies and in fact it is a private system. That pillar conditions the amount of the future pension benefits for younger beneficiaries on their individual contribution of work. In other words, it is dependent on the amount of premiums and decisions made by investment pension funds managing the contributions collected in individual pension accounts. There is no constant indexation rate in the second pillar. The Treasury does not guarantee maintaining the capital at a certain level. The capital accumulated in the insurance funds under management of pension funds is increased by the return of investment performed by OFE managers or decreased by losses in the investment process. According to the most recent data, as at 31 December 2015 in Poland there were 1,054 occupational pension schemes within the second pillar, 689 of which were in a form of a group life insurance contract with an insurance capital fund, 332 were in a form of a contract on the transfer of employees' contributions by the employer to the investment fund and 33 in a form of an occupational pension fund. The value of assets accumulated in the occupational pension schemes was PLN 10.6 billion (EUR 2.4 billion). The occupational pension schemes covered 392.6 thousand persons which accounted for 2.41% of the total number of persons employed. The average basic annual contribution per one member of the occupational pension scheme was PLN 3,660 (EUR 875). The situation on the market of pension benefits included in the second pillar has not changed for many years now. The number of the created occupational pension schemes remains at the level of thirty schemes annually. In 2014 there were twenty-nine registered schemes, and in 2015 there were twenty-five of them.

The third pillar creates for the insured, who are subject to one of those two pillars of the pension scheme (the first conducted by the State Social Security Agency and the second managed by pension funds), a further opportunity of voluntary pension insurance. The creation of the third pillar of the old-age pension insurance was an indication for the insured, that the state reduces its share in financing social security benefits. The third pillar of the old-age pension scheme provides an additional opportunity for the insured to extend social benefits of pension scheme through personal savings voluntarily transferred into the Individual Retirement Account (IRA), and since 2011 also into Personal Old Age Security Account (POASC). In the third pillar there are 858.7 thousand persons which account for 5.3% of the number of employed persons (data as at 31 December 2015). The value of the market of Individual Retirement Accounts (IKE) was PLN 5.7 billion (EUR 1.36 billion). The individual retirement accounts are kept by five financial institutions under a contract concluded by a person saving with: an investment fund, an entity conducting a brokerage business, an insurance company, a bank or any pension fund. The greatest number of individual retirement accounts is operated by insurance companies (573.1 thousand) and by investment funds (205.5 thousand).

Individual Retirement Security Accounts (IKZE) were held by 597.6 thousand persons (data as at 31 December 2015). The market of the accounts assessed in terms of the allocated assets had a value of PLN 622 million (EUR 148 million). An average payment into an individual retirement security account was PLN 2.6 thousand (EUR 622).

The presented data concerning the second and the third pillar of the retirement system prove that the pillars, from their beginning, lack dynamics. As regards voluntary schemes they receive little attention in Poland. A major problem is a non-active IKE and IKZE account, ratio which is 31% and 24%, respectively.

In the new system of pension insurance, a limit on earnings, which are the basis for the assessment of amount of contribution to the mandatory insurance schemes, was introduced. The amount of contributions cannot be larger than thirty average salary rates. The introduction of this limitation for the insured in investment in the insurance system discharged to the Social Security Fund (managed by State Social Security Agency) has resulted in a loss of capital in the form of collected premiums in the amount of PLN 5.2 billion (EUR 1,244 billion) in 2010 to PLN 6.2 (EUR 1.48 billion) in 2013 *in the scale of the entire country*. In respect to that the State Social Security Agency has estimated that the loss will increase to PLN 7.3 billion (EUR 1.75 billion) in 2016. (Review of the pension system, *supra*, p. 11).

Both pension systems (pay-as-you-go and funded) have functioned since 1999. They still operate simultaneously and will do so for several dozen years to run. For this reason, unbalancing the Social Insurance Fund, from which part of the collected funds from pension contributions is transferred into open retirement funds, forced the Polish government to take measures to reduce the costs of managing II pillar capital. This was done by way of a reduction in the fee charged by the Pension Fund from payments in respect of premiums transferred from State Social Security Agency to OFE from 7% to 3.5%. Also the amount of fees that OFE charged for the management of OFE has been limited to the level of PLN 186 million registered annually. Previously, these charges treated as management's profit were not dependent upon the financial performance and achieved the amount of more than 70% of the total cost of Pension Fund for the retiree.

By introducing these constraints and reducing the amount of the contribution from State Social Security Agency to open retirement funds, the state was released from the obligation to take out loans in order to balance social insurance fund administered by the State Social Security Agency. The reduction of contributions transferred from the Social Insurance Institution to pension funds was offset by the increase in the limit on share capital investment accumulated in the funds managed by Pension Fund to 90% of assets. In 2013, this limit is 47.5%. In 2014, it will be increased to 50%, and in the following years is bound to increase each year by 2% up until 2034.

Introduced in 1998, the reform could include only newly employed persons to go on a pension after several dozen of years in employment. The reform of the pension plan did not include persons born before 1949. Persons born after 1948 but before 1969 have been formally covered by the ZUS pension system but they were also allowed to voluntarily join the new (OFE) funded pension scheme. Nonetheless, those born after 1968 have been covered by insurance in the second and third pillar of the funded pension scheme. From the base of future pension benefits of the persons entitled, there are contributions paid in the amount of 12.22% for Social Insurance Institutions and 7.3% for open retirement fund. The premiums of all employees who joined the scheme before 1999 were considered as initial capital, and they contributed to the individual pension accounts of those persons in the Social Security Agency.

Concluding reflections on the competence of public and private insurance institutions in Poland today it should be mentioned that the currently existing mixed nature of the pension scheme is a major cause of imbalance in revenue and expenditure of State Social Security Agency (ZUS). For this reason, the Polish Social Insurance Fund requires subsidies from the state budget. The establishment of the funded pension scheme pillar was not accompanied by an increase in the provision of insurance premiums paid by the Social Insurance Institution, but by Pension Fund managing open retirement funds. The current deficit in Social Insurance Fund results from the obligation of the present working generation to the generation of recipients receiving pensions paid under the old system. This is a long-term commitment because in 2060 will see retired persons receiving means only from the first (pay-as-you-go) pillar of the pension scheme. Only after this date will all the insured be covered by the benefits derived from the other – second (funded) and so de facto and de jure the only pillar of the pension scheme. With the increase in the number of funded pension scheme beneficiaries, the role of private institutions in the national social insurance scheme will be increasing. However, for almost half of the next century a public institution – the State Social Security Agency will exert a decisive influence on the management of the Social Insurance Fund.

Part II. Contribution and Financing

Chapter 1. Contribution Regulations for Employees

§1. Field of Application

I. Territorial Field of Application

54. Polish social security legislation applies within Polish territory. Coverage by social security depends on either employment by a Polish undertaking or contribution to the social security fund by Polish citizens working abroad. The physical presence in Poland of an insured person is not a necessary prerequisite for coverage by the national social security scheme. Nor does employment at a Polish undertaking serve as an indicator for such coverage. Three decrees issued in December 1998 by the Council of Ministers of 30 December 1998 (*Journal of Laws*, No. 165, item 1197 as amended); the Minister of Labour and Social Policy of 18 December 1998 (*Journal of Laws*, No. 161, item 1106 as amended); the Minister of Labour and Social Policy of 14 December 1998 (*Journal of Laws*, No. 153, item 1005) regulate the legal duty to contribute to the social security fund in social security dues by and for workers employed by Polish undertakings and other individuals performing work under the civil type of contract other than contracts to achieve particular effects. The open retirement funds membership agreement obligates the insured, who has elected a fund, to pay insurance premiums into the pool of capital from which retirement benefits are paid out. According to the above-mentioned legal regulations, the link with Polish territory must exist for both the worker who has to perform work at a Polish undertaking either in Poland or outside Polish territory and for the employer, who has to be legally established in Poland. Workers' nationality does not play any role at all in the case of a non-Polish citizen with a work permit in Poland. The very same principle applies to employers who are not holders of Polish passports. Both the place of registration of the company headquarters and the place of residence of the worker play an important role in social security while they are located on Polish soil. All seamen are covered by the Polish social security scheme on the condition they sail under the Polish flag or are employed by a company sailing under the Polish flag.

II. Personal Field of Application

55. The social security system is based upon the system of social security dues (contributions) paid by all employees (with exception of judges and prosecutors) and employers employed either on an employment contract or on a civil type of contract with the exception of a contract to perform particular work. Employers are under legal obligation to submit to the local social security agency a list of employed workers and individuals under the civil type of contract together with a list of monthly earnings.

56. When introducing the reform of pension law, the legislature allowed the insured persons who already had been paying social insurance premiums to choose one of the previously mentioned systems of pension insurance: the pay-as-you-go or funded scheme during the transition period. After several years of experience in parallel operating both insurance systems, the state authorities realized that the majority of the insured were not interested in making the choice on the fund from which pensions will be paid and left the decision in the hands of the insurance institutions. Pension funds which managed the funded pension scheme used professional salesmen to undertake activities in order to gain members for OPF. No decision on choosing one of the two pension schemes: pay-as-you-go or funded scheme meant that the insured with the Social Security born after 1948 but before 1969 neither did not want to change affiliation between two alternative pension funds nor did not take decision on choosing between existing different insurance methods. This forced the use of a Social Security lottery which assigned the insured individuals to the pension scheme. As part of the general social insurance scheme, there exist unique schemes as well.

They are based on a defined pension scheme, just like the common pension system, but the pension benefits are calculated according to more favourable conversion of the pension. Miners are the ones who benefit from the favourable scheme. They are also the only group of persons covered by the universal social insurance who are entitled to an early retirement. Certain categories of employees are allowed the early termination of the work activity by bridging pension plans and teachers' compensation benefits. However, in contrast to mining the teachers' bridging pensions and compensation, benefits are not financed from the capital accumulated in their account in the Social Insurance Fund. Moreover, the method of calculating insurance benefits granted to teachers is the same as the one used by the Social Insurance Institution when calculating the benefits of universal pension schemes. The unique situation of miners stems from historical and political reasons. The socialist authorities in Poland tried to valorize miners' importance for the economy, as they generated significant foreign exchange, and compensate for disturbance and above-average risks to the health and life at work. Miners are a well-organized, influential professional group, accustomed to the use of political pressure on the authority of the state and they often resort to those means. After the change of political system in Poland, no political party ruling the country has been able to effectively carry out the reforms of pension schemes and adjust the mining insurance benefit rights to the universally applicable pension system. In addition to the general pension scheme, there also operate separate Agricultural Social Insurance Fund (ASIF), funds for professional military and paramilitary organizations (police and other uniformed services (fire brigade, prison), judges and prosecutors).

57. The following categories of employed people are covered by the social security schemes (retirement, invalidity, sickness, and industrial injury) on which behalf both insured and their employers must contribute in social security dues:

- employees and workers;
- individuals drawing 'sportive stipends' not covered by social security schemes under other titles (such as work or study);
- individuals performing work on the basis of the civil type of contract;
- members of agriculture cooperatives;
- businessmen acting on their own and individuals cooperating with them;
- advocates;
- the spouses of employees delegated to international (such as the United Nations) or Polish missions abroad;
- individuals taking personal care of a handicapped child.

58. An employee and their employers are obliged to pay a contribution to the social security fund in social security dues on behalf of any employed person regardless of written contract of employment. According to Article 29, section 3 of the Labour Code, an employment contract might come either in oral or written form. If an employment contract is concluded in oral form, an employer is under legal obligation to issue an affidavit within seven days of the conclusion of the employment contract in which the terms and conditions of such a contract would be stated. Therefore, there is no issue of illegal employment. If an employer ceases to submit such affidavits, then either an employee himself/herself or a labour inspector acting on behalf of the employee may bring legal action against the employer in the labour court. The court order will accept as legal evidence that a particular individual was employed and that therefore the employee and his/her employer were obliged to contribute in social security dues to the social security fund.

59. The duty to submit social security dues as contributions to the social security fund extends to all branches of the compulsory national social security system: disability insurance, old-age pensions, occupational diseases and industrial injuries, family allowances, and unemployment.

The field of application of the contributions system to the social security fund is determined in such a way that any type of work is covered, as long as it is performed either under an employment contract or under the civil type of contract, with the exception of the contract to get a particular result. The compulsory national social security scheme is based on the principle of forced solidarity of gainfully employed members of Polish society. That system comes under the criticism of more productive members of the society who are not willing to financially support other less active individuals. The current Polish social security system is characterized by a limited amount of benefits and an unlimited amount of contributions, except in retirement and invalidity insurance less than the maximum set up by the state (thirty monthly prospected wages). Therefore, due to the lack of a relationship between input (in social security dues) and output (in social security benefits), it is hard to define the current Polish social security system as based on the insurance principle.

60. Mining pensions are paid out from the public Social Insurance Fund. Miners and their employers – mines or mining companies – pay identical contributions to the social security fund as other insured employees covered by the social security fund. The mining pensions are calculated on contribution assessment basis applying favourable conversion rate of the employment period of working underground. Moreover, the miners have the right to retire early. Due to privileged treatment by the social security regulations, the retirement pensions and disability pensions are almost twice as high as average retirement pensions and disability pensions paid out to other insured individuals. This is feasible due to subsidizing of the benefits from the state budget. In 2012, the expenditures on mining pensions totalled at PLN 8.8 billion (EUR 2.2 billion).

61. The pension system of public servants is functioning independently from the public pension system. Pension benefits in this system are paid out from the state budget. The remuneration of public servants called emolument (uposażenie) is not subject to the obligation of paying contributions on social security. In 2012, the expenditures from state budget on public servants' pensions (army, police, system of justice) amounted to over PLN 10 billion. In 2012, provisions of the law concerning pensions of civil servants were changed. The minimal period of service of fifteen years was extended to twenty-five years. Moreover, the minimal age that entitles the public servants of twenty-five years of service to pension was raised to fifty-five years.

62. The old age and invalidity insurance of the farmers is financed in majority of budgetary grants from the treasury funds, supplemented in small degree from premiums paid by the farmers. In 2012, the government subsidy to farmer insurance system (ASIF) amounted to PLN 15.6 billion (EUR 3.72 billion). Contributions from farmers premiums amounted to PLN 1.5 billion (EUR 0.36 billion), being almost 10% of government subsidy to ASIF. Whereas the amount of paid out pensions amounted to PLN 11.5 billion in 2012.

63. According to data collected by the Central Statistical Office in 2011, 9,123,563 people collected social security benefits. Total amount of monies paid to beneficiaries out of various social security funds is as high as PLN 177,304 million (EUR 42,315 millions). There are: 5,237,000 old-age pensioners; 1,210,900 recipients of invalidity benefits; and 1,349,000 beneficiaries drawing survivor's pensions. Retirees and pensioners as per cent of total population run as high as – 23.7%. The average monthly social security benefits are as follows:

Retirement	PLN 1,783.06 (EUR 425.55)
Disability pension	PLN 1,323.19 (EUR 315.79)
Family pension	PLN 1,543.14 (EUR 368.29)

§2. Calculation of Contributions

64. Polish social security legislation dictates that employees and employers pay a percentage of their wages as social contributions to be paid as social security dues. Since 1999, an amount of social security dues is divided between different types of social security funds. In addition, social security dues to retirement and invalidity funds are each financed on an equal basis by the insured and their employers. Social security dues to sickness and industrial injury benefits are paid exclusively by employers.

The minimal social security due paid monthly for retirement insurance is as high as 19.52% of basic wages –'the base'. The basic amount out of which the social security contributions for retirement insurance (an old-age pension and invalidity benefit) is paid since 1 March 2013 cannot be lower than PLN 3,080.84 (EUR 735.28). The average wage in the third quarter of 2012 (July through September 2012 was PLN 3,510.22 = EUR 837.76). A total of 7.3% of the social security dues contributed to the retirement insurance is transferred by the State Social Security Agency to the retirement fund. Division of social security dues in two parts is obligatory to those insured who were born after 31 December 1968. Thirteen per cent must be paid for retirement insurance and 8.75% for health insurance (since 1 January 2006).

65. Unemployment benefit and vocational benefit are paid out of the Labour Fund, which is the separate fund from the social security fund. The Labour Fund is financed by employers who since 1 June 2005 are obliged to contribute monthly to this fund up to 2.45% of the base, which serves as an indicator of contribution to the social security fund. Contributions to both funds (the Social Security Fund and the Labour Fund) are paid at the same time by employers.

66. Employees working abroad who want to be covered by the national social security scheme are obliged by the Law of 14 December 1994 on employment and countervailing unemployment to contribute to both funds (the Social Security Fund and the Labour Fund) in social security dues. The contribution to the Social Security Fund is calculated in the same way that the contribution is calculated from wage earners employed in Poland with provision that the minimum base for contribution in social security dues paid by a worker employed abroad cannot be lower than 100% of the national monthly wage. The contribution to the Labour Fund by workers employed abroad is equal to 12% of the average monthly wage paid in Poland.

67. The basis for calculating the social security dues of wages earners out of employment relationship is the gross wage of the worker as well as the benefit paid in kind to the worker.

68. The gross wage is the wage actually paid by an employer to the particular employee before the deduction of taxes and other financial obligations imposed upon an employee by public regulations. The gross wage is a fictitious wage that an employer must report to an employee, giving him/her an amount earned on a monthly basis. The gross wage is not a wage paid by an employer to an employee. An employee receives a net wage that consists of the gross wage from which public contributions, mostly taxes, are being deducted. An employee cannot include social security dues in the gross wage. Those dues are paid by an employer exclusively. From the social point of view, trade unions demanding higher wages for employees from time to time come up with the argument that those wages should include social security dues. The economic concept of the gross wage does not include social security dues even though they must be taken into account as the real cost of the employment of a particular worker. Social security contributions are not calculated on the basis of the real cost of employment. They are counted as regular payments of an employer to an employee as a regular remuneration for work performed month after the month.

69. A legal definition of wage is not given by the Labour Code. Article 78 of the Labour Code provides that a wage should reflect the type of work, qualifications of the employee, and the quantity and quality of work performed. Polish labour law states that a wage is a compensation given to a hired person (an employee) for his/her services. If labour is treated as a commodity, the wage is regarded as the prize. One may add that the wage is a remuneration paid by an employer to an employee on a regular (monthly) basis.

Taking that information into account, one must conclude that Polish employers cannot easily escape from paying their contributions in social security dues to the various social security funds. The minister of economy and labour created the draft regulation according to which an employer must pay in social security dues from various financial privileges provided to his employees (perks) such as reimbursement for hotel expenses and a higher cost of living, using private car for work purposes (mostly managers), etc. This proposal means that the state government wants employers to contribute to the social security funds in social security dues on the basis of any kind of privilege provided to employees by the employer.

70. The decree of the Minister of Labour and Social Policy of 18 December 1998 on the particularities to establish bases for social security dues (*Journal of Laws of 1889*, No. 161, item 1106 as amended) states that bases of calculating social security dues cover all financial gains as listed by the taxation regulations with thirty-two exceptions listed in paragraph 2. The list of exempted benefits from contribution payment to the social security funds embraces – amongst others – the following payments in cash by an employer to his employees:

(a) bonuses for extensive services provided by a particular employee to the employer. Bonuses are paid on the basis of twenty, twenty-five, thirty, thirty-five, forty, forty-five, and fifty years of employment services;
(b) bonuses paid by an employer to retired workers, or workers who are not able to perform work any longer due to disability or other deficiencies of body;
(c) compensation for unused leaves of absence from work such as holidays. According to the Labour Code, such compensation can be paid only to those workers who are not in the position to use their legal rights to holidays in kind. Among those workers, the Labour Code lists those who are not able to demand holidays due to the fact of termination of their employment contract;
(d) compensation paid to relatives of workers who have passed away. This compensation might be included into the basis on which social security contributions are calculated only in situations in which the beneficiary is considered as a person whose income must be counted as the ground for estimation of social security dues;
(e) compensation for travelling expenses with the possibility that such expenses can be taken into account due to most recent legislative proposals;
(f) provisions for protective clothing and work equipment, and allowances paid by an employer to employees who decide to bear on their own the cost of protective devices;
(g) compensation for unjustified or illegal termination of the contract of employment;
(h) allowances paid to workers in lieu of providing working clothes and equipment;

(i) compensation for accommodation and food when work is performed outside the place of residence of the worker.

The financial base in Polish zlotys for social security dues and social security contributions for certain categories of insured people changes from month to month. The latest information presented by the Social Security Agency present the following figures (zloty – PLN 1 = EUR 4.2) on 31 December 2009.

§3. Reductions and Exemptions

71. Social security dues are paid on a monthly basis. Therefore, a reduction in the amount of compulsory contributions is granted in periods in which work was not performed by an employee on a full monthly basis. If an employee is under contract of employment for a period of less than thirty days during a particular month, the social security dues are reduced according to the number of days the parties were bound by the employment contract in the particular month. One day under the employment contract counts as 1/30 of the month.

72. Exempted from contributions to the Labour Fund are enterprises with the legal status of 'protective work'– in which the disabled are employed as well as enterprises run by the following organizations: the Polish Association of Deaf People, the Polish Association of Blind, the Association of Blind Soldiers, the Association for Protection of Blind, The Shelter for the Blind in Laski near Warsaw (Article 53, section 4 of the Act of 22 December 1995 amending the Act on Employment and Countervail of Unemployment).

§4. Contributions on Benefits

73. Social security dues are paid on wages by workers still active on the labour market. Social security benefits were paid upon the retirement of active workers. This idea was dropped by the previous political system. The new political regime based on strict economic foundations reintroduced a legal duty to contribute to the social security fund on all wages earned by social security beneficiaries. Beneficiaries of the social security system are also obliged to pay taxes from their earned income. It does not matter whether or not social security beneficiaries are not eligible for any social security benefits because they are already drawing those types of benefits. They are under the legal obligation to contribute as any other active worker to social security. Despite their income from the social security fund, the law treats them as fully active workers if they decide to continue with their work on a part-time basis.

§5. Administration

74. All the obligatory social security schemes, with the exception of schemes introduced for the above-mentioned category of workers, are administrated by the state Social Security Agency (Zakład Ubezpieczeń Społecznych – ZUS).

Short-time social insurance benefits, for example, sickness benefits, are administered by employers in both state-owned enterprises and private employers. State-owned enterprises are also obliged to pay for damages caused by industrial accidents or occupational disease. In the case of private employers, such a duty relies on the state Social Security Agency.

The Social Security Agency is charged with the collection of contributions and the distribution of contributions over long-term benefits. The Social Security Agency is considered a public institution set up by the government as a central branch of the government, which enjoys administrative autonomy. The Agency is under the scrutiny of the Board of Overseers and the Minister of Social Policy.

Both central and local boards of overseers carry out important functions. Among them are control, judicial, and advisory functions. The board is entitled to make suggestions related to any type of activity carried out by the agency, rule over the decisions made by the agency (as a matter of fact the board works an appellate tribunal from the decisions made in individual cases), and file a petition to the President of the Security Agency demanding immediate discharging of the Director of the local branch of the agency.

The Social Security Agency administers all social security matters of self-employed people, together with sickness and benefit caused by industrial injuries and occupational diseases. It also manages alimony allowances for all employed or self-employed mothers taking care of children neglected by their fathers.

Social assistance is provided for those in need by the public centres run by local (municipal) government.

All social security benefits, with the exception of damage caused by industrial accidents or occupational diseases during work performed in state-owned enterprises, must be claimed either from the Social Security Agency or from one of the agencies run by the respective administrative branches of the central government, for example, police officers by the Ministry of Interior, railroad workers by the Ministry of Transportation, etc. This statement applies respectively to long- and short-time benefits, even though the latter ones are administered by state-owned enterprises themselves. Those enterprises act on the principle of contracting agent (a substitute) of the local branch of the Social Security Agency.

75. Due to the idea of unification of various social security schemes, the new constitution and by-laws of the State Social Security Agency (ZUS) were introduced by the decree of the Minister of Labour and Social Policy of 13 January 2011 (*Journal of Laws of 2011*, No. 18, item 93) on the new law defining the legal and administration status as well as scope of power of the State Social Security Agency (ZUS). According to the law on the social security agency, the State Social Security Agency must be an independent administrative body within the government. It must enjoy legal entity. Thus, the social security agency will participate in legal disputes as an independent governmental institution. Having been awarded independence from the central government, the State Social Security Agency could act as an owner towards any property which so far is under its administration only.

76. The State Social Security Agency is run by a board containing eighteen members. Half of the board should represent insured people. Five members must represent employers, and four of the board members will act as representatives of the state government. Members of the board are to be elected by trade union organizations (members representing the interest of insured people), employers confederations (those who sit on the board as employers representatives), and appointed by the prime minister (members representing the government) to six-year term. The first term, however, is to be cut to two years only.

77. The state security agency is run on a day-to-day basis by its director general. Within the director's scope of power, the following prerogatives are laid down: hiring and firing his deputies, the head of the medical examiners, branch directors, and the director of the foreign branch of social security benefits. The director general is appointed to his position by the prime minister. Only the minister of and social policy is entitled to submit a motion for the above-mentioned nomination.

78. The scope of power of the social security agency is broad and important. The State Social Security Agency is responsible for the administration of social security benefits coming out of different schemes. In particular, the State Social Security Agency is empowered to: (a) declare the duty to insure; (b) make a judgment as to whether or not insured individuals are able to keep working or if they are eligible for disability benefits; (c) collect social security dues, and run different social security funds; and (d) oversee any other institutions, both state-owned or private in any matter related to the above-mentioned activity connected with social security benefit.

The social security agency is responsible as an exclusive agent to run the state's compulsory social security schemes. The agency is also empowered to manage any additional social security scheme. It is interpreted as an indication that the supplementary, private social insurance schemes could be introduced by any parties and trusted to run as their agent by the state social security administration.

79. The most important purpose of the activity of the State Social Security Agency is management of the general social security fund. The fund is put up by the contributions from social security dues, grant-in-aid from the governmental treasury office, and income from any industrious activity of the State Social Security Agency. Social security benefits are paid out of the social security fund, along with the other expenditures of the social security agency.

80. Within the social security fund, three separate funds are created under which separate social insurance schemes are covered. These three funds are: (a) the retirement and disability pension fund; (b) the sickness, birth, and death benefits fund; and (c) the industrial injury benefit fund.

81. Acting as an independent governmental agency, the social security agency is overseen by the minister of labour and social security. The minister is allowed to control the social security agency and conduct a survey as to whether or not its activity is handled properly both from the point of view of social security laws and social policy directives. The bill declares that any administrative decision taken by the social security agency contrary to the rules of social security law is null and void. The statement of the minister of labour and social policy taken within thirty days from the day the decision was published declares a voidance of such decision.

One of the peculiar signs of the former Polish social policy was the growing number of young people drawing cash from the disability fund. It is necessary to stress that there were no significant differences in the levels of cash drawn from the retirement pension fund and the disability fund. The majority of social problems related to a tight labour market were frequently resolved by granting general permits to go into early retirement. Since the money was paid out of the state budget, the social security benefits were treated by beneficiaries not as benefits but as assistance. In the past, due to the high inflation, ad hoc measures were applied to keep the real value of limited benefits. Even government policy is based on the principle of mechanical equality of the working population; however, due to loopholes in the statutes on retirement pension and disability benefit, some people were able to manage far more from average social security benefits.

82. After 1989, the leading issue of social policy and social security laws was how to finance social security benefits. Thus the major choice of future social policy in Poland was to maintain proper relationships between input and output to and from the social security fund. A financially sound social security fund managed by an independent governmental institution (social security agency) should guarantee payment of benefits as high as 75% of the previous income earned by the beneficiary active on the labour market. Therefore, social policy choices and social security features in Poland could be brought down to the two important questions mentioned above: sound financing and effective management of social security funds out of which benefits in cash are paid to those who are not able to perform due to old age, disability, injury, sickness, birth, maternity, or the death of the main wage earner of the family.

83. Financial troubles of the social security scheme shaped too much by the socialist government after the Second World War clearly demonstrated the economic, organizational, and legal limits of the social policymakers' image. Policymaking for social security in socialist Poland had always been conducted as if social policymakers could predict that everyone in need would be 100% taken care of out of the funds coming from the state budget. The appearance of collapse of the social security fund, which was no longer supported by donations from the state's budget, not only required that painful action be taken as quickly possible, but it also forced an obvious recognition – which is also painful to the budgets of employed and members of their families – that a close relationship between social security dues and social security benefits is inescapable.

Chapter 2. Contributions for Public Sector Workers

84. Military personnel, police officers, prison and border guards, and civil servants are covered by social security; however, technically speaking, they are treated only partially as employed. Their terms and conditions of service are regulated by different statutory regulations that belong to administrative law and to not labour law. Since these groups of workers perform various services directly for various branches of the state government, they are far better protected than other workers. Military personnel and police officers are covered by distinctive statutory regulations on injuries while performing services for the state. Injured civil servants are covered by the statutory act on industrial injuries, which covers all legal matters concerning rights to benefits for all injured workers. The other two categories of injured public sector workers – military and paramilitary personnel – are covered by two separate statutory acts: 16 December 1972 on Beneficiaries Injured During Military Service (*Journal of Laws*, No. 53, item 342 as amended) and 16 December 1972 on Beneficiaries Injured While Performing Police Duties (*Journal of Laws*, No. 53, item 345 as amended). Those two statutory regulations use a similar concept of industrial injury and provide the same type of social security benefits in cash and in kind in cases of an industrial accident. The word 'industrial' is used to describe any accident that occurred during professional service provided by public sector workers. However, military personnel and police officers cannot be called either 'employees' or 'workers'.

85. Differences between public sector workers and other workers as far as the social security system is concerned can be seen in the following areas:

- financing social security schemes;
- ways of legal regulation of conditions to acquire legal rights to social security benefits;
- administration of social security benefits.

86. Public sector workers are directly employed by the state. Therefore the state guarantees their social benefits in case of lack of possibility of continuing service. Since the state plays two roles at the same time in the case of public sector workers – as both employer and provider of social security benefits – the state government ceases to tax itself on social security benefits paid to their own functionaries. It is understood that the state does not use a regular insurance technique while taking care of the social needs of its servants. Social schemes for public sector workers are found on the basis of the supply type of technique. The state is under the legal duty to provide (supply) social benefits to public sector workers who are in need due to the occurrence of any risks covered by social security laws.

87. Legal conditions required for acquisition of social security rights by public sector workers are set separately by the state in statutory regulations. All categories of public sector workers are covered by separate acts. Legal rights to social security benefits of professional military personnel are regulated by the Act of 19 December 1993 (*Journal of Laws of 2004*, No. 12, item 10 as amended by the Act of 6 May 2005, *Journal of Laws of 2005*, No. 130, item 1085). The rights of other paramilitary functionaries, such as police officers, prison and border guards, and firefighters, are regulated by the Act of 18 February 1994 (*Journal of Laws*, No. 53, item 214). Social security rights of other categories of civil servants employed by either the state or local government are regulated by statutory acts for which their application extends to all segments of the working population. The only distinction is based on the technique of legal regulation. Social security acts that apply directly to all categories of employed people with the exception of public sector workers are applied to the latter category of employed people because separate statutory acts that regulate the legal status of separate categories of public sector workers expand the scope of application of common social security regulation to various categories of public sector workers: central state government, local government, and the judiciary.

Chapter 3. Contributions for the Self-Employed

§1. The General Concept of Self-Employment under Polish Social Security Law

88. Due to the ideological principles of the previous political system, the vast majority of the working population was gainfully employed in various state-owned enterprises. Therefore, the state acted as both direct and indirect employer. Those members of Polish society who worked for the state were, and – as a matter of fact – still are, employed either under an individual contract of employment, or under an administrative act of the sovereign (the state) – a nomination.

For a long period of time, the socialist government failed to recognize a tiny minority of the population that was employed in the so-called non-socialized system of the state economy.

Eventually, the state came to the conclusion that in the so-called private sector of economy, some individuals are employed under employment contracts with individual employers. As workers employed in the private sector, those individuals were included in the general social security scheme developed to cover all employees regardless of the type of employer: public or private. In the end, the state government, in its constant and restless drive towards total regulation of various parts of social life of virtually all segments of the fabric of Polish society, concluded that private sector employers (patrons) also should be covered by the social security schemes adopted by the state legislature.

Moreover, the state government recognized the necessity of providing social security protection to those individuals who were not employed either by the state or by private employers. Those people were considered by the state as acting in the national labour market in a dual capacity: as employees and as employers at the same time.

Naturally, some of the above-mentioned categories of employees and employers produced goods or delivered services exclusively to the state-owned enterprises. As close collaborators of the state-owned enterprises, they were covered by the Social Security Regulations issued on 19 December 1975. Since the last category of insured people – producers – have their own customer (the state) for which they deliver goods or provide services on the principle of exclusivity, they cannot be included in this report as either self-employed or employed by the state-owned enterprise. Thus, the Act of 19 December 1975 created a peculiar category of semi-self-employed beneficiaries of the state social security system. People who fell into this category were covered by the social security regulations issued to guarantee social security benefits to workers and employees performing work under an individual contract of employment.

Obviously, in this monograph there will be no references to the social security provisions introduced to cover workers if those provisions are not being adopted in order to provide social security protection to those people who perform work outside an employment relationship. This method used to distinguish the special category of beneficiaries who can be called 'self-employed' fails to provide a clear division between groups of people called 'semi-self-employed' and 'self-employed'.

There is no problem in making a distinction between those people who are employed under a contract of employment and those who are not. There were serious problems, however, if one tried to analyse the latter category – those people who could not be treated by the State Social Security Agency as employed. Within this category, certain groups of beneficiaries of various social security schemes were distinguished. One had to list: advocates, individual farmers, artists and artisans, along with individual producers who delivered goods or provided services exclusively for the state-owned enterprises. The last category of individuals could not be presented as wage earners, however, they were being paid regularly for goods delivered and services provided. Since they did not operate on a market but instead work under a civil type of contract only for one customer (the state-owned enterprise), they were treated for the sake of discussion as semi-self-employed. Still, the last statement does not bring us closer to a conclusion. What was a general concept of self-employment under provisions of the Polish social security law?

According to the general concept of the social security regulations in Poland, the self-employed person is either producing goods or providing services to unknown customers at his/her own risk. Therefore, individual farmers are considered as self-employed only if they deliver their agricultural products to an open market. However, they cannot fall within the category of self-employed if they make a deal with the state food agency according to which they are obliged to provide a certain amount of agricultural products per year. If individual farmers contracted their services, they must be treated as semi-self-employed. The same principle applies to artisans and advocates employed in legal cooperatives, law firms, or in their own private practice.

§2. Field of Application

I. Territorial Field of Application

89. For the self-employed, the Statutory Act of 13 October 1998 (*Journal of Laws* of 1998, No. 137, item 1118 as amended) states that that act applies to all individuals engaged in any type of professional activity. Among the members of cooperatives, individuals performing services on the basis of the civil contract, entrepreneurs engaged in any activity outside agriculture, artisans and writers are listed.

The Act of 13 October 1998 as any other act concerning social security benefits applies within national boundaries. Since 1 January 1999, the Polish Social Security Law is uniformed. The social security regulations concerning self-employed people is no longer a separate scheme. It is included in the general scheme for which coverage extends to the twenty-one categories of active professionals listed in Article 6, paragraph 1 of the Act of 13 October 1998. Therefore, there is no historical remnant of the distant past when Polish territory was under the influence of foreign social security regulations, mostly German and Austrian.

II. Personal Field of Application

90. The real self-employed group in Poland contains advocates running private legal offices, artists, artisans, and individual farmers producing for unknown customers.

There is also one more category of beneficiaries that does not fit into the picture. That group consists of members of the clergy. They cannot be considered as employed, semi-self-employed or self-employed. The kind of service they provide to members of their church districts put them into a special category of servants.

91. There is no major problem concerning delimitation of different categories of self-employed. Distinction between writers, artists, private businessmen and individual farmers is based on the type of work provided by the insured person.

92. All groups of employed, semi-self-employed and self-employed people are subject to the general social security scheme organized for wage earners. There is one general social security scheme introduced by the Act of 13 October 1998. In separate statutory regulations related to various occupational schemes, there is always a reference that in matters that are not separately regulated by a given occupational social security scheme, the general social security scheme applies. A similar arrangement no longer applies to other categories of insured people, who are covered either by semi-self-employed or self-employed social security regulations. The only exception to this rule is the advocates. Those who carry on with their profession in organizational form of legal cooperatives are treated by the social security regulations like any other employees and are covered by law that applies directly to the employees. The others who conduct their private activities in other legal forms, particularly in their private offices, are treated as self-employed engaged in activity other than agriculture. That strange statement is based on distinction between two types of professional activities recognized by the social security regulations: agriculture and non-agriculture.

There are different techniques that are used for application of the general social security scheme to various groups of employed, semi-self-employed or self-employed covered by separate social security schemes. Those techniques fall into one of the two listed below categories:

(a) simple technique that limits itself only to a general declaration that a particular group of self-employed (e.g., advocates), or employed (e.g., civil servants) considered by the social security law as a separate group of insured is covered by the general social security scheme;
(b) sophisticated technique that breaks up a social security scheme into two separate groups:

  - the general social security scheme;
  - the social security scheme that serves as an occupational indicator of particular regulations either separate ones, or regulations that state conditions under which particular regulations provided by the general social security scheme are applied to the particular group of insured individuals.

Thus, under the present system, self-employed people are at the same time subjected to the general social security scheme established to cover primarily wage earners.

Although, at the same time, certain specific rules apply to different categories of self-employed people.

According to that rule, insured individuals engaged at their private houses on behalf of state-owned enterprises and other entrepreneurs are under legal obligation to contribute in social security dues to the retirement and invalidity social security schemes. As a result of that obligation, they are covered by only those two social security schemes. They may, if they choose to do so, contribute on a voluntary basis to the sickness fund. They are not covered, though, by social security schemes in cases of industrial injury and occupational diseases. Some categories of employed, on the basis of the civil law contract regulated by the Article 734 and Article 750 of the Civil Code, are partially excluded from an obligation to contribute to various social security funds.

93. The legal protection of beneficiaries covered by the social security scheme for self-employed people is carried out along the same lines of protection structured organized for people covered by the general social security scheme as provided.

94. As one may see, there are few differences between the general social security scheme and the scheme developed for social security protection of self-employed people. Since both schemes are constructed along the same or similar lines as far as territorial scope of application, administration, finances, and legal protection of insured people and beneficiaries are concerned, the only differences may be seen in legal requirements that are prescribed by the social security scheme for self-employed people.

Chapter 4. Other Contributions

95. Individuals who are not covered by any of the above-mentioned main contribution schemes can be included in the social security system by decision of the president of the state Social Security Agency. Article 73, paragraph 3, section 6 of the Statutory Act of 13 October 1998 as amended empowers the president of the State Social Security Agency to issue a decision by which employees and other people falling under the scope of personal coverage by the Act of 13 October 1998 who, however, do not meet the legal requirements provided by this act, and – due to their incapacity for work, or their age – are not able to report to work may be granted social security benefits which disregard their lack of competence required by statutory regulations.

Chapter 5. Government Funding

96. Subsidies out of the general state budget constitute part of the funding of social security benefits (Article 52, section 1, items 3, 8 and Article 53, section 1 of the Act of 13 October 1998 as amended). Those subsidies may be used by the Social Security Agency to support social security benefits guaranteed by the state.

97. Since 1 January 1999, the state does not provide medical care free of charge. Prior to that date, the scope of cost-free healthcare assistance provided by the state was rather limited as far as both personal scope of application and type of services was concerned. An order issued by the Ministry of Health and Social Assistance on 18 August 1962 (*Journal of Laws*, No. 55, item 277 as amended) listed categories of patients and types of diseases that could be treated at the state's expense. Another order issued by the same minister on 19 January 1994 (*Journal of Laws*, No. 14, item 50) listed healthcare services in kind that were provided to retired individuals and members of their families free of charge. Since 1 April 2003, the Act of 6 February 1997 on common health insurance (*Journal of Laws of 1997*, No. 75, item 468 as amended) introduced common, compulsory health insurance financed by social security dues.

Part III. Healthcare

Chapter 1. Field of Application

§1. Territorial Field of Application

98. As a rule, entitlement to healthcare is given to those individuals who are subject to the legal obligation to pay contributions in social security dues to the social security fund. Since everyone is obliged to contribute in social security dues to the healthcare fund, the coverage by the healthcare insurance is the broadest one.

Modern industrialized societies view healthcare as a different form of commodity that could be sold on the open market. For this reason, industrially advanced societies introduced national health insurance schemes.

99. In post-Second World War Poland, the national healthcare scheme was introduced as a significant part of political changes. As a matter of ideological and political principle, the socialist government declared that every citizen is entitled to enjoy the right to health protection. That is why government institutions perceived healthcare to be its obligation to deliver to citizens for free. On the other hand, many citizens became aware of their right to healthcare and displayed a tendency to abuse it. Realization of that right was less than complete. It was so because of financial resources that could be used for improvement of the level of this very important human right were allocated to suit other purposes.

100. It is common knowledge that no country in the world regardless of its political system and economic condition is as healthy as it could be. Within natural limits set by biology (genetic factors) or climate every nation chooses its own level of health by its evaluation of death rate compared with other priorities. Even if no country in the world does as much for the sick as it is technically capable of doing, it is worth examining past and present policies in order to answer the question whether it is still possible to do more to improve the standard of health of the society. This question is especially important to answer during a period of major political changes.

§2. Personal Field of Application

101. The past Polish healthcare system was inflexible, ineffective, heavily influenced by politics of the socialist system, shaped by the socialist government and run by a bureaucratic, highly hierarchical state organization. The visible hand of government substantially influenced by political propaganda full of slogans such as 'every one is entitled to free healthcare' (which did not take into consideration that there is no such thing as 'free healthcare'; someone must pay for it) resulted in a deterioration of healthcare services and caused wastage of resources, both material and human.

102. As far as a modern healthcare system is concerned, it is necessary to solve the following problems in order to meet the highest standard of healthcare: coverage, quality, organization and behaviour of potential recipients. The present Polish healthcare system is comprehensive, covers the vast majority of the society, is uneven as far as quality is concerned, is non-competitive, totally depended on the state support, controlled by bureaucrats and abused by better connected patients. It has been under common criticism since the mid-1970s.

103. The quality of the services provided by the state healthcare system was especially attacked. In the new political environment it was necessary to assess which health system is more favourable to society: public or private? It was also necessary to decide which attitude (competitive or regulatory) should prevail. Other questions facing the democratic government contained: the extent of monopoly power within various domains (such as, for example, hospitals) of the healthcare system in Poland. The monopoly power of hospitals run by the public authorities did not allow them to use monopoly returns earned on rent or profit when treating wealthier consumers to subsidize treatment of less well-to-do and poor patients. Hospitals in Poland were officially treated as charitable institutions, devoted to the care of patients supported by state contributions. They did not charge for services they provide, regardless of the cost of those services. Therefore, it was easy to discover that non-profit oriented hospitals are much less efficient than they should be. Thus, a fundamental question was asked: should the private profit-seeking hospitals be allowed to exist? This question dealt with the idea of the privatization of the national healthcare system. It raised numerous problems, such as: what can one expect from private healthcare institutions and private insurers; to what authority those institutions should be responsive: state or private?; are they going be more effective than the present public one in carrying out their duties, controlling costs and the quality of services provided?; should government maintain a uniform national scheme of healthcare?; what would be the possible consequences of supplementary, private healthcare schemes on the well-being of the society?

104. Any kind of healthcare scheme seemed possible: public, private and mixed. My task as an author is to examine past and present healthcare systems in Poland in order to make a proposal that suits the ideal, which is a guarantee to achieve a maximum life expectancy set up by natural forces.

§3. Pre-Second World War Polish Healthcare

105. Before Second World War, Poland did not enjoy a uniform healthcare system. Healthcare services in capitalist Poland were divided between different independent subsystems. The central control of health problems was in two separate departments of the government: the Ministry of Labour and Social Welfare and the Ministry of Interior. The principal responsibility of the Ministry of Labour and Social Welfare was to oversee the work of the preventive personal services throughout the country: child hygiene clinics, health centres, anti-tuberculosis work centres, anti-venereal clinics and anti-alcoholic dispensaries.

Child hygiene clinics were either official or private organizations. Public organizations were organized at special health centres run and supervised by the Ministry of Interior.

In the mid-thirties more than 150 health centres existed in Poland organized for the purpose of providing consultations for infants and their mothers, and to cope with tuberculosis. Anti-tuberculosis work centres were directed by the Department of Health of the Ministry of Interior. They were set up to fight tuberculosis. Anti-venereal clinics were organized in some towns. They were situated in health centres. The ambulatories for sickness insurance provided treatment of venereal diseases. Anti-alcoholic dispensaries, six of them, were located at health centres. Those hospitals and ambulatories care centres were financed and controlled by local government. Apart from public healthcare institutions, various hospitals, dispensaries, and sanatoria operated by private charitable organizations as well as religious bodies existed.

106. Separate coverage was set up for workers and their families employed by the industry and trade. This insurance paid for most of the costs of a private physician's care and drugs. In mining, healthcare was provided by salaried doctors in organized dispensaries. The rest of the insured persons obtained medical services from private practitioners.

It was estimated that between First and Second World Wars, only 15% of the Polish population had some kind of health insurance protection. This system was inadequate. It appeared to an external examiner as too rapidly improvised. The relation of insurance work to the work of the municipal and state hospitals was listed as not satisfactory. The hospital beds were found inadequate for national needs. As the worst feature of the ambulatories was mentioned the uncontrolled access of insured patients to any doctor they may select. Free choice of doctors at the ambulatories precluded any accurate registration of cases.

The majority of the population obtained medical care privately. Most physicians were in private practice; they were paid by fee for their services proved. The majority of doctors practised in urban areas.

107. Taking into consideration that two-thirds of the population lived in rural areas, it was necessary to encourage doctors to move to the countryside and practise medicine. In order to support doctors who decided to move to rural areas, consumer cooperatives were organized in some rural communities with responsibility to pay physicians a part-time salary.

§4. Public Healthcare System in Post-Second World War Socialist Poland

108. After Second World War, a public, unlimited and comprehensive healthcare system was introduced. It covered a working segment of the population. The new socialist government introduced a policy that called for medical free of charge service to all citizens. With the exception for a fee of 30% of an official price of prescription for drugs for out-patients, no charges were made for healthcare services under the public programme. Since someone had to pay for those services, the state and local governments volunteered to do so. As an effect of the new policy based on political changes that took place in Poland after 1945, the government took over all health facilities run by local and private organizations. Total control over healthcare institutions was exercised by the Ministry of Health and Social Welfare. The Ministry of Health even controlled school health services and the education of health personnel. To suit the last purpose, medical schools were transferred from the universities into separate academies of medicine. Those academies were supervised not by the Ministry of Higher Education as universities but by the omnipotent Ministry of Health and Social Welfare.

109. In 1951, private pharmacies were nationalized and assigned to the supervision of the above-mentioned ministry. With the exception of few special segments of the populations considered vital to the maintenance of the political system such as: military personnel, police force, judicial personnel, and – for historical reasons – railroad workers, the Ministry of Health and Social Welfare bore sole responsibility for maintaining and supervising the whole healthcare system.

110. The Ministry of Health and Social Welfare was the central authority for the programmes of public health and welfare. The Ministry took responsibility for healthcare and rehabilitation, sanitary inspection, education and research in the medical field, social welfare, pharmacy and medical technology, personnel, legal and social matters of physicians, nurses and other people employed at any institution of the so-called integrated health service. The Ministry of Health and Social Welfare was responsible for national planning, the setting of both health and medical standards, programme coordination, and production of drugs and health supplies.

111. Until 14 January 1992 when the new Law on Integrated Health Services was introduced, the Ministry of Health and Social Welfare used to work through regional units established in each of the provinces. The provincial health department was an administrative structure that took sole responsibility for all programmes run by the Ministry of Health and Social Welfare. The organizational framework of healthcare within the country and its provinces was based, and still is – according to newest regulation, on subdivision of territory into local areas of integrated health services (ZOZ, to use the abbreviation of the legal terms in Polish). A unique feature of the Polish structure of healthcare was the combination of health and social welfare services at each administrative jurisdiction.

Another characteristic phenomenon of the past organizational structure of health services in Poland was the pattern of administrative and political controlling authorities to which the director and his deputy of the integrated health service were obliged to report. There were some vertical lines of professional supervision from larger to smaller departments starting from the top: departments of the Ministry of Health and Social Welfare and going to the bottom: units in the smallest integrated health services located in rural areas. There were also horizontal lines of operational responsibility from departments located on each level (central – at the Ministry of Health and Social

Welfare; provincial – big integrated health services; local – small integrated health services) to the proper governmental authorities at each level.

112. Each integrated health service had at least one hospital and several ambulatories, and long-term facilities with a wide range of specialty services, all under the medical director. All integrated health services came directly under the authority of the provincial health director.

His/her official title was the provincial physician. A provincial physician was subordinated directly to the national physician, a medical doctor acting in a civil servant capacity, employed by the Ministry of Health and Social Welfare.

113. The sanitary-epidemiological services (Sanepid) were separate from the units of the integrated health services. However, at the provincial level, the provincial sanitary inspector, to whom all the local sanitary-epidemiological stations reported maintained a liaison with the provincial health inspector.

114. The general control of drugs and supervision of pharmacies was the responsibility of a chief pharmacist in the provincial health department. This same department was also responsible for registration and maintaining control over the professional conduct of physicians, nurses, and other medical personnel.

115. It was common practice that in heavily industrialized provinces units of integrated health services were organized to provide healthcare to the workers and members of their families employed at local factories. Such factory-based health services were called 'special integrated health services' in contrast to the usual local units of integrated health services structured on a territorial basis.

116. In provinces in which universities were located, special units of integrated health services were organized for students and university professors and members of the staff. Both, factory- and university-based integrated health services were responsible directly to the provincial level of health administration.

There were also organized 'specialized units of integrated health services'. Those units served as the referral centres for several provinces within the region. The multi-province units of integrated health services focused on a specialized branch of medicine, treating patients with heart disease, or cancer.

117. One of the unique features of the Polish healthcare system is separate organization of emergency services. On average the emergency services were included in the scope of professional interest of the local units of the integrated health services. Typically, in municipalities there was a tradition of emergency care provided by the branch stations located in each district. Internists and surgeons were assigned to specially equipped ambulances as well to duties at treatment centres. Staffs of nurses, drivers and technicians were organized for twenty-four hours of duty. Their task was to provide free services to all victims of accidents and emergencies that occurred within the administrative jurisdiction.

118. Integrated health services served in Poland till mid-January 1992 as basic institutions providing day-to-day services personal health service to the general population. Since the integrated healthcare units contained hospital and ambulatories, they were able to provide primary healthcare in areas of internal medicine, paediatrics, obstetrics-gynaecology, and dentistry. General integrated healthcare units were also responsible for providing health services to elementary schools located within an area.

119. The most distinctive feature of the former Polish healthcare system was the integration of hospitals, ambulatories, emergency units, school health services, and – in some areas – industrial health clinics under single, unified direction.

120. Specialized healthcare services such as occupational health services, mental health services, sanitary-epidemiological services and emergency healthcare services were provided by specialized institutions. Provinces in which substantial industry was located created specialized industrial health programmes. Also larger industrial plants employed a range of medical specialists and provided specialized laboratory equipment in addition to the general physician service available. Industry-wide health services included pre-employment assessment and job placement, periodic medical examination in relation to specific work hazards, the care of sickness and industrial injury. Several national institutes of occupational health located in Lublin (rural and agricultural hygiene), Lódz (radiological exposure), Katowice (with reference to mining and heavy industry), and Gdańsk (marine medicine) set standards for occupational health services and provided training opportunities for physicians and nurses specialized in providing occupational health services.

Health services for mental diseases were separate from the integrated health services. In each province, there was a director of mental health services who supervised all psychiatric care provided in all medical institutions, throughout the province. The National Research Institute for Mental Health in Warsaw served as a teaching and advisory institution to all psychiatric clinics and hospitals on the nation-wide scale.

Environmental hygiene services were also the responsibility of a special system healthcare that was independent of the personal healthcare services. The integration of preventive and curative services was achieved by placing unified authority for both personal health services and sanitary-epidemiological services in the hands of the provisional directors of departments of health and social welfare. At the provincial level, the sanitary inspector was regarded as a deputy director of the health and social welfare department. At the national level, all sanitary-epidemiological services were run by the deputy minister of health and social welfare and the national sanitary inspector. At the local level, the director of sanitary-epidemiological station (Sanepid) was obliged to cooperate with the director of the local institution of the integrated health service. His/her duties included such matters as control over an environmental sanitation, housing, factory hygiene and health education. The director of the local Sanepid station was obliged to deal with major hygienic and epidemiological problems such as: food contamination, typhoid fever, tuberculosis, malnutrition, streptococcal infections disorders, factory contaminants, air pollution and viral hepatitis.

121. There were more than 640 hospitals in Poland (two hospitals per 100,000 inhabitants). Those hospitals provided exactly 5.6 beds per 1,000 population. Of the above-mentioned hospitals, more than 500 were the hospitals providing care within provinces. The remaining hospitals were either referral hospitals or hospitals whose main task was to provide healthcare to a specific segment of population. Therefore, the hospital system was structured on a four-tier basis. The most advanced and highly developed hospitals were connected with the medical academies and research institutions. Five years ago, forty-six of this type of hospitals existed in Poland.

Their primary task was to serve as a referral and consultative centre for the hospitals located in the provinces in which one of the ten functioning academies of medicine was situated and to other hospitals located in three or four provinces around the main province hosting an academy of medicine. In each province, there was a principle hospital located in the local capital or main city in province.

As was mentioned in the previous item there was a principle hospital for each local institution of integrated health service. There were hospitals located in small towns and rural areas. There were more than twenty hospitals operated by the Ministry of Defence, the Ministry of Interior and the Ministry of Transportation.

In addition to the hospitals mentioned above, there was a diversity of specialized hospitals provided primarily psychiatric services, anti-tuberculosis sanatoria and other respiratory diseases. Besides hospitals, a variety of facilities provide medical and personal healthcare on an in-patient basis. Among those institutions were homes for the chronically ill (over 150 homes) and homes for the aged (more than 100 homes) that provided healthcare on a long-term basis.

122. Ambulatory care was provided at rural health stations, primary healthcare centres, polyclinics, and out-patients departments. Rural health stations and primary health centres staffed by one or two physicians and associated staff provided first-contact health services, both preventive and therapeutic free of charge to practically anyone in need.

123. More specialized ambulatory care services were provided by both polyclinics and out-patients departments of hospitals. Their ambulatory services included services of surgeons, ophthalmologists, ear-nose-throat specialists, dermatologists, neurologists, cardio logical specialists, psychiatrists and others. The level of specialists varied. Some polyclinics and out-patients departments provided a wide range of specialists while the others limited itself to only one highly specialized field of medicine, for example, cancer.

124. Decisions concerning drug production and distribution were made by a state-owned pharmaceutical enterprise called 'Cefarm-Polfa' in collaboration with the Ministry of Health and Social Welfare. Due to the shortage of hard currency, the general policy was to produce all recommended drugs domestically to the greatest extent possible.

125. There were more than 68,000 physicians in Poland in the 1980s. There were three levels of physician specialization: general practitioner, specialist of second degree and specialist of first degree. A general practitioner is a doctor who provides all type of medical services within a health service area. Approximately one general practitioner was available for 4,000 patients. The second degree specialists involve physicians specializing in paediatrics, obstetrics, internal medicine and general surgery. The first degree was employed at provincial hospitals and clinics.

Two levels of specialization of nurses were common in Poland, full nurse and assistant nurse. There were more than forty full nurses and three assistant nurses per 10,000 inhabitants. In addition to this type of supportive medical personnel, there were five midwives and physician's assistants per 10,000 population.

126. The majority of physicians and almost 100% of supportive medical personnel were employed by governmental healthcare institutions. Since the available public resources (hospitals, ambulatories) could not meet the needs of the population, physicians treated patients privately, in private offices. Thirty per cent of physicians were free to engage in private practice after completing their working per day rate in the public healthcare institutions. After retirement, they were permitted to engage in private practice on a full-time basis.

It was quite common for physicians to engage in semi-private practice in so-called medical cooperatives. More than 20% of physicians engaged in this type of medical activity on a part-time basis. People who were not satisfied with the official healthcare services provided by the government were attracted by unrestricted freedom of choice of doctors in medical cooperatives. Since medical cooperatives existed only in large towns and provincial capitals, they contained the best specialists in the particular field of medicine. Therefore, it was quite a common understanding among prospective patients that only the best qualified specialists bearing the first degree of specialization, of then associate professors and professors employed at local academy of medicine were allowed to practise medicine as members of medical cooperatives.

127. The general pattern of providing healthcare in Poland was similar to the pattern of treating patients by hospitals in Western European countries. Poland had a low discharge rate and a long average length of stay of patients in hospital. It is because in Poland the physician who treated the patient before and after hospitalization was not the physician who treated during hospitalization. Thus, the common tendency was to keep the patient at the hospital until his/her full recovery.

128. In terms of the quantity of basic resources for health services during the post-Second World War years, Poland, ruled by a socialist government, succeeded in attaining the highest production in the world as far as physicians, nurses, hospital beds and supportive medical personnel is concerned. However, due to the shortage of family doctors, public health nurses, medical researches, social workers and medical administrators the Polish healthcare system was considered incomplete, uneven, and lacking in a kind of day-to-day managerial know-how.

Under the socialist government, healthcare services were highly centralized and unified. To provide healthcare was seen as the sole responsibility of the state. In the limited areas of private and semi-private medical practice, the state felt obliged to display its official attitude towards private and semi-private practitioners. At best it was an attitude of tolerance since it was not able to provide an adequate healthcare service for all segments of the society.

The quality of healthcare was poor. Polish healthcare institutions were limited on budget and short in facilities. With minor exceptions, the general practitioners worked with a minimum of equipment and assistance. Therefore, it was a common practice among general practitioners to refer the majority of cases, except the most straightforward ones, to provincial specialists, and relied heavily on injections and prescriptions of palliative medicine. Medical facilities tended to be old and rather worn out. Patients' accommodation was crowded, rudimentary, and totally lacking in privacy. The most common rule was multi-beds wards. Due to the very low salaries, the inadequacy of resources for the basic maintenance of mechanical healthcare facilities was considered quite a problem largely contributed to the professional problems.

Among those problems listed as professionals were: barely adequate technical equipment, short supplies of supporting personnel, unsatisfactory research facilities, low salaries of medical personnel and a heavy daily patient load. The majority of the physicians were specialists. Therefore, few general practitioners were overloaded and constituted a very weak foundation for the work of single skill experts.

The social and economic status of doctors and other health workers was low. The physicians suffered from low public esteem, poor pay in the national system, lack of appropriate reward and limited intellectual stimulation. It is fair to say that the average physician was overworked, did not have enough (if any) time for studying professional literature, and as an effect of these negative factors was engaged in routine medical practice.

129. As a result, the healthcare system, which on the one hand was generally easily accessible (with the exception of some remote areas of the country), was on the other hand also considered ineffective. Since healthcare was provided to almost all members of the society for free, patients did not develop a sense of owning the system. They lacked any choice as far as the selection of doctors in public healthcare facilities was concerned. As a matter of principle, the patients understood that the heavily structured, highly bureaucratic governmental structure of healthcare was unable to provide them with more sophisticated medical care.

130. The past socialist government did not express enough concern in matters of the quality of the healthcare system. During political crises in 1956, 1968, 1976 and 1980, the healthcare service was the subject of criticism. Any of the political reviews of the health system usually ended up with identification of the same problems: shortage of medical personnel, inadequate technical equipment, low quality of medical care, severe shortage of drugs and poor organization of the health services. Those obstacles within health service that could not be overcome by the socialist government caused a major failure of healthcare policies after Second World War.

There were the other good reasons for the failure of the state health policies heavily influenced by the socialist politics. One of them was almost total lack of integration and coordination between primary care and more advanced both technologically and scientifically hospitals. On average, primary care remained under-developed. Physicians employed at the provincial hospitals did trust diagnoses presented by their counterparts working at the primary care institutions.

Total disregard of prevention that was supposed to be one of the main features of the Polish healthcare system was another explanation for the failure of the healthcare system. Separate but better quality healthcare services for some segments of the more well-to-do members of society, such as the government elite, functionaries of the political party apparatus, the army and police officers contributed to the division of two classes of the society: those whose healthcare needs were taken better care off, and the rest of the national population.

Total centralization of the decision-making process combined with the unusual influence of certain pressure groups caused a lot of chaos in the administration of different healthcare programmes. All of this contributed largely to inefficiency, corruption and the inequality of healthcare services.

Bearing in mind economic difficulties that severely affected the healthcare system, one should not be surprised that almost forty-five years of socialist rule in Poland could be characterized as more than four decades of drastic and disturbing changes to the previous, pre-Second World War healthcare services based on the concept of mutual contribution of insured people and unfulfilled social promises.

§5. Problems of Healthcare in Democratic Poland

131. The problems of healthcare were considered vital to the striking workers at Gdansk shipyard. One of the twenty-one conditions presented by Solidarity to the government in 1980 in Gdansk called for improvement both of the working conditions in the health service and the demand for better (proper) medical care for working people. In the report entitled 'The state of health and healthcare of Polish population' prepared by experts of the Solidarity trade union and published at the beginning of 1981 the tasks for the 1980s in the field of healthcare were clearly indicated: reduction of the mortality rate, in particularly among infants, reduction of viral hepatitis, tuberculosis, and hospital bed infection, evaluation of the industrial health service and fighting the problem of alcoholism.

132. It is obvious that due to the poor state of the healthcare system in contemporary Poland, and due to the level of deterioration of the national health, the government, regardless of the economic situation, could not afford not to try to solve the problem of healthcare services. What was really done by the new government to solve this issue? The only piece of statutory legislation concerning healthcare institutions was the Act of 30 August 1991 (*Journal of Laws*, No. 91, item 408). This act maintained the old structure introduced by the previous socialist government. It altered it a little bit. The statutory regulation of 1991 even used the old socialist legal terminology as far as the title of healthcare institutions was concerned. The Act of 30 August 1991 imitates the previous legislation and calls basic health institutions integrated healthcare services (zakłady opieki zdrowotnej – ZOZ).

133. There are some changes, though. It is permitted to set up integrated health services by different agencies of the central and local state organizations. That means that the integrated health organizations are not agencies of the state as such. They are treated by the state as agencies of different authorities. The central administrative organs of the state are the only one of three governmental institutions that are in a position to form integrated health services. The other two contained: governors of provinces and local authorities.

Moreover, the above-mentioned administrative organizations are not the only ones that are allowed to form integrated health services. This is an important change; since the new law was introduced, it broke state monopoly to form and run the integrated health services.

The integrated health services are formed by private and public bodies. Among those bodies the law listed: churches and religious organizations, insurance agencies, foundations and charitable organizations, foreign institutions operating on Polish soil and private individuals.

134. The integrated health services are formed in order to provide medical, ambulatory, and educational services to the population without any additional cost except paid in social security dues contributed to the health insurance. Those dues are gradually expanding. During the period of January 2004 till 31 December 2004, all insured members of the population were obliged to contribute to the health insurance in social security dues as high as 8.25% of the basis. During the year, 1 January 2005–31 December 2005, social security contribution rose to the 8.5% of the basis. In 2006, it gained 8.75%; there is higher base out of which social contributions to the health insurance must be paid. This base cannot be lower than PLN 1,818.93 (EUR 454.73). The social security contribution to the health insurance in 2009 was PLN 156.52 (EUR 118). The ultimate goal is to reach 9% of the basis for social security dues. It is necessary to make the health insurance system self-financed, which means free of charge from any additional payments for health services. There is an exception from the rule of unpaid medical services. The Act of 30 August 1991 provided that medical services to a person under the influence of alcohol should be charged regardless of such a person's rights to free medical care. The same was applied for the person whose illness was caused by the use of alcohol.

135. The Minister of Health and Social Welfare maintains administrative control over the integrated healthcare services. The minister in particular states the conditions for facilities used by the integrated health services that should be met by those institutions. The minister also states the medical and legal requirements that must be met by directors and managers of the integrated health services. The minister proscribes the legal conditions for registration of each integrated health service station within the governor of one of the provinces. Last but not least the minister of Health and Social Welfare states the administrative conditions with respect to the medical documentation that should be collected in each medical case treated by the particular station of the integrated health services.

The minister of Health and Social Welfare in democratic Poland does not enjoy the same tremendous power that was used by its socialist predecessor. The role of the ministry was not described in the Act of 30 August 1992 since this Act does not deal with the scope of administrative power of the state organ for taking responsibility for health and social welfare but regulates only functions of the basic healthcare institutions in the country.

136. One of the most characteristic features of the new legislation is a broad definition of the integrated health services. According to the Act of 30 August 1991, the integrated health services could be set up in one of the seven legal entities listed in Article 2, section 1. The most important ones are: hospitals, ambulatories, immediate care units. As one can see there is nothing new, except terminology, as far as the administrative fashion in which healthcare institutions are structured in democratic Poland.

The Act deals particularly with the legal status of the public integrated health services. A public integrated healthcare unit is managed by its director who is appointed by the public organ that created this particular institution. A supervisory board, created by the public integrated health services unit and made up of representatives of the proper public organs, controls the director.

Each particular integrated health service unit is financially independent. One cannot derive any arguments as far as finances of the integrated health services are concerned from the statement presented above in matter of social security dues to the insurance health services. The public integrated health services charge for the medical services provided for the insured segment of the general public that public institutions that decided to form the particular integrated health service unit. Those members of the public who are not covered by the national health insurance plan are obliged to pay a fee for medical services.

137. The Act of 30 August 1991 focus on the legal rights of the patients and corresponding with these rights the legal obligations of the hospitals, clinics, and ambulatories. The law guarantees a patient the legal right to: sufficient medical care accordingly with the standard of medical knowledge, the right to refrain from particular medical treatment, the right to get information concerning the patient's state of health, the right to die with dignity.

The integrated healthcare service is under obligation to provide all necessary medical treatment, guarantee proper accommodation and board to all patients, furnish their religious need and, guarantee them all type of contact with outside world. One of the most important obligations on the part of the integrated health services is the obligation to secure the patient's privacy and guarantee his/her dignity while providing him/her medical treatment.

138. The quality of the health services depends on the professional qualifications of the physicians. The Act of 30 August 1992 is not concerned with the qualifications of the medical personnel. The law provides that medical services must be provided by physicians with proper medical qualifications. Therefore, the democratic government is accepting legal regulations introduced by the socialist government on 17 May 1989 (the Act on Medical Chambers, *Journal of Laws*, No. 30, item 158). The statute concerning professional qualifications attained in European Union Member States passed on 18 March 2008 (*Journal of Laws of 2008*, No. 63, item 394) regulates the demands placed on such professional work as is stipulated in the appendix to Directive 2005/36/WE, from the 7 September 2005 (*Official Journal of the European Union* L255, 30 September 2005, page 22 with amendments), within Poland by citizens of other EU Member States, the Swiss Confederation as well the Member States to the European Free Trade Association (EFTA).

The act sets up an independent chamber of physicians that takes full responsibility for professional conduct of its members. Due to the compulsory membership in the chamber of physicians, the independent, self-governing body of physicians controls the professional behaviour of all medical doctors practising in Poland. The chamber of physicians represents the professional interest of the medical community. Therefore, it serves as an important pressure group whose responsibility is to take care of professional interests of the medical community.

The socialist government neglected the interests of both groups: physicians and patients. On the very last day of its rule (the Act of 26 May 1989 came into effect on 1 January 1990) the socialist government yielded to the pressure brought upon it by different factions of society, including the Solidarity trade union, and allowed the professional representation of physicians to take care of their own matters. There is a possibility, though, that the interests of the patients will come into collision with the professional interest of the physicians. A recent statement made by the council of the national medical association concerning abortion issue is a clear example that such conflict of interests is possible (The council of the national medical association declared that abortion, technically legal, should not be performed by any physician).

139. The democratic government is basically carrying on the policies of the unified, self-financed integrated healthcare introduced by the socialist government.

§6. Healthcare Policy Choices and Healthcare Features

140. The former and present healthcare systems were and still are based on the idea of national healthcare insurance. This plan extends its coverage to virtually every member of society. In order to support this system, the government gave up the idea of collection taxes to pay everyone's medical bills. Instead of taxes, the state government set up the national health insurance fund financed out of separate social security dues that aimed to guarantee the integrated healthcare institutions self-sufficiency. All members of the society regardless of their other legal obligations under the national social security scheme are under legal obligation to contribute in social security dues to the healthcare insurance. Thus, those who are insured under two more different titles are obliged to contribute in social security dues separately to the health insurance. The former system of financing the national healthcare insurance out of the taxes has been changed to the system based on social security dues connected with an obligation for some of the insured individuals to contribute more than once.

The physicians are obliged to deliver basic medical services regardless of what the scheme would pay. The Act of 6 February 1997 distinguishes between medical services that must be provided free of charge, those that are partially and totally paid by patients. As it proved, the quality of healthcare deteriorated since the government did not fully support the medical services provided by the public healthcare system. As an effect of this failure, the level of health services gradually and systematically deteriorated.

141. The democratic government made a point to bring Poland back to Europe. In the matter of healthcare, this statement means that European patterns of healthcare would be introduced.

There are four main ways in that the healthcare system could be structured:

(a) *pay or play*; this system is based on the private insurance concept. The employers, however, are obliged by the state to either provide basic medical coverage for their employees and members of their families or pay into the public healthcare fund to help the government to do so;

(b) *tax credits and vouchers*; this system provides that every member of society gets either a full or partial tax credit, or a tax supported voucher to buy either public or private healthcare coverage;

(c) *a managed market*; this system is based on the idea of bargaining over the cost of medical services. Both employers and the government are obliged to bargain with differently managed healthcare plans provided by insurance companies, physician's associations, or hospitals that decided to provide for profit affordable healthcare to all members of society. This system is based on the idea of competition and profit-making between the public, private and mixed institutions setup to provide efficient healthcare to different segments of society;

(d) *universal healthcare*; this system guarantees total coverage to all members of society. All residents regardless of their citizenship are entitled to healthcare that is mainly public. The healthcare system is mainly founded by the government from taxes. Patients are allowed to choose their doctors, who are mainly paid by the government. The universal, public healthcare system did not work well in

> Poland. Therefore, it is feasible to advocate the major change in management of the market system of healthcare. The basic insurance contracts provided either by the public or private institutions are obliged to offer healthcare service benefits rather than cash indemnities regardless of the hospital's charges. Pre-admission testing and out-patient services such as: accidental injury and minor surgery, medical emergencies, diagnostic testing, physical therapy, kidney dialysis and chemotherapy treatments must be covered in insurance certificates. In addition to the compulsory healthcare scheme, public or private institutions may offer supplementary variable healthcare services for unlimited amount. Those benefits may include the services of a physician, surgeon, physiotherapist, nursing house care, care in the house after hospitalization, ambulance services, prosthetic appliances, blood transfusions, prescription drugs, rental or payment for durable equipment, therapy treatments, diagnostic x-rays, laboratory services, catastrophic illness coverage, coverage for licensed practical nursing care in the hospital, treatment of nervous and mental conditions, drug addiction and alcoholism.

It is hard to predict in which direction the healthcare system in democratic Poland is most probably going to develop. One may observe in the mid of 2005 the major tension between the Minister of Health and the president of the National Health Fund developed in matters of financing and management of health services. The state resumes only partial financial responsibility for financial debts caused by the Act of Parliament, which in issuing the act brought a legal obligation on the part of the integrated health institutions to increase the monthly wages paid to the medical employees for PLN 203 (EUR 50). One may, however, discover that the development of a new model of healthcare is not going to proceed according to pattern proscribed by the ILO: stage No. 1 – creation of the independent statutory body; stage No. 2 – transition from administrative to negotiated allocation of resources; stage No. 3 – changing the status of providers; stage No. 4 – achieving the new paradigm.

§7. Prospective Healthcare System

142. From 1 January 1999, the national Polish healthcare system is regulated by the Act of 6 February 1997 on common healthcare. This act introduces a compulsory healthcare system that covers all segments of the population: employed, self-employed, students and people performing any functions for society such as, for example, military services, and also unemployed.

All segments of the population, Polish citizens and foreigners legally residing in Poland are obliged to contribute to healthcare insurance in social security dues, each of 2.45% of the base. The principle of 9% of the social security due contributed on behalf of every insured individual is transferred to the healthcare insurance system was not yet realized.

Out of the healthcare system the cost of all healthcare services is covered with the exceptions of plastic surgery. Services provided by dentists are also covered by the healthcare system, providing insured people contribute additional dues in order to reimburse the cost of materials. The healthcare system does not cover the cost of maintaining a patient in hospital; therefore, all insured people are obliged to contribute a sum that covers a cost of bed and lodging in hospital for a maximum period of ten days on yearly basis.

Healthcare services are provided by mutual fund-holding organizations (kasy chorych) that enter into contract with local physicians' associations. Insured individuals enjoy freedom of choice of both the fund-holding organization and the medical examiner with whom the particular fund-holding organization entered into contract concerning medical services.

Basic drugs mentioned by the Minister of Health on the free of charge drug list are free of charge for people covered by the healthcare system after they pay a lump sum declared by the ministry of health and welfare. Any additional drugs are sold to people covered by the healthcare system for either 30% or 50% of their nominal cost.

Chapter 2. Conditions

143. Health insurance covers each employed person. It also covers family members of the employee as well as retirees and their families. There are no conditions that must be met in order to benefit from the health insurance system. Article 70, section 2 of the Polish Constitution guarantees free of charge health insurance to all persons covered by separate statutory regulations providing social security coverage.

144. All insured individuals are provided social security identification that the employer confirms on a quarterly basis with healthcare institutions that the person asking for medical help is employed and automatically covered by one of the above-mentioned social security schemes.

145. There is proposal to introduce the waiting period before an insured person is entitled to healthcare benefits. Help is provided to all people in need immediately from the time of their employment contract becoming effective. Also, unemployed people enjoy health protection in the case of illness.

Chapter 3. Drugs

146. The Act of 27 September 1991 (*Journal of Laws*, 1994, No. 94, item 422 as amended) states the conditions of payment for drugs prescribed by medical personnel. Only privileged categories of patients treated in hospitals enjoy the right to free of charge drugs and medical materials. Other categories of patients must bear the cost of drugs. The amount of payment depends on the legal status of patient and runs from 0.5% of the minimum monthly wage to 100%. The cost of the majority of drugs runs as high as 30% or 50% of the market value.

Part IV. Family Allowances

Chapter 1. Field of Application

§1. Territorial Field of Application

147. Family allowance is paid to Polish citizens residing in Poland and foreigners with a legal residence permit (Article 1, section 2 of the Act of 1 December 1994 on family and care allowances, *Journal of Laws*, 1995, No. 4, item 17 as amended). That act was amended and its scope of regulation was extended to childcare allowances by the Act of 17 December 1998 on old-age and invalidity pensions (*Journal of Laws of 1998*, No. 162, item 1118) enforced since 1 January 1999. The Act of 28 November 2003 on family allowances (*Journal of Laws of 2006*, No. 139, item 992 as amended) established regulations upon which family allowances are paid to qualified categories of insured individuals.

Family allowance is paid to the Polish citizens, citizens of the European Union Member States, and foreigners legally residing in Poland (Article 1, section 2).

§2. Personal Field of Application

148. Family allowance is paid to those beneficiaries whose income per capita on members of their families does not exceed PLN 504 (EUR 126) monthly wage (Article 5, section 1). The field of application of family allowance is very wide.

Chapter 2. Dependent Children

149. The insured person is the one who by virtue of social security coverage is entitled to family allowances if he/she takes care of children.

150. In order to be entitled to family allowances, an insured person must take care of a child who satisfies several conditions set by the Statutory Regulation of 28 November 2003 (Article 6, section 1).

A child must have a certain relationship to the insured person. He/she must be within a certain age and related conditions. The child must be either the natural or adopted child of the insured person or of his/her spouse. Grandchildren, nephews, nieces, brothers, sisters, and other children placed into the legal custody of the insured person can qualify for family benefits. Children placed at boarding schools also qualify for family allowances if the insured person who takes legal care of them bears the cost of their education.

151. Family allowance is granted for children within a certain age limit. Family allowances are granted for children up to the age of 18. In cases where the child continues their education after the age of 18, a family allowance is paid until the child's education is completed, but not beyond, however, the year in which the child is 21 years old. Family allowance is paid to qualified person (parents or guardians) in favour of disabled children who continue their education for an additional three years. The same condition applies in cases where the child continues education at any higher institution of learning.

152. Certain categories of children are disqualified from family allowance by the Act of 28 November 2003. Article 7 provides that family allowance is not paid to children who decide to get married. The other categories excluded by law from family benefits include children granted financial support by public institutions such as a full boarding house, military school or penitentiary institution.

153. Adults are also qualified to draw family benefits under the following conditions. A spouse, either female or male, is entitled to family benefit if such a person takes care of a child entitled to a nursing allowance. Family allowance is related to the nursing allowance in Poland. The nursing allowance is a kind of social security benefit that may be drawn by children up to 16 years old who cannot live independently and who require the constant support and help of the other person. Children over 16 are also entitled to a nursing allowance if they are pronounced as invalid and their incapacity to work is a considerable one. The nursing allowance is also paid to minor disabled individuals whose disability was caused before they turned 21 years of age.

154. Adults who are over 75 years of age are also entitled to a nursing allowance of PLN 144 monthly (EUR 34.29).

155. Only adults with their own means of financial support (with incomes equal to or exceeding the level of minimum social security benefits paid on a monthly basis) and children supported by the state (patients of nursing houses or clients of penitentiary institutions) are excluded from nursing allowances for the time during which their needs are being taken care of.

156. The beneficiary of both family allowance and nursery allowance is either an eligible child or adult who is qualified by the Act of 28 November 2003. Family allowance and nursery allowance is paid separately or jointly, depends on the family situation of the eligible person to an individual who is drawing either wages (an employee) or long-term social security benefits (old-age pension, invalidity benefit, unemployment benefit).

157. One beneficiary is entitled only to one family allowance or nursery allowance. Family allowance is paid to a person who takes care of a child eligible for allowance. This condition is formally regulated by provision of Article 27, section 2 of the Act of 28 November 2003, which states the legal right to claim family and nursery allowance by person in whose household the eligible child stays. The law does not set any legal condition of permanent residence; therefore, family allowance must be paid to the person in whose household a child eligible for benefit resides in that particular month. Family and nursery allowances are paid on a monthly basis. If the child resides in a common household maintained by both parents or legal custodian(s), the family allowance and nursery allowance is paid to that custodian who demands it, declaring himself/herself as the main wage earner of the family.

158. Adult children are not in a position to demand payment of family allowances directly to themselves, even if they live outside their families and support themselves. They are still treated as beneficiaries exclusively, and their legal guardians are entitled to collect family allowances.

Chapter 3. Amount of the Benefit

159. Family allowance in Poland is composed of a basic amount. It is paid on a flat rate basis. Each beneficiary (child or spouse) is entitled to certain amount of Polish zlotys paid on a monthly basis. The Act of 28 November 2003 (*Journal of Laws of 2006*, No. 139, item 992) stated the amount of family allowances depends on the age of child. The basic rate of the family allowance is rather limited: PLN 44 (EUR 11) for child up to 5 years of age; PLN 56 (EUR 14) for child 5–18 years of age; PLN 65 (EUR 16.25) for child older than 18 and younger than 24 years of age. There are seven additional cash benefits paid to those qualified individuals who are entitled to family allowance. Those additional cash benefit are paid for certain occasions listed in Article 8 of the Act of 28 November 2003, such as: birth of child (PLN 1,000 = EUR 238.10 paid one time), starting education (PLN 100 = EUR 23.81 paid once a year in September), expenses related to education and rehabilitation of invalid child (PLN 50–PLN 70 = EUR 11.40–EUR 16.67 paid monthly), and bringing up the child by a single parent (PLN 170 = EUR 40.48 paid on a monthly basis). The amount of the nursery allowance is as high as PLN 144 = EUR 34.29. The Tripartite Council for Social and Economic Matters is entrusted with the right to estimate the level of family allowances. The first estimation was scheduled on 1 September 2006 (Article 18, section 2). If the Tripartite Council does not decide for each year on the new level of family benefits before 15 June of the most current, the right to declare an amount of those benefits is entrusted by the Act of 28 November 2003 to the Council of Ministers.

160. Family allowance is calculated per month. If a child is entitled to family allowance at any time during the month, he/she will receive the full monthly amount declared by the president of the State Social Security Agency.

Chapter 4. Payment

161. Family allowance is paid only to those main wage earners in the family whose monthly income within the family does not exceed the per-person certain amount established by the government.

162. Nursery allowance is also related to the economic situation of the family in which the beneficiary is taken care of. It is paid only if the monthly income per person does not exceed figure given by the Council of Ministers.

163. Family and nursery allowances that should be paid for any month must be paid before the end of the month. In case of an incorrect calculation of allowance, or any other mistake that should be placed on an institution responsible for payment of allowances, the family allowance should be paid back for the past three years. In case of lack of payment of family and nursery allowances, a statutory three-year time limitation to family and nursery allowance is paid.

Part V. Incapacity to Work

Chapter 1. Field of Application

§1. Territorial Field of Application

164. The condition of residence in Poland applies in principle to payment of different short-term payment of cash benefit for incapacity to work covered by the Statutory Regulation of 25 June 1999 on the social security cash benefits paid in case of illness and maternity (*Journal of Laws of 1999*, No. 60, item 636 as amended). At the time of application for benefits paid in case of incapacity to work, the beneficiary must reside in Poland. Those benefits are paid to those insured individuals who are covered by the Act of 13 October 1998 on the National Social Security Scheme (*Journal of Laws of 1998*, No. 137, item 887 as amended) on the assumption that the beneficiary unable to work was employed in Poland.

The act of 25 June 1999 does not provide that short-term social security benefits paid in the case of incapacity for work cannot be applied to foreign citizens working in Poland for foreign or international offices, spouses or next of kin employed by their husband or a close relative who runs an independent business and, therefore, are treated by social security legislation as a self-employed person. Since the day of accession of Poland to the European Union (1 May 2004), the right to social security benefits of the citizens of the Member States of the European Union covered by the Polish national social security scheme is coordinated and regulated by the regulation 1408/72.

§2. Personal Field of Application

165. As far as short-term social security benefits paid in cash are concerned, the personal field of application is the same as it applies for the contribution obligation, paid by the wage earner employed under an employment contract and self-employed people. Public sector employees do not pay contributions for the risk of incapacity to work. They continue to draw wages during sickness periods.

166. There is a certain extension that certain contribution-free periods, such as periods of unemployment, are taken into account for entitlement of cash benefits paid in case of sickness. There are also periods of voluntary continuation of insurance when an insurance period runs out. Self-employed people and the immediate members of their families may extend the insurance period for an additional six months after his/ her insurance runs out.

Chapter 2. Benefits

167. The cash benefits branch of insurance in case of incapacity for work provides for one-off and covers several different risks, such as:

- death (one-off funeral benefit);
- sickness (short-term benefit);
- extended period of illness with a good chance of recuperation (short-term rehabilitation benefit);
- reduction in work ability (short-term benefit);
- birth (one-off benefit);
- maternity (short-term benefit paid to females before and after giving birth to child);
- obligation to take care of a child (short-term benefit);
- leave of absence from work with the purpose of bringing up a small child (short-term benefit).

168. With the exception of funeral benefit, the rest of the above-listed social security benefits amalgamates in the legal system into one type of social insurance paid in the case of incapacity to continue work for a period that lasts from a few days (e.g., obligation to take care of a child) to several years (e.g., leave of absence with the purpose of bringing up a child).

§1. Funeral Benefit

169. This one-off social security benefit was introduced with the purpose of guaranteeing any member of society that in the case of death of a remaining relative, they would be in a position to meet the cost of a decent funeral. Funeral benefit was introduced to reduce the risk of burial at public expense out of funds covered by public assistance, which is associated with lack of decent burial.

170. Funeral benefit is paid to the person responsible for bearing the cost of the funeral of a wage earner, an employed person who passes away during an unpaid leave of absence from work, or an insured worker drawing short-term social security benefit due to illness or maternity.

Funeral benefit is also paid to reimburse the cost of funeral of a family member of an employed person who is not working. In the latter case, an important condition must be met; the family member who is not working should maintain a common household with an employed beneficiary, or the last one should make a significant contribution to the cost of living for the deceased family member.

171. The amount of funeral benefit is as high as 200% of the average monthly income of the wage earner. The amount of funeral benefit is valorized on a quarterly basis. In 2008, the amount of funeral benefit was PLN 5,734 (EUR 1,365.24). Its amount covers the cost of a simple burial ceremony. It does not cover the cost of the monument that is traditionally erected by members of the family of the deceased person at the graveside at the cemetery.

172. Funeral benefit is paid to the person or people who have borne the expense. In the latter case, funeral benefit is divided by the social security agency between the individuals responsible for meeting the cost of burial.

173. When a funeral ceremony is organized and financed by either the state agency or the employer, the remaining relatives – spouse, children, grandchildren, brothers, and sisters – are still entitled to funeral benefit. The same right is enjoyed by people who have lived in the same household with the deceased person until his/her death.

174. Funeral benefit is paid separately from compensation in the case of death during the state of employment paid to the family members of a deceased worker. This compensation in the case of death is regulated in the Labour Code.

§2. Birth Benefit

175. Only female workers are entitled to birth benefit. The Act of 25 June 1999 does not associate the right to birth benefit with giving birth to a child. A female worker who adopts a child is also entitled to birth benefit if she earns the right to maternity benefit.

176. Employment status is the most important factor taken into consideration during the decision-making process concerning payment of birth benefit. Female employees maintain their legal status during leave of absence with the purpose of taking care of and bringing up a child. Therefore, if she gives birth to a second child during a leave of absence period granted to take care of an older child, she does not lose her right to birth benefit after giving birth to a second child.

177. There are some exceptions from the rule according to which birth benefit must be paid to an employed female. Birth benefit is also paid to a former female worker who was discharged due to redundancy. It is also paid to either a wrongfully or unjustly terminated worker who was awarded compensation by the labour court.

Birth benefit is awarded either to currently employed females, or – under certain conditions specified above – to formerly employed female workers.

178. An absolute exception from the principle that birth benefit is associated with the employment status of its recipient is the regulation according to which birth benefit is paid to the wife of a worker who is not working if the spouses maintain a marital economic community. The concept of a marital economic community differs significantly from the notion of maintaining a common household. A married couple who live together and therefore maintain a common household do not necessarily maintain a marital economic community and vice versa. The Act of 25 June 1999 focuses on a marital economic community between spouses who might not live together in the same household.

179. Birth benefit is paid to a female for the birth of any child. The amount of birth benefit is as high as 20% of the average monthly wage.

The rate of birth benefit is not high. The purpose of such a benefit is to help a female who either gave birth or adopted a child to cope with the sudden expenses that must be borne in an expanding family. The tradition in Poland under former times was that either the local state government or an employer was obliged to provide help in the form of in-kind benefits to a female worker who gave birth to a child. That arrangement was one of the most spectacular examples illustrating the thesis that the state takes care of its working population. Under the current situation, limited birth benefit paid in cash is only taken as an example of the moderate prenatal policy of the state government. Additions to the family allowance of PLN 60.73 (EUR 14.46) can amount to PLN 999.97 (EUR 238.09).

§3. Incapacity to Work

I. Wage Earners

180. The other benefits of this branch that cover a short-term incapacity to work are paid in the case of sickness, maternity and bringing up children.

A. Sickness Benefit

181. Sickness benefit is paid to an employee who cannot continue to work due to illness. The illness must occur during the period the parties (employee and employer) are bound by an employment contract. The Act of 25 June 1999 treats sickness on an equal basis with the situation in which an employee cannot continue working due to the fact he/she was defined as a person unable to work by the sanitation authority or was placed for anti-alcohol or anti-drug treatment in hospital.

182. Sickness benefit is paid to a worker who became ill during a period of employment. However, the law provides that sickness benefit is paid to an individual formerly employed who became ill within a certain period after termination of an employment contract: within three months in the case of certain diseases listed in Article 7, item 2 of the Act of 25 June 1999, or within fourteen days in the case of any other illness. In the latter case, the former worker must be ill for at least thirty consecutive days.

The right to sickness benefit is also vested for a former worker who decides to start a business activity and is covered by the social security scheme for self-employed people. It does not cover those who decide to register as unemployed. In the last case, an unemployed individual is covered by a separate regulation concerning rights to short-time benefits in case of sickness of unemployed individuals.

Sickness benefit is not paid to former workers whose employment contract was terminated because such an employee has drawn all his/her rights to sickness benefit. The law provides for special protection for sick workers for a period during which social security benefits in the case of sickness are paid. After completion of that period, a sick worker is no longer under the special umbrella of intensive protection against the termination of an employment contract by an employer. After nine or twelve months of sickness, an employer is free to terminate an employment contract without notice due to absence from work.

Sickness benefit also is not paid to a former employee who has become eligible either for an old-age pension or invalidity benefit. Such an individual is covered by a separate insurance scheme.

183. The right to sickness benefit is related to an employment period of thirty days in case of obligatory coverage and 180 days in case of voluntary social security coverage regardless of whether the parties (an employee and an employer) concluded an employment contract for an indefinite period. The title to insurance (employment relationship for indefinite or definite period of time, or self-employment) is regulated by labour law.

The Act of 25 June 1999 introduces a waiting period of one month during which an employee covered by compulsory social security scheme must perform his/her activities for an employer to qualify for sickness benefit. In case of voluntary coverage by the social security, a waiting period is extended to 180 days (Article 4, section 1). This condition does not apply to incapacity to work caused by industrial injury or occupational disease. In the latter cases, an employee employed for a definite period qualifies immediately from the day employment contract was concluded for sickness benefit. It also does not apply to those insured individuals with the compulsory ten years of social security seniority.

184. Sickness benefits may be drawn for six months. In the case of tuberculosis, the sickness benefit is extended to nine months. Sickness benefit covers the risk of incapacity to work caused by one type of disease. Periods during which an employee is not able to perform work due to the same disease are counted as running continuously if, between the end of the period of sickness and the beginning of the new period of sickness caused by the same disease, there is a break that does not extend to a period longer than one month.

185. The period of six or nine months during which an employee is allowed to draw sickness benefit may be extended for an additional three months based on a physician's decision that during that extended period an employee has a good chance to recover.

186. Sickness benefit is paid on a monthly basis. It is as high as 80% of the monthly income of the sick employee paid by his/her employer on a regular basis. This 80% principle does not apply to female employees who became ill during the period of pregnancy. It also does not apply to employees whose incapacity to work was caused by either industrial injury or occupational disease. After ninety days of continuous incapacity to work during the same illness, the sickness benefit reaches 100% of the monthly wage paid to the employee directly before the employee became ill.

It must be added that the Labour Code introduced new regulations, according to which for the first thirty-three days starting from the day of incapacity to work caused by illness, the employer has the sole and exclusive financial risk of bearing the cost of employment of an employee unable to perform work. Sickness benefit is paid from the first day not covered by the social type of risk placed upon an employer by the labour law.

187. The amount of sickness benefit should reflect the wages lost by an employee during the period of sickness. A sickness benefit is, after all, a surrogate of lost wages. Therefore, a sickness benefit is calculated on the principle of regular wages earned by the sick employee during the six months preceding the day on which an employee became eligible to draw sickness benefit.

In the case of high fluctuation of wages during the previous six months, the basis for calculating sickness benefit is taken from a period longer than the last twelve months.

In the case that the right to sickness benefit was established before a six- or twelve-month period is taken into account while estimating the amount of sickness benefit, the Act of 25 June 1999 takes into account an average monthly salary paid to the insured person. The Act of 25 June 1999 does not set a maximum limit for the amount on which behalf the basis for such a benefit is established. The current social security regulation on sickness benefits dropped the idea used by the previous statutory regulation according to which the basis could not exceed 250% of the average monthly wage on the national level. Under the previous regulation, all groups of employees' wages were taken into account, while calculating the basis for counting sickness benefit on which social security dues were paid had to be taken into consideration during the process of calculating the amount of sickness benefit.

After six months, the basis on which sickness benefit was calculated comes under the process of valorization. Normally, the valorization process takes into consideration the depreciation of the value of any payment from the social security fund between the third quarter of the current year and second quarter of previous year, the fourth quarter of the current year and the first quarter of the previous year, the third quarter of the current year and the first quarter of the previous year, the second quarter of the previous year and the fourth quarter of the previous year.

An indicator used for the purpose of valorization of social security benefits of any type is declared by the president of the State Social Security Agency and published in a legal gazette (*Monitor Polski*).

188. Sickness benefit plays a certain function. Its main and ultimate goal is to provide an income to those workers who because of illness are not able to carry out their regular duties as employees. The primary function of sickness benefit is to guarantee income to those employees who cannot earn their wages due to reasons beyond their control.

Sickness benefit plays an important function as a compensatory type of social security benefit. Its role is to compensate the loss of salary of the working wage earner. Therefore, sickness benefit is considered as a surrogate of lost wages. Thus, sickness benefit cannot be paid during the period in which an employee is entitled to earn wages. It is also not paid during a period in which an employee is not legally entitled to claim wage payment. Those periods are listed in Article 12, sections 1 and 2 of the Act of 25 June 1999. Those periods include unpaid leave of absence from work and periods spent at a penitentiary. The latter periods are considered as spent at the tax payer's expense.

189. Normally, sickness benefit should not be used as a disciplinary measure. However, the Act of 25 June 1999 establishes several exceptions from that principle. The law provides for a possibility of stripping an employee of the legal right to sickness benefit in the following situations:

- during a period in which an employee is suspended from his/her regular working duties because of suspicion of being affected by a particular disease either refuses to accept a sufficient work offer submitted to him/her by an employment agency or neglects his/her duty to register within seven days at the employment agency;
- when incapacity to work was caused by an employee himself/herself who, acting purposely, took part in a fight and as a result was injured. The very same condition for disqualification applies to an employee who was sentenced by a court or magistrate for committing a crime that resulted in causing a state of incapacity to work.

190. Provisions concerning sickness benefit play an important disciplinary function. The Act of 25 June 1999 provides that an employee who caused his/ her incapacity to work by overusing alcohol does not qualify for sickness benefit during the first five days counting from the first day of his/her inability to work.

191. An employee drawing sickness benefit is not allowed to perform any type of work or pursue any type of activity that may cause the prolongation of the state of incapacity to work. Abuse of this regulation causes automatic stoppage of the legal right to sickness benefit.

B. Rehabilitation Benefit

192. Usually an employee who has used up his/her sickness benefit must either resume his/her work or cease working and claim an invalidity benefit. Rehabilitation benefit is the type of benefit that gives an additional chance for recuperation to those employees who have not yet fully recovered from illness and who do not qualify for invalidity benefit. Rehabilitation benefit is the type of social security benefit that should be placed between short- and long-term benefits paid out of the social security fund.

193. Rehabilitation benefit is provided exclusively on a physician's recommendation. The medical examiner must pass a judgment whether or not the patient's health shows any positive signs of recuperation. The doctor's opinion must be approved by a decision made by the committee whose task is to screen the state of health of candidates for invalidity benefits.

194. Rehabilitation benefit is paid for a maximum period of twelve months. It starts from the day after the last day the sickness benefit was used up by an ill employee. The amount of rehabilitation benefit is equal to 75% of the wage, which is taken into account as the basis for calculation of the amount of sickness benefit.

Only in the cases where incapacity to work was caused by industrial injury or occupational disease or incapacity to work affects a pregnant employee does the amount of rehabilitation benefit rise up to 100% of the previous wage earned by injured worker.

195. An employee who recovers during the period in which he/she was drawing a rehabilitation benefit enjoys the legal right to be reengaged in his/her previous post. The law requires that such an employee must make a request immediately after the day his/her right to draw rehabilitation benefit stopped.

196. Quite often the level of productivity of an employee who has recovered from illness is lower than the productivity of a regular worker. Therefore the Act of 25 June 1999 introduced a social security benefit paid in cash to those employees who are employed either at professional rehabilitation centre or at an adjusted place of work. This benefit serves the purpose of guaranteeing a regular standard of wages earned on a monthly basis by a worker whose productivity is lower due to such a worker re-entering the labour market after a sickness period.

197. This benefit, which has the role of providing a reconvalescent employee with a steady income regardless of his/her productivity, may be paid for a maximum period of twenty-four months. It is based on comparison of average wages paid during the last three months before an employee qualifies for such benefit.

C. Maternity Benefit

198. A female worker is entitled to maternity benefit if she either gives birth to a child or adopts a child during the period of her employment. Even an unemployed female is entitled to maternity benefit if she gave birth to a child or an adopted child during a period of leave of absence from work for the purpose of taking care of a child born earlier. Technically, leave of absence with the purpose of taking care of a small child is considered as a continuation of an employment relationship. However, a female worker may decide to cease the employment relationship for the purpose of taking care of her small child. If she gives birth to another child during a period that does not exceed the period of either paid or unpaid leave of absence, she is entitled to maternity benefit.

A female worker made redundant while pregnant also enjoys a legal right to maternity benefit until the day of confinement.

199. Maternity benefit is paid on a monthly basis. It is equal to 100% of the wage earned by the pregnant female worker. Maternity benefit is paid during the entire period of maternity leave of absence from work, which lasts up to twenty, thirty-one, thirty-three, thirty-five, or thirty-seven weeks. The period of maternity leave of absence is regulated by the Labour Code. Its length depends on the number of children born during the act of birth and the number of times the female worker has given birth. In accordance with the newly amended Labour Code, as of the 1 January 2010 (*Journal of Laws of 2009*, No. 237, item 1654), employees (the mother and, in certain situations, the father of the child), have the right to additional leave, which carries the same conditions as maternity leave. This is stipulated in the following:

- Article 183(1)(1) of the Labour Code (twenty weeks for the care of one child), up to twenty-two weeks in 2010 and 2011, to twenty-four weeks in 2012 and 2013.
- Article 183(1)(2) of the Labour Code (thirty-one weeks for the simultaneous care of two children), up to thirty-four weeks in 2010 and 2011, to thirty-five weeks in 2012 and 2013.
- Article 183(1)(3) of the Labour Code (thirty-three weeks for the simultaneous care of three children), up to thirty-four weeks in 2010 and 2011, to thirty-five weeks in 2012 and 2013.

Parents of children born in 2009 also have the right to this additional leave if on the 1 January 2010 maternity leave was granted.

From 1 January 2010, fathers have the right to one-week paternity leave. This leave should be taken within the first year of the child's birth.

200. On 17 June 2013, the law came into force amending the law – Labour Code and some other laws, passed on 28 May 2013 (*Journal of Laws* of 2013, item 675). The above-mentioned law granted to employees (men and women) the right to additional maternity leave from six to eight weeks immediately after the use of maternity leave (Article 182 1 § 1 of the Labour Code). Immediately after the use of a full additional maternity leave, the employee is entitled to parental leave for up to twenty-six weeks, regardless of the number of children born at one birth (Article 182 1a § 1 of the Labour Code). The employer is obliged to grant the employee such leave. The parental leave can be simultaneously used by both the child's parents. It is granted once or can be divided up into three parts, none of which may be shorter than eight weeks. Each part of the holiday should fall directly one after the other (Article 182 1a § 2 of the Labour Code). The above holiday entitlement granted to the child's biological parents is also granted to persons who have adopted a child or children for education and have the legal status of the family (Article 182 4 §§ 1–2 of the Labour Code). Employees who use additional maternity leave and parental leave have the right to opt out of this leave in whole or in part, and return to work (Article 179 2 § 1, Article 179 3 § 1 of the Labour Code). During the period of maternity leave and additional maternity leave, parents of the child are entitled to maternity allowance equal to 100% of the base of the benefit that is in the amount equal to the remuneration received by an employee during their work. During parental leave, the child's parents have one-month maternity allowance equal to 60% of the basis of such a claim. An insured person who is not an employee, but is engaged in business on their own account has the right to receive benefits during maternity leave and parental leave at 80% of the base assessment of that benefit which is the declared income of the business.

201. The act of 24 July 2015 on the amendment of the Labour Code and certain other acts entered into force on 2 January 2016. It amended the provisions of Chapter VIII of the Labour Code governing the parental rights of employees (Journal of Laws of 2015, item 1268). The act specifies the types of leaves for the insured persons – employees and other insured persons performing work not under an employment relationship, a mother, a childcarer, and a father or a legal guardian of a child. This is a maternity leave and a parental leave. The maternity leave is granted depending on the number of children born at one birth: one, two, three, four, five and more, and amounts to twenty, thirty-one, thirty-three, thirty-five, thirty-seven weeks, according to the number of children born. After an employee has taken at least fourteen weeks of the maternity leave, the remaining part of the leave may be taken by the employee-father raising the child. After the maternity leave has been taken or a maternity allowance for a period corresponding to the period of maternity leave has been received, the employee is entitled – depending on the number of children born at one birth – to a parental leave up to thirty-two or thirty-four weeks. The parental leave may be taken jointly by both parents. They can take it at the same time. The parental leave can be taken all at once or in parts, not later than by the end of the calendar year in which the child reaches the age of 6. An employee-father raising a child, is entitled to a paternity leave up to two weeks, however only until the child is twenty-four months old. In the case of adoption of a child, a father is entitled to the paternity leave within a period of twenty-four months after the decision on the adoption has become final and valid, until the adopted child is 7 years old at the latest. An employee who has been employed for at least six months is entitled to a child-care leave in order to take a personal care of his child. The child-care leave entitlement is thirty-six months. It is granted for a period not longer than by the end of the calendar year in which the child reaches the age of 6. During the said leaves the persons who raise children and are covered by the social insurance in respect of sickness and maternity as specified in the act of 15 May 2014 amending the act on the social security cash benefits in respect of sickness and maternity (Journal of Laws z 2014 r., item 159), are entitled to allowances.

202. The act of 11 February 2016 on the state assistance in raising children published on 17 February 2016, entered into force on the first day of the month following its adoption. On 1 April 2016 a right to the child benefit was granted for the second and each subsequent child at the amount of PLN 500 per each of the mentioned children. The above entitlement was granted to the Polish citizens and foreigners legally residing in the territory of Poland for a period during which they should receive the child benefit. The child benefit is granted to a mother, father, an actual guardian or a legal guardian of a child. The purpose of this benefit is to partially cover the expenses connected with raising children, including taking care of children and satisfaction of their vital needs. The child benefit is payable until a child reaches 18 years of age. The poor families in which the family income per person does not exceed PLN 1,200 (EUR 287) are entitled to the child benefit also for the first child. The entitlement to the child benefit for the second and the subsequent children in the family is not dependent on the wealth of the family. A phenomenon observed during the first period after introduction of the child benefit was resignation from work by low paid women who were entitled to the child benefit.

203. Incapacity to work may be caused not only by the poor state of health of the worker but also by the worker's duty to take care of a dependent who is unable to function on his/her own and who is a member of the worker's immediate family. The Act of 25 June 1999 takes for granted the very basic fact that members of the family must take care of themselves and show their care for each other.

The social security benefit that enables people to take care of a member of family in need is paid in the following situation:

- an employee must take care of a child up to 8 years old during a period of unexpected disturbance in the kindergarten, or the primary activity of the school normally attended by that child;
- sickness or maternity duties of the parent who takes care of another child within the family on a regular basis;
- hospitalization of the parent who takes care of the child;
- sickness of a child up to 14 years old;
- sickness of another member of the family: parents, parents-in-law, grandparents, grandchildren, brothers and sisters, and children over 14 years old who stay with an employee entitled to social security benefit in the same household.

204. The social security benefit paid for the purpose of taking care of a member of family in need is paid up to sixty days in the case a minor child having to be taken care of. When care must be provided by an adult member of the family, the social security benefit is paid for fourteen days. The maximum number of days per year in which an employee is entitled to draw social security benefit paid to workers who are taking care of members of family is as high as sixty days.

205. The Act of 25 June 1999 sets a rate for social security benefit at 80% of the monthly wage earned by an employee obliged to take care of a member of his/ her family. This social security benefit is paid on the condition that there is no adult member of the family who could relieve a parent from his/her duty to take care of a member of family. Only in the case of illness of a small child of up to 2 years is the mother entitled to draw social security benefit paid to parents who take care of children regardless of the fact that there are other members of a family who take care of a sick small child. The law acts on the presumption that only the mother may provide proper care of a child not older than 2 years.

D. Childcare Leave of Absence

206. Social security benefits paid to one of the parents who decides to bring up a small child is regulated by the Labour Code (Articles 186–187[5]). The leave of absence is granted to either a female or male worker to suit her/his purpose of taking care of a small child (up to 4 years old). A request for parental leave of absence may be presented by a worker with a minimum seniority of six months. The waiting period for an activation of the right to present a request for the parental leave of absence is not limited to those working parents who are employed at least for six months by an employer whom they ask for the leave of absence. Any worker employed by various employers may claim he/she accumulated the required period of seniority if the total number of working months exceeds the legal minimum set by the Labour Code.

Parental leave of absence is granted for up to three years before the child is 4 years old. In cases where the child has to have special treatment, the leave of absence is granted to take care of a child under 18 years. Parental leave of absence may be taken in four parts by an eligible parent. The decision about who takes parental leave of absence is left to the parents. The Labour Code provides that the maximum three-year period for taking care of one child should be decided between eligible parents. An employer cannot allow granting a leave of absence for one child for a period longer than three years, regardless of the amount of leave of absence taken by either parent.

207. During parental leave of absence, a worker taking care of a small child is entitled to the social security benefit that enables a parent, who temporarily ceases to work in order to provide care to her/his child, to support himself/herself during the period of parental leave of absence. It is important to note that the right to social security benefit is paid during a limited period of time. A parent who is taking care of one child is entitled to draw social security benefit for up to twenty-four months. A female worker who is listed as a single mother is entitled to draw social security benefit for up to thirty-six months. Social security benefit is paid for the same period to a parent taking care of at least two children. The right to draw the social security benefit up to seventy-two months is extended to a parent taking care of a disabled child.

5. *Journal of Law*, No. 106, item 457 as amended.

208. The right to draw parental leave of absence benefit depended on the economic status of the family. Social security benefit was paid only to those workers on parental leave of absence living in a family whose monthly income per family member did not exceed 25% of the average national monthly wages in the previous year. Social security benefit paid to workers on parental leave of absence was presented in flat figures. According to the Ordinance of the Council of Ministers of 28 May 1996 on parental leave of absence and benefits paid to the eligible employees taking those leaves, a parent on leave of absence was entitled to PLN 179.90 = EUR 42.83 in social security benefit. A single mother on leave of absence was entitled to PLN 286.10 = EUR 68.12 in social security benefit. The social security benefit paid to a parent on leave of absence was systematically valorized. Information concerning valorization of family allowances was applicable to the social security benefit paid to working parents on leave of absence for the purpose of taking care of a small child. The Labour Code (Article 186–Article 186^8) does not mention parental social allowances. However, childcare leave is not again unpaid as it once was in 1968 when the very first regulation on maternity (not parental) childcare was introduced. During childcare leave, employees (either the mother of the child, father of the child, the legal guardian of the child or the de facto guardian) have the right to an allowance. This benefit has been granted by the Family Benefits Act, passed on the 23 November 2003 (*Journal of Law* 2006, No. 139, item 992). This allowance carries a family benefit characteristic. It is granted for a period of twenty-four, thirty-six, or seventy-two calendar months (Article 10(1)). The right to this childcare additional allowance while making use of a thirty-six-month childcare leave is granted to those employees who are taking care of more than one child born during the one delivery.

Employees entitled to seventy-two weeks of childcare leave are those whose child is disabled. The additional allowance amounts to PLN 400 = EUR 95.24 per month. The allowance paid for care that does not amount to one full calendar month is calculated at 1/30 of the allowance for each day of care. Should childcare leave be used by both parents or legal guardians of the child, the allowance is granted to only one of the parents, based on the premise of the one child being taken care of.

The additional allowance is not granted to the following employees: those who during childcare leave are carrying out other paid employment, those whose child is in a childcare facility for at least five days per week (either in a day nursery or in day care) or those who have ceased personal care of their child. Placing a child in a care facility due to health or therapeutic reasons or if the child is disabled, does not disentitle an employee on childcare leave from being granted the additional allowance.

II. Self-Employed

209. There is no differentiation between wage-earners and self-employed people in matters concerning one-off and short-term social security benefit paid in the case of incapacity to work. The Act of 25 June 1999 provides that self-employed people covered by the Act of 13 October 1998 are entitled to all social security benefits both paid in kind and in cash to insured employees such as:

- health insurance;
- sickness benefits, rehabilitation benefits, birth benefits, and maternity benefits;
- death benefits.

Chapter 3. Certification of Incapacity to Work

210. As already mentioned, the incapacity to work must be certified by a physician. The worker enjoys the liberty to choose any doctor he/she wants. At the end of the visit, the worker receives a certificate in legal form. The worker must submit the certificate to the employer or send it to the employer by mail. An employer is trusted with the task of managing funds out of which social security benefits, both one-off and short-term, are paid. In fact, an employer advances funds paid to an insured worker from its own budget. An employer presents a financial statement to the social security agency for reimbursement of funds advanced to an employee.

That system of payment of social security benefits was developed during the period in which the State Social Security Agency cooperated with the state-owned enterprises. After 1989, the majority of state-owned enterprise went into the process of privatization or commercialization. The system, however, remains basically the same. Those employers who did not present their employees to the State Social Security Agency on an individual basis are trusted with the task of forwarding social security benefit to eligible workers. Only those employers who report their employees to the State Social Security Agency on an individual basis are obliged to forward certificates of incapacity to work to the branch office of the social security agency that takes care of the payment of social security benefit. The latter category includes small and medium-sized private employers. Self-employed people receive their benefits and allowances directly from the local branch of the State Social Security Agency.

211. In the case of disagreement between the worker and employer concerning the worker's state of incapacity to work, the worker is entitled to apply directly to the local branch of the State Social Security Agency to get a certificate of his/her incapacity to work and a statement concerning his/her right to one of the above-mentioned social security benefits.

Any decision issued by the State Social Security Agency in the matter of social security benefit is treated by the social security regulations as an administrative type of decision that may be challenged in a court of law adjudicating social security cases (the social security court).

Chapter 4. Benefits

212. As already mentioned, the amount of social security benefit paid in the case of incapacity to work is not fixed by law. The Act of 25 June 1999 only establishes a relationship presented in percentages between the salary earned by an employee incapable to work and the amount of social security benefit paid to the worker affected by one of the risks covered by the Act of 13 October 1998.

213. The same principle of proportionality between the level of benefit and earned income applies to self-employed people. There is no direct relation, though, between the monthly wage earned and the amount of social security benefit because self-employed people do not earn wages. The social security regulations on self-employed people establish an indirect link between the level of income and the amount of social security benefit. Since there is a direct link between social security dues and the economic basis on which those dues are calculated, which is monthly income earned and declared as the basis for the purpose of calculation of social security benefit, the amount of social security benefit paid to self-employed people depends on the amount of income declared by such a person as an economic basis for calculation of social security dues.

214. One-off social security benefits: birth and death benefits are paid immediately after the risks that are covered by social security law (birth, or death) occurred. The other social security benefit paid by employers should be paid on a monthly basis on the same day's wages are usually paid. Social security benefits paid by the local branch of the State Social Security Agency must be paid immediately after presentation of certification of incapacity to work by the insured individual. Currently, social security benefits must pay at the latest within thirty days starting from the day an affidavit of incapacity to work was submitted by the insured person to the local office of the State Social Security Agency.

215. Social security benefits should be paid to an individual eligible to receive those benefits or to another person entitled to the collect the salary of the insured worker. Upon the request of the insured beneficiary, social security benefit may be paid to any other person. If the insured beneficiary is hospitalized social security benefit is paid to his/her spouse or a person taking care of the beneficiary's child.

216. In the case of error, either in matters of right to social security benefit or the amount of such a benefit, made by an institution responsible for payment of social security benefit, the beneficiary is obliged to pay back to the social security agency the benefit forwarded to him/her but only if the mistake was his/her fault.

217. The social security law introduces a six-month statutory limit on the right to claim social security benefits by an insured individual. Statutory limitation starts from the day on which an insured person may present a legal demand for any benefit to which a beneficiary has become eligible.

Chapter 5. Conditions

218. On average, the conditions for entitlement to cash benefits for incapacity to work are the same as for healthcare benefits. Any working person is automatically covered by the national insurance scheme from the day he/she started to work. With the exception mentioned earlier concerning the right of self-employed individuals performing work on the basis of a civil type of contract, applying for sickness benefit, there is no waiting period treated by social security legislation as precondition to acquire cash benefits.

Contribution documents (an affidavit concerning the state of health of the insured individual, or his/her family situation) should be presented to the decision-making authority: an employer or the State Social Security Agency. Lack of grounds for exclusion to some of the social security benefits, such as sickness benefit, serves as another legal condition for entitlement.

219. Only a professionally active person is entitled to social security benefit paid in case of incapacity to work. Therefore, entitlement to social benefits covering the risk of incapacity to work ceases to exist after the insured person has earned the right to an old-age pension, or invalidity benefit. An individual entitled to either an old-age pension, or invalidity benefit could carry on working. In that case, he/she is entitled to social security benefits paid in case of sickness, or other risks covered by one-off or short-time social branch of social security.

220. During the period of incapacity to work, the beneficiary puts himself or herself at the disposal of his/her employer or the local branch of the State Social Security Agency. Both institutions – the employer and the social security agency – are allowed to check up on beneficiaries to make certain they use social security benefits according to the rules established by the social security regulations.

Chapter 6. Accumulation Rules

221. The general rule, already mentioned in this chapter, is that social security benefit is not due when compensation for the same risk provided for by any other branch of the compulsory, national social security scheme. An additional, private insurance scheme, which is still rather limited in Poland, can be combined with national social security benefit.

222. As already mentioned, there cannot be accumulation of wages and social security benefit. As a matter of principle, the social security benefits are considered a surrogate of wages. Social security benefits are paid exclusively in situations in which an insured person cannot carry on with earning wages because of his/her incapacity to work.

Part VI. Industrial Accidents and Occupational Diseases

Chapter 1. Field of Application

§1. Territorial Field of Application

223. The Statutory Regulation of 30 October 2002 (*Journal of Laws of 2002*, No. 199, item 1673 as amended) protects wage earners against occupational hazards. The law applies to industrial accidents and occupational diseases created during the period of employment of a professional activity listed in Article 3, section 2 of that act of an injured worker within the territory of Poland.

224. There is a significant extension, though, in the field of territorial application of the statutory regulation where occupational hazard is concerned. The Act of 30 October 2002 applies to all injured workers covered by the industrial injury scheme who are performing their tasks in Poland as well as abroad for Polish enterprises. The territorial field of application is extended to Polish citizens who are employed outside Poland and who are employed under employment contracts for enterprises owned by Poles.

225. The Statutory Regulation of 30 October 2002 applies to any employment relationship in which a Polish citizen enters within Polish territory regardless of the legal status of the employer.

§2. Personal Field of Application

226. The Act of 20 October 2002 applies to those insured individuals who are wage earners or self-employed covered by the part of the national social security system related to the old-age pension and insurance in case of incapacity to work (Article 12, section 1 of the Act of 13 October 1998). According to Article 12, section 2 of that act, the Law of 30 October 2002 does not apply to:

- unemployed while drawing unemployment benefits;
- individuals employed under the civil law type of contracts;

- member of military forces, carrier military personnel and members of the paramilitary forces (policemen, prison guards, border control, etc.);
- employees on parental leaves;
- persons drawing social assistance.

The Act of 30 October 2002 does not apply either to those individuals who may be covered on their request by the national social security scheme.

227. The Act of 30 October 2002 is strict. It deals only with injured individuals who come under the category of employed and professionally active. They claim benefits either from their employers or the State Social Security Agency.

228. Semi-self-employed individuals performing work under a civil contract for legal entities or other individuals are also protected against occupational hazard by the Act of 30 October 2002. They claim benefits from either legal entities or individuals for whom they perform work regulated by a civil contract.

229. Self-employed people are covered for occupational risk by the Act of 30 October 2002. They claim benefit from the State Social Security Agency.

230. Injured enlisted men, members of the military, police forces, border and prison guards, and individual farmers are covered by separate statutory regulations.

231. The territorial and personal field of application regulated in the statutory acts listed above is the same as the field of application stated in the Act of 30 October 2002. The same statement applies to the concept of accidents with the exception that accidents regulated by separate statutory acts are not called ‘industrial’. They are legally related to the activity performed by the insured person, conditions of eligibility, and payment and amount of benefit.

Chapter 2. Concept of 'Industrial Accident'

§1. Accident

232. The legal definition of 'industrial accident' is presented in Article 3, section 1 of the Act of 30 October 2002. According to that definition, industrial accident is a sudden occurrence caused by an outside factor that results in injury. This sudden accident created by an external force must be linked to the work performed by the injured worker.

233. The Act of 30 October 2002 distinguishes between an accident during work and an accident that is known as a type of work accident (Article 3, section 2).

234. One of the most distinguishing features of any of those above-mentioned accidents is the sudden occurrence and the injury. A victim of an industrial accident must prove the relationship between the sudden occurrence and the injury. It is not required by law to prove the abnormal nature of the sudden accident. An accident may be caused by regular conditions of work. It is required, though, to prove that an accident was caused by an external force.

235. This concept of an outside factor is quite important. It has caused many different interpretations of the Supreme Court. Depending on individual circumstances, the legal condition of an external force that caused an industrial accident is met if the cause of accident was created by any biological factor that developed in the body of the injured worker. The best example to illustrate this statement is an accident accused by either heart attack or brain collapse. These accidents are created by factors that cannot be easily located outside the human body. Therefore, the Supreme Court created a theory under which any circumstances existing in a working environment hostile to the human body that result in a sudden malfunction of human organs qualifies as an industrial accident. Therefore, stress caused by the working environment that results in heart attack may be considered as an industrial accident.

236. An accident qualifies as 'sudden' if it occurs within one working day.

237. An accident qualifies as a work accident even if it does not cause incapacity to work of the employee affected by the industrial accident. The Act of 30 October 2002 makes a legal distinction between industrial accident and the social security benefit paid when such an accident occurs. Normally, an industrial accident results in incapacity to work or death. In that situation, an injured worker or his/her family is entitled to compensation and/or invalidity benefit. However, an industrial accident may not cause any damage to the human body. Lack of a result does not disturb an injured worker to require an official acknowledgment that the incident that occurred legally qualifies as an industrial accident. An injured worker has a legal interest in getting an affidavit with legal classification of the incident as an industrial accident. Such affidavit may be useful in the future in case the state of health of the injured worker deteriorates. The legal classification of the incident may be used as the basis for bringing a claim for compensation caused by an accident qualified by the act of 30 October 2002 as an industrial injury.

§2. Link to the Contract of Employment

238. An incident becomes an industrial accident if it shows a juridical link with an employment contract. The concept of 'juridical' link is the most peculiar idea created by the Act of 30 October 2002. The juridical link means that there is no necessity to establish any direct link between the place and time of work and the industrial accident. The juridical link is the type of link that is related to the employment contract or certain type of professional activity performed by insured person. This means that an injured worker was performing his/her regular duties under the authority of an employer. Therefore, the juridical link between an accident and the employment contract exists when the worker was injured while he/she was performing his/her regular duties under the employment contract. The juridical link also exists when an injured worker was carrying out orders given to him/her by an employer. If a worker was injured while acting within the best interest of an employer or showing initiative, such an accident qualifies as an industrial accident. The Act of 30 October 2002 does not require proof that an injured worker was acting under the supervision of an employer. Under an employment contract, the legal possibility of supervision will suffice as proof, even if the actual supervision is not possible. Such a legal concept of an industrial accident implies that the accident may occur outside the regular place of work as long as one may consider the worker to have been performing his/her duty and, therefore, placed under the legal possibility of supervision of the employer.

An accident that occurs during an official break is also considered as a work accident. It does not matter whether or not the break or work stoppage was legitimate. By making an unauthorized work stoppage, the worker does not break a juridical link with the employment contract. The Act of 30 October 2002 does not require the existence of a direct link between work performance and the accident. Therefore, an accident on the way from the gate to the actual place of work is considered as the work accident, not an accident on the way to work. Such an accident happens at the place of work, not on the way to work. An accident that occurred during the period of getting tools ready for work to be performed is treated by the social security law as a work accident.

239. There is a general rule established in Article 6 of the Civil Code that applies also to the legal regulations concerning industrial injuries. The burden of proof is placed upon the party that claims a certain legal status. However, the victim of an industrial accident does not have to carry the burden of proof that the accident that happened during the regular course of employment was caused by the implementation of the worker's regular duty. The Act of 30 October 2002 assumes that every accident happening during the performance of duty under an employment contract arises out of that contract. It is the legal duty of the employer or the State Social Security Agency to prove otherwise. Such a burden of proof contrasts with relationship that is taken for granted between an accident and an employment contract, which may only be made by either an employer or the State Social Security Agency by way of showing that the injury occurred during activities not related in any way with employment duties that must be carried out by an employee. For example, an employee injured while performing some functions contracted on his/her own for a third person on work premises, during company time, and using an employer's tools cannot claim such an accident as a work accident regulated by the Act of 30 October 2002. In an example given, the juridical link between an accident and the contract of employment is lost. The proceedings on how to determine the circumstances and causes of accidents occurring within the workplace, as well as how such accidents are to be documented and how the scope of information relating to such accident is entered into the accidents log, is described by the Order of the Council of Ministers, handed down on the 1 July 2009, concerning the Determination of the Circumstances and Causes of Accidents Within the Workplace (*Journal of Laws of 2009*, No. 105, item 870).

240. The injured worker's own fault in causing an injury does not change anything in the process of legal classification of the accident as a work accident. The Act of 30 October 2002 disqualifies an injured worker or his/her family in case of death caused by an accident only from social security benefit paid to the victim of industrial injury or his/her survivors. An accident caused by the worker's own fault remains a work accident if it shows any juridical link to the contract of employment under which the injured worker acted.

Alcohol consumed by an injured worker always brings up the question of the injured worker's own fault in causing the work accident. The Act 30 of October 2002 sets a legal obligation upon an injured worker to put himself/herself for a test that is designed to establish the amount of alcohol consumed. The law does not disqualify an accident as a work accident if the victim of such an accident was under the influence of alcohol. The law disqualifies an injured worker from any social security benefit paid to victims of work accidents who by the fact of consuming alcohol caused to a great extent the work accident.

241. In some cases, the link between the work accident and the employment contract is limited. It happens when a worker is injured in the course of complying with an obligation to serve in a paramilitary organization existing on the company premises, or serving in a voluntary firefighters brigade organized by an employer. Those accidents are treated by the Act of 30 October 2002 as accidents equal to work accidents as far as legal consequences are concerned. The very same conclusion is applied to accidents that occurred during a worker's involvement in trade organizations or political parties functioning on company premises.

Involvement in any of those organizations is made possible because those organizations exist in the enterprise at which the injured worker was employed. In tackling the problem of linkage of work accident to the contract of employment, one may conclude that an indirect link exists between a work accident and the employment contract. After all, had it not been for the contract of employment with the particular employee, the work would not be involved in the type of activity described in Article 3, section 3 of the Act of 30 October 2002, which eventually included an industrial injury.

242. There is a far more clearer link between an employment contract and an accident that occurred during work-related travel. An accident that occurred during such official journey on which an employer sent an employee is treated equally with a work accident defined in Article 3, section 1 of the Act of 30 October 2002.

243. An employer's risk does not extend to all acts of a worker's behaviour who is delegated by an employer to perform some professional tasks outside the place of employment. In cases where the accident is due to the worker's behaviour not connected with his/her professional duties, such an accident cannot be treated on an equal footing with a work accident. By engaging himself/herself with a type of activity not connected with a type of work an employee was delegated by an employer to perform, the worker cuts the link between an employment contract and an accident.

§3. Accidents on the Way to Work

244. The Act of 30 October 2002 does not define an accident that occurred on the way to and from work. Article 57(b), section 1 of the Act of 17 December 1998 as amended by Article 44 of the Act of 30 October 2002 defines the accidents on the way to and from work and workers injured on the way to and from work. Generally, the way to and from work is defined as the normal route a worker typically takes when commuting between his/her place of residence and the place where the work is performed. Deviations from a regular route are acceptable if justified by circumstances. As examples of decisions concerning work accidents which occurred on the way to and from work, the following cases are given:

- an accident occurring on the way to or from the supermarket, or to a restaurant in which the worker goes to buy food or to eat;
- an accident occurring on the way to or from the school in which the worker has enrolled himself/herself for training;
- an accident occurring on the way to and from the doctor's office to which the worker has gone for medical treatment;
- an accident occurring on the way to and from school or kindergarten to which an injured worker has gone to collect children;
- an accident occurring on the way to and from the state office building to which the worker has gone to deal with some administrative matter.

245. One of the issues under legal debate is the point of departure in the case of an accident on the way to work and the point of arrival in the case of an accident outside work. The point of departure to work and arrival from work must be the place of residence of the injured worker. Jurisdiction puts an emphasis on a worker's intent to make the place of residence the centre of living. Therefore, a place where an injured worker stays occasionally does not qualify as a place of residence within the meaning of the Act of 30 October 2002.

246. The journey to work starts and ends when the worker crosses the threshold of his home (building or apartment).

247. The 'regular' way to and from work does not have to be the shortest or the most direct way. For example, a longer route with better public transport between the worker's residence and the place of work is treated by the judiciary as the 'normal' way to work.

248. The worker is allowed to make stops on the way to and from work. Any interruptions are treated by the judiciary as part of the 'normal' route taken by the worker to and from work if they are justified by a legitimate reason.

§4. Other Legal Definitions of 'Industrial Accidents'

249. The Act of 30 October 2002 introduces three additional legal definitions of industrial accidents. The act defines accidents that result in the death of an injured worker. The 'mortal' industrial accident is an accident that causes the death of the injured worker either immediately or within the six months after the work accident has occurred (Article 3, section 4 of the Act of 30 October 2002).

250. The second legal definition deals with 'serious' accidents. Any industrial accident that results in heavy damage to human body is considered as a 'serious' accident. Article 3, section 5 of the Act of 30 October 2002 lists damages considered by the law as heavy. Among them, the following damages to human body are listed:

- permanent disturbance in the process of the normal functioning of the human body;
- lost of vision, sound, and ability to communication;
- incurable illness or illness that threatens life;
- permanent mental illness;
- permanent or major illness that affects in impossibility of accepting and carrying out any work assignment or effects in permanent serious destruction of the body of the injured worker.

251. The third legal definition introduced by the Act of 30 October 2002 deals with a work accident that affects more than two workers. Such an accident is called an accident with a greater number of victims 'the group accident' (Article 3, section 6). The difference between a work accident that affects one victim only and the 'group accident' is related to an employer's duty. An employer on whose premises at least two victims of one work accident are listed is under a legal obligation to notify the proper state authorities, primarily the labour inspector and district attorney's office.

Chapter 3. Concept of 'Occupational Disease'

252. Occupational diseases are defined by an official list of diseases issued by the state government. Article 237, paragraph 1, item 2 of the Labour Code serves as an official basis for issuing this list. The official diseases list is a long and casuistic list of diseases and products causing diseases, including most of the known occupation-related sickness.

253. It is vital that the particular disease is included in the official list of diseases. Otherwise, the most common sicknesses among a particular profession cannot be treated by the Act of 30 October 2002 as an occupational disease. According to Polish social security regulations, the victim of a disease that is not included in the official list of occupational diseases is not allowed to prove the occupational nature of that disease. If the particular disease is not listed, it cannot be considered as an occupational disease under the legal regulation of the Act of 30 October 2002.

254. The victim of an occupational disease must prove that the given disease has been registered as an occupational disease. The victim also must prove that he/she was exposed to the risks of that occupational disease. An official list of occupational diseases lists professions that are exposed to the particular risks covered by regulations protecting against certain occupational diseases. The newest list is comprised of twenty-six work-related illnesses and forms part of an appendix to the Order on Work Related Illnesses of the Council of Ministers, handed down on 30 June 2009 (*Journal of Laws of 2009*, No. 105, item 869).

Chapter 4. Medical Care

255. Effective 1 January 2003, a victim of an industrial accident is not entitled to medical care free of charge. However, the cost of his/her medical treatment is covered by the industrial injury fund (Article 23 of the Act of 30 October 2002). An injured worker receives medical care from the State Social Security Agency. This care is paid for by the State Social Security Agency itself. The Act of 30 October 2002 does not declare that medical service to the victims of industrial injuries is provided for free. The drugs used by the victims of industrial accidents are not provided free of charge any longer. Their cost is also covered by the social security agency out of the above separate industrial insurance fund.

Since there is nothing such as free service of any kind, someone must bear the cost of free medical and drug service provided by the state to victims of industrial accidents. The Act of 30 October 2002 shifted the burden of expenses for medicare of victims of industrial injuries from the taxpayers to the special type of fund.

Chapter 5. Incapacity to Work

256. Incapacity to work caused by an industrial accident may be permanent or temporary. It also makes an injured worker totally or partially unfit for work.

257. The worker who has been injured on the job is allowed to get one-off social security benefit – one-off compensation for either a death within the family or invalidity pension paid to injured workers.

258. An invalidity payment that comes as legal compensation for a work accident is either paid directly to the beneficiary or to the beneficiary's family.

259. Permanent incapacity to work caused by a work accident enables an injured worker to function normally. Temporary, long-lasting incapacity to work is defined as unfitness to work that lasts longer than six months but, according to medical knowledge, presents a chance for the recovery of health. As a matter of principle, any injury that causes any damages to biological functions of the human body can be treated as temporary, long-lasting incapacity to work.

260. A distinction between permanent and temporary incapacity to work is made by the Act of 30 October 2002 to establish two categories of injured workers. One category is entitled to the one-off compensation for damages caused by a work accident. Permanently and temporarily injured workers with long-lasting incapacity to work are entitled to compensation for each per cent of damage. The amount of compensation for each percentage of damage to the body of the worker injured in the work accident is declared by Article 12, section 1 of the Act of 30 October 2002. The amount of compensation runs as high as 20% of average national monthly wages for each per cent of damage. However, from 1 April 2005 until 31 March 2006, an injured employee received 18% of average national monthly wages per each percentage of damage (PLN 4.12 = EUR 1.03). In case of total incapacity to work, a victim of industrial injury received PLN 8,013 (EUR 2003.25). From 1 April 2006 until March 2007, that amount of compensation increased by 1%. An injured worker received an increase in compensation 20% of average monthly wages for each additional 1% of damages that exceeds additional 10%. For instance, if an injured employee received 360% of the average national monthly wage or 20% damage caused by the industrial accident (18% for each percentage of 20% damage), he/she would receive additional 180% of that average wage if – due to the earlier industrial injury – his/her state of health deteriorated by at least an additional 10%. On the 8 March 2013, the Minister for Labour and Social Policies announced the following one-off compensation amounts for accidents at the workplace or for work-related illnesses (The Polish Monitor 2012, item 164). It is valid from 1 April 2012 until 31 March 2014 (PLN 4.19= EUR 1.00):

- PLN 704 (EUR 168.01) for each per cent of determined damage to the health of the worker that is either permanent or long-term.
- PLN 704 for each per cent of permanent or long-term increase of damage by at least ten points.
- PLN 12,326 (EUR 2,941.76) for the complete inability to carry out work as well as an inability to live independently.

- PLN 31,690 (EUR 7,653.24) as a one-off compensation entitlement for a beneficiary of the deceased (who was either insured or a pensioner), the beneficiary not being a spouse or an offspring of the deceased.
- PLN 63,390 (EUR 15,128.87) as a one-off compensation entitlement for the following beneficiaries: spouse or offspring, two or more offspring, spouse and one or more offspring. Should the compensation be paid out to three or more beneficiaries, the amount of the compensation increases by PLN 12,326 (EUR 2,941.76).

261. A worker with a minor injury caused by an industrial accident also can expect the one-off compensation. He/she can expect to receive more than 20% of the supplementary benefit paid to those injured workers whose health has deteriorated as a result of the work accident. The victim of a work accident is eligible for the invalidity benefit paid during the period of incapacity to work. Any victim of a work accident, even one whose health has deteriorated as a result of such an accident less than the required minimum (10%), is entitled to the invalidity benefit paid during the period of incapacity to work. The only difference between permanently and temporary injured workers is such that the first are eligible for permanent benefits while the latter qualify for temporary invalidity benefits issued for the period shown in the decision of the local branch of the State Social Security Agency acting on behalf of the recommendation of its medical adviser.

262. The one-off compensation calculated on behalf of the amount of damage caused by a work accident is not treated by the law as established forever. The nature of the injuries caused by the work accident is determined when the health condition of the victim of the work accident has stabilized. The State Social Security Agency acting on the recommendation of its medical advisor expresses the degree of incapacity to work by presenting it in a percentage figure between 0 and 100. If the victim does not agree with the estimation given by the State Social Security Agency, he/she may challenge that decision. Another medical examiner reviews the estimation made by the medical expert called by the insurer. After all, the legal battle between lawyers representing contrary interests (the victim and the insurer) is fought between various medical experts. Legal knowledge is helpful to the extent that it may help to create a state of doubt concerning unfavourable medical opinions and demanding the calling of the other experts with the hope they might look at the case on more favourable terms.

263. While determining the percentage of incapacity to work, the State Social Security Agency must concentrate on the future position of an injured worker on the labour market, not on the actual loss of currently earned wages. A worker may be declared as permanently disabled, even though he/she may be employed on a full-time basis and may be earning a normal salary. On the other hand, a worker may be declared as temporary unable to work with a percentage of incapacity below 10%, and even such a minor work accident may effect in termination of current employment and may cause great difficulties in finding another job. The percentage of work incapacity must reflect the average future earning capacity of an injured worker.

264. As already mentioned, the percentage of incapacity to work determines the state of health and capacity to work of an injured worker at the date on which an estimation was made. The state of the injured worker may improve or may deteriorate. In the first case, the worker who has accepted a certain amount of compensation for the injury caused by the work accident is not obliged in any way to pay back to his/her employer, or to the State Social Security Agency, the amount of the one-off compensatory benefit, constituting a multiplication of the percentage in which his/her state of health has improved and the basic figure presented by the ministry of labour and social policy paid for each percentage of the industrial injury.

An inverse situation, in which the state of an injured worker's health has deteriorated with the passing of time from the day of the work accident, is foreseeable. Any linkage established between the work accident and a higher degree of incapacity to work must result in a higher percentage of the one-off compensation benefit for the injury caused by the work accident.

265. Invalidity benefit is paid to an injured worker – the victim of a work accident. The Act of 30 October 2002 distinguishes between permanent and temporary invalidity benefit paid to a work accident victim. Besides those two types of invalidity benefits, there is also educational benefit paid to the victim of the work accident.

266. Permanent invalidity benefit is paid to the victim of a work accident permanently unable to carry on with work.

Temporary invalidity benefit is paid in the case where the incapacity to work is temporary. Depending upon the health status and prospects for placing an injured worker back in the labour market, the temporary invalidity benefit either ceases or becomes a permanent one.

Educational invalidity benefit is paid to the victim of a work accident if the victim is pronounced incapable of continuing the type of work that was carried out during the time when the work accident occurred but if the victim is capable of performing another type of work for which, at the present time, the victim of the work accident does not have the necessary qualifications. Usually educational invalidity benefit is paid for a six-month period. It may be extended up to thirty months if the conditions of particular training require more time for teaching and practice.

267. The Act of 30 October 2002 provides a minimum amount for invalidity benefits paid to a victim of a work accident. The invalidity benefit paid to the worker injured in the work accident cannot be lower than either 80% or 60% of the basis taken during the process of calculation of the old-age pension and invalidity benefits. A higher platform (80%) for establishment of the minimum invalidity benefit is used during the process of calculating the invalidity benefits for victims classified as victims who are totally unable to work. A lower platform (60%) is used for calculation of the minimum amount of those victims who are temporarily unable to carry on with their work. The educational invalidity benefit cannot be lower than 100% of the basis taken during the process of calculation of the old-age pension and invalidity benefits.

Chapter 6. Death

268. When the victim of a work accident or occupational disease passes away as a result of such an accident or disease, the members of the victim's family are entitled to the social security benefit designed for the family of deceased worker.

269. The Act of 30 October 2002 lists members of the family entitled to such benefit (Article 13, section 2). This list includes: the surviving spouse, natural and adopted children, stepchildren, grandchildren, parents, stepmother, and stepfather if classified to receive the family benefit under the general provisions of the Act of 17 December 1998.

270. Family benefit paid to victims of work accidents eligible for family benefit is calculated on the percentage of the basic amount of income, which serves as the platform for calculation of any type of social security benefits not presented in the flat figures. The amount of family benefit to the members of the family of the deceased worker varies according to the numbers of members of the family entitled to such a benefit. Strangely enough, the type of family relationship between the survivor (beneficiary) and the victim of the accident is not important at all during the process of calculation of the amount of the family benefit. The Act of 30 October 2002 treats all members of the family who survive the victim of the work accident as equally eligible to family benefit. According to Article 73, section 1 of the Act of 17 December 1998, monthly family benefit paid to the survivors of the victim of the work accident runs as high as:

- 85% of the basis serving as the platform for calculation of the invalidity benefit if only one member of the family is eligible for family rent;
- 90% if at least two members of family are eligible for such a social security benefit;
- 95% if at least three members of the family are eligible.

271. Survivors entitled to family benefit are also entitled to a one-off compensation. Those members of the family of the deceased worker who are entitled to the family benefit are also entitled to the one-off compensation. The general rule reads as follows: a one-off compensation is paid to those eligible members of the family of the deceased worker who lived together with him/her in the same household during his/her last days.

272. The amount of the one-off compensation for the death of a worker who is the victim of a work accident is established by the Article 14, section 1 of the Act of 30 October 2002. The amount of compensation reads as follows: in the case of death as a result of a work accident or an occupational disease the amount of compensation depends on the number of the members of immediate family who have survived the victim of the work accident and the kind of relationship between the deceased worker and his/her immediate family members. An amount as high as eighteen times the national average of monthly wages is paid if the deceased worker was survived by a spouse or a child (PLN 63,390 = EUR 15,128.87). Fifty per cent of that amount is paid when the deceased worker was survived by the other member of his/her family

(PLN 31,695 = EUR 7,564.43). An additional amount of 3.5 times national average (PLN 12,326 = EUR 2,941.76) is paid to any additional family members of the deceased worker who survived the victim of the work accident.

Chapter 7. Prevention of Occupational Diseases

273. The former Act on Industrial Injury and Occupational Diseases of 12 June 1975 did not deal with the prevention of occupational disease. The Labour Code, though, provides for preventive measures, consisting of a temporary removal of a worker exposed to an occupational hazard from his/her place of work with an entitlement to the same social security benefit as is paid in the case of incapacity to work. After all, a worker exposed to occupational hazards cannot perform his/her professional tasks any longer. The act of removal of the endangered worker from the workplace is considered an important preventive measure in the Polish social law system. The Act of 30 October 2002 states that 1% of the social security dues contributed to the industrial injury fund must be spent to support the preventive measures in places of work.

274. The worker exposed to occupational hazard is entitled to vocational retraining. He/she will receive for a period of three years the supplementary benefit between the wages earned during the period of last six months before removal from the work post and the earning received after retraining.

275. The employer who disregards medical opinion and continues to employ a worker after having been warned of the hazard to the worker's health may be sentenced by the labour inspector to an administrative fine and may be found responsible for any damages caused by further exposure of the worker to the occupational hazard.

Chapter 8. Supplementary Benefits

276. A worker who is the victim of a work accident and who was negatively affected by the accident, diminishing his/her work capacity, is entitled to supplementary benefit if he/she continues to work and achieves earnings reduced by 10% on a monthly basis. Supplementary benefit is paid exclusively to the injured worker who decides to carry on with his/her job. A worker who draws social security benefit paid to victims of work accidents cannot be awarded supplementary benefit.

Supplementary benefit covers the difference in wages earned by the worker before and after the industrial injury. The amount of supplementary benefit cannot exceed 30% of the wage earned by the worker before the date of the work accident. Supplementary benefit may be paid for a period not exceeding three years.

277. A victim of a work accident is entitled to such supplementary benefits as:

- nursery benefit;
- health service paid out by the social security agency from the industrial injury fund;
- compensation for damage to any personal belongings being in the possession of an injured worker during the time an accident occurred. This statement does not apply to any vehicles: cars or motorbikes.

All the above-mentioned benefits are provided to both injured workers and victims of work accidents regardless of their right to invalidity benefits.

Chapter 9. No-Fault Insurance

278. One of the most distinctive features of the Polish social law is the total social risk put upon the employer by legal regulations. Therefore, an employer cannot escape the social risk connected with the necessity to employ workers to carry out regular tasks in an enterprise run by the employer on a daily basis. Therefore, an employer cannot shift the legal responsibility for the damages caused by the work accident to a third party – an insurance agency.

Chapter 10. Civil Liability

279. Until 1 January 1990, the Act of 12 June 1975 was the sole legal source on which any claim for damages made for any work accident could be presented. The compensation awarded on behalf of the Act of 12 June 1975 was the only compensation provided by Polish social law that should repay all damages caused by the industrial injury regardless of real damage. Since 1 January 1990, the legal situation has changed. Those workers who became victims of work accidents may sue their employers for damages not covered by the Act of 12 June 1975. The same statement applies to the Act of 30 October 2002. The only condition introduced by the judiciary is that those damages should occur after 1 January 1990 regardless of the date of the work accident.

Chapter 11. Accumulation Rules

280. The Act of 30 October 2002 contains only two rules concerning the accumulation of social security benefits with other benefits paid out of other social security schemes. Rule number one deals with the combination of one-off compensation with other similar types of benefits such as death benefit and burial grants paid in the case of the death of either an employed or a previously employed individual.

Rule number two deals with the accumulation of invalidity benefits paid to the victim of a work accident and an old-age pension. This accumulation of benefits paid out of different social security schemes is made possible by the fact that the worker injured in a work accident may continue to work and earn his/her right to an old-age pension benefit. The Act of 30 October 2002 establishes the rule according to which such a person who earned his/her rights to two separate benefits paid out of different social security schemes may combine one full benefit with 50% of the other. Therefore, a victim of a work accident is entitled to 100% of invalidity and 50% of the old-age pension, or 100% of the old-age pension and 50% of invalidity benefit.

The very same rule applies in the case where invalidity benefit paid to victims of work accidents are being combined with social security benefits paid to individual farmers who turn over their farms to either a successor or a local government in exchange for the right to an old-age pension.

281. The most spectacular rule not yet mentioned is that invalidity benefit paid to the victims of work accidents may be freely accumulated with wages. The Act of 30 October 2002 establishes a set of legal regulations that deal in abstract terms with workers affected by industrial injury. The law provides standard compensation for the abstract loss of possibilities on the labour market. The law does not deal with the particular situation of an injured worker who is able to place himself/herself back on the labour market and earn 100% of their former income paid in the form of wages.

Part VII. Unemployment

Chapter 1. Provision of Work

§1. The Role of the State in Administering the Labour Market

282. Any modern state bears certain obligations to cope with unemployment. The present democratic government in Poland cannot, and as matter of fact does not try to, excuse itself from tackling this issue. The Act on the Promotion of Employment and the Institutions of the Labour Market of 20 April 2004 is just another major piece of legislation adopted in recent years that faces the issue of unemployment. However, the law does not formulate a legal or political obligation of the state government to cope with the problem of unemployment. It only makes the Council of Ministers responsible for formulating social programmes in matters of 'promotion of employment, curing the effects of unemployment and providing active professional measures' (Article 3, section 1). The Act of 20 April 2004 provides only that legal regulations define the tasks of the state in areas of employment, countervail of unemployment and pacification of the effects of unemployment. The law does not guarantee anyone the right to work or freedom from unemployment. It sets up only legal and administrative measures to cope with the issue of unemployment. Among those measures the law mentions the state employment agency and its council, local government organizations, and the state labour fund. The major purpose of those state organizations is to create an administrative framework that enables the unemployed to cope effectively with the question of unemployment. The Act of 20 April 2004, however, does not leave to the above-mentioned state agencies with any freedom to come up with institutions that are, to the best knowledge of state organs, sufficient to cope with the unemployment question in particular labour markets. The law creates a uniform system of state employment agencies and state employment councils. Apart from the state employment agencies, the law provides that certain tasks can be performed by so-called voluntary labour detachments which are considered by the law also as organizations of the state. Needless to say, the labour fund is *expressis verbis* considered a financial organization run by the state. Therefore, the state has become – since 1 December 1991 – a major force, both political and administrative, that has imposed upon itself the legal obligation to conduct a fight against unemployment. The Act of 20 April 2004 does not mention trade unions and employer organizations as jointly responsible with the state to countervail unemployment. However, it states that 'the social dialogue institutions' are being considered as 'the institutions of the labour market' (Article 6, section 1, item 5). It also includes social partners into the national and local councils for employment (Articles 21–23).

283. The state decided to regulate the issue of unemployment benefits for the first time at the end of 1989. The first democratic government introduced the law on massive layoffs. For political reasons, the state government decided to postpone the latter piece of legislation until the law concerning employment and unemployment was introduced. After a short while, it turned out that the state employment agencies registered as unemployed people who decided by themselves to stay at out of work for various reasons, mostly family reasons. Taking advantage of the new legislation, they felt free to remain out of work and get paid for it. This situation, from both an economic and a social point of view, was unacceptable. Therefore, on 14 December 1994, new regulations concerning unemployment benefit were introduced. That act was amended by the Act of 6 December 1996. Then it was replaced by the Act of 20 April 2004. This piece of legislation creates at the present time the most current legal and administrative framework for the battle against unemployment.

284. The state government did not limit its legal actions to the creation of state administrative agencies and councils able (according to the government estimate) to cope with the issue of unemployment. The state also set up a number of programmes for the sole purpose of countervailing unemployment. Among those programmes are: vocational training, public service employment, supported-work experiments, job creation efforts, youth training detachments, housing benefits and loans presented to those individuals who decide to resettle and start private businesses.

§2. Employment Agencies and Councils and Their Role in Labour Mediation, Vocational Training, and Direct Work Provision

285. By decision of the previous Act of 14 December 1994, the central employment agency was created as an administrative body to cope with unemployment. The central employment agency was located within the bureaucratic structure of the ministry of economy and labour. The head of the central employment agency was appointed and demoted by the Prime Minister on request submitted by the minister of labour and social policy. The structure and principles according to which the central employment agency and its territorial branches function were set up by the ordinance issued by the minister of labour and social policy.

286. The structure of the central employment agency was highly centralized. At the national level, the national employment agency was responsible for carrying out the tasks defined by the Act of 14 December 1994. At a lower level, the branch offices, located in each of the forty-nine administrative departments into which Polish territory was divided, were responsible for implementation of social policy priorities set up at a national level. The basic work was carried out by local employment agencies. Thus, the structure of the employment agency was three-tiered.

287. The Act of 14 December 1994 did not define the legal scope of power and the scope of administrative responsibility of the central employment agency. The Act transferred this power to the minister of labour and social policy. It was unusual, though, that the Act of 14 December 1994 itself chose to specify the legal scope of power and described an administrative responsibilities of branch and local employment agencies. The Act, however, stated that the sole responsibility for carrying on legal and administrative responsibilities in the field of employment and unemployment was vested in the minister of labour and social policy (Article 4, section 1). The central, branch, and local employment agencies are treated by the Act of 14 December 1994 only as supportive administrative bodies.

They reported directly (in case of the central employment agency) and indirectly (in case of branch and local employment agencies) to the minister of labour and social policy. The later administrative organ acted also as a coordinator of manpower policy on the national level. Therefore, all governmental institutions, such as housing authorities and headquarters of voluntary labour detachments, were obliged to proceed accordingly with directives and ordinances issued by the minister of labour and social policy. The law was particularly careful in putting the minister of labour and social policy in a position of the state organ that maintained legal control over any state agencies dealing with social policy issues (Article 2, section 2).

288. According to the customs prevailing in the public sector, the Act of 14 December 1994 defined only the scope of power of the head of branch and local employment agencies. The law did not list all the legal responsibilities and administrative duties of the heads of the branch and local employment agencies. The list for the head of the branch employment agency contained fifteen items. Respectively, fourteen items were listed as responsibilities of the head of the local employment agency.

289. The head of the branch employment agency took certain legal and administrative responsibilities towards:

(a) the minister of labour and social policy;
(b) the branch employment council;
(c) the state educational agency;
(d) local employment agencies.

It also bore legal responsibilities towards prospective employees and employers.

290. As far as legal and administrative responsibilities towards the minister of labour and social policy were concerned, the head of the branch employment agency was in charge of writing proposals and evaluating results in the field of social policy on particular territory. Those proposals were submitted to the minister of labour and social policy at his request.

291. The head of the branch employment agency presented to the minister of labour and social policy proposals concerning the amount of finance to be transferred from the labour fund for the disposal of employment agencies situated on particular territory administered by the branch office. Naturally, the head of the branch employment office was also responsible for submitting reports to the minister of labour and social policy on the amount of monies distributed from the labour fund in a given territory.

292. The head of the branch employment agency was obliged to cooperate with the local employment council in taking administrative measures against unemployment. This statement gave a limited freedom to executive and advisory branches of administrative powers of the state government to apply methods listed in the Act of 14 December 1994 only.

293. The legislative body of the state government, by making such a statement, expressed limited faith in the ability of the branch administrative offices to prepare and implement additional measures designed to fight unemployment. Lack of trust displayed by one state organ against another was one of the major weaknesses of the current legal regulations adopted to fight unemployment.

294. The Act of 14 December 1994 particularly mentioned as the responsibility of executive and advisory administrative organs efforts to gain additional job slots, set up vocational training centres, and create jobs for disabled people.

295. The head of the branch employment agency was obliged to cooperate with a branch office of the central state educational agency in order to make plans concerning vocational training and retraining of unemployed individuals.

296. As far as activity of local employment agencies was concerned, the prime responsibility of the head of the branch employment agency was coordination of activities in which local employment agencies were engaged. The head of the branch employment agency was in a position to control the amount of activities both from an organizational and a financial point of view. It was up to him to decide upon the number and the scope of the territorial power of local employment agencies. Before deciding how many local employment agencies must be created within a particular territorial jurisdiction, the head of the branch employment agency must discuss his ideas with a governor.

297. Real power was vested in the hands of the head of the branch employment agency in financial matters. The head of the branch employment agency distributed to local employment offices monies transferred from the central labour fund. He (the head) was also empowered to control the way monies were spent by his subordinating local employment agencies.

The head of the branch employment agency was responsible for organizing and maintaining the labour exchange on the territories controlled by neighbourhood offices. No one knew what it meant, since the scope of power of the branch employment agency was restricted to one territory of the forty-nine territories into which Poland was divided. It may mean that the heads of particular branch employment agencies were free to enter into any type of agreement with their respective partners they choose. It meant that the heads of each of the forty-nine branch employment agencies were free to enter into any bilateral or multilateral agreements they choose. In a highly decentralized society, which is not the case in Poland, such a statement could open unlimited opportunities for alliances between various regions. In Poland, this particular item of the Act of 14 December 1994 was a dead letter of the statutory regulations. At the utmost, it gave authority to two neighbouring departments to enter into a kind of legal agreement to cooperate in matters related to transfer of manpower across the state line.

298. The current Act of 20 April 2004 disbanded the central state institution responsible for employment policy, diminished the role of the governors as representatives of the central government, and divided the tasks in the field of employment between local governments. It made the heads of the local governments: regions and districts (marszadek województwa, starosta) who control the branch employment agencies located at the district and regional level responsible for coordination of activities of various institutions that provide social services in the field of employment.

299. The head of the district or region who controls the branch employment agency (later called 'the head of the local employment agency') is vested with direct legal power as far as employment of foreigners in Poland is concerned. He issues administrative decisions concerning permission for employment of foreign subjects on Polish soil. He also accepts declarations of Polish individuals who decide to enter into employment contract abroad. The latter administrative duty serves strictly statistical purposes. As far as the present Polish legal regulations are concerned, there is no requirement for citizens to get permission from the state government as a legal precondition of entering into an employment contract abroad.

300. The head of the regional local employment agency is obliged to provide help to jobless people and furnish them with work. The very same obligation is imposed upon the head of the local employment agency as far as the need for employers to find employees is concerned. Thus, the Act of 20 April 2004 puts the head of the local employment agency in a position in which he must accommodate the needs of both parties to the employment contract, both the employees and the employers.

301. The head of the local employment agency is also obliged to take up necessary measures to prevent negative effects of massive layoffs. In particular, the head of the local employment agency must do his best to gain new job positions and to organize vocational training or retraining.

302. In order to comply with his obligations, the head of the local employment agency registers unemployed and jobless persons seeking employment. He may present to these people offers to enter into new employment, accept vocational training, public service employment or supported-work experiments. If none of the above-mentioned opportunities exist, the head of the local employment agency is in a position to make decisions concerning payment of unemployment benefit to jobless people.

303. An initiative to set up vocational training as well as a decision concerning financing such training lies in the hands of the head of the local employment agency. He is also responsible for the creation of additional jobs within the state sector of the economy. This particular provision of the Act of 20 April 2004 gives a legal power to the head of the local employment agency to start a supported-work experiment.

304. The head of the local employment agency is also empowered to help unemployed people to start their own business ventures. He may do so by giving an order to his subordinate office to issue a one-off only financial loan out of the labour fund.

305. The head of the local employment agency is also responsible for setting up and financing public service employment within the local jurisdiction. His legal and administrative responsibilities also cover activities such as: conducting vocational training for jobless and job seeking people, financing severance payments to those employees who lost their jobs due to massive layoffs, financing the salaries of youth workers employed to get professional experience and on-the-job training, financing stipends paid to students of vocational schools during the job training, and administrating monies paid out of mobility flows that enable unemployed people to move to different places located away from their residence in order to get a job.

306. The head of the local employment agency is obliged to cooperate with advisory local labour councils in order to initiate and maintain the most effective social policy enabling the state administrative bodies to fight against unemployment. In particular, cooperation of the executive and advisory body is required by the Act of 20 April 2004 in the case of decision making concerning distribution of monies paid out of the labour fund.

307. The Act of 20 April 2004 maintained the idea of the labour council created by the previous Act of 14 December 1994. The national labour council is located as an advisory organ to the minister of economy and labour. Members of the national labour council are appointed for a period of four years by the minister of labour and social policy out of representatives of social partners, national non-governmental organizations. The Committee for Labour and Social Policy of the Polish Academy of Sciences nominates its representatives to participate in the national labour council.

308. All types of labour councils were created by law as advisory administrative organs that may present opinions in employment issues. The national labour council is obliged by the law to criticize any draft regulations concerning employment matters. The national labour council also may submit a formal requirement to the proper state authority to issue the necessary legal regulations in the field of employment and unemployment.

309. The central labour council may present its opinion in all matters related to activity of the labour fund. In particular, the council may criticize both programmes and annual reports presented by officials representing the labour fund.

The central labour council is obliged to submit to the minister of labour and social policy on a regular basis reports and information on its activity and activities of branch and local labour councils.

310. Labour councils are set up as advisory bodies whose function is not limited to presenting opinions in matters of social policy but enjoy a power of introducing new ideas in matters related to social policy issues and maintain a formal control over activities carried out by the proper state administrative authorities set up by law in order to fight against unemployment.

311. The legal and administrative functions of labour councils set up at the state branch and local administrative offices are similar to those performed at the national level by the central labour council. The major difference between the national council and local labour councils is territorial jurisdiction. The scope of jurisdiction of the central labour council extends to the whole Polish territory while the scope of jurisdiction of branch and local councils covers respectively only limited geographic territory.

312. The Act of 20 April 2004 creates the following manpower programmes, called 'labour market services' (Article 35, section 1) designed to fight against unemployment and provide social policy of full and productive employment:

(a) labour exchange;
(b) EURES service;
(c) vocational training;
(d) public service employment;
(e) the supported-work experiments;
(f) job creation programme.

Those measures represent the type of in-kind administrative tools designed to fight unemployment in opposition to financial measures, which cover both unemployment benefit and loans out of the labour fund.

313. The labour exchange programme is designed to help to find work for jobless people who are looking for work. In order to fulfil this task, the state employment agency is obliged to furnish with information concerning job vacancies to both candidates setting up an employment relationship: employees and prospective employers.

The labour exchange is provided free of charge. This activity provided by the state employment agency is conducted on the four following principles:

(1) the principle of availability of labour exchange to all people looking for work and to employers looking for workers;
(2) the principle of freedom in using services provided by the state employment agency;
(3) the principle of equality; the state employment agency is obliged to serve all people looking for work regardless of their nationality, membership in political organizations, and associations, gender, creed, age, sexual orientation, ethnic origin;
(4) the principle of openness; the state employment agency is obliged to post each vacancy in such a way that all people who are looking for jobs are in a position to get acquainted with offers presented by employers.

314. The EURES service is designed to find work for jobless citizens of the European Union who are looking for job in Poland.

315. Local state employment agencies are obliged to register unemployed people who are looking for work.

The state local employment agency is obliged to present an employment offer or organize vocational training for those unemployed people who are looking for work and are hard to employ. The category of 'hard to employ' covers: the unemployed who are younger than 25 years of age, the permanently unemployed, the unemployed who are older than 50 years of age, the unemployed who do not possess any professional qualifications, the unemployed who by themselves take care at least of one child not older than 7 years, and the handicapped unemployed (Article 49). Vocational training may be organized for twelve months. Since 1 January 1995, important changes were made in regulations concerning amount of benefits provided for people covered by unemployment regulations. During this entire period, a trainee was entitled to draw a vocational benefit, which used to run under previous regulation (the Act of 16 October 1991) to 80% of his/her last salary. The Act of 16 October 1991 stated a minimum (40% of average monthly salary) and a maximum (110% of average monthly salary) amount of vocational benefit. Unemployed graduates were entitled to vocational benefits which do not exceed 115% of unemployment benefits provided for them by legal regulations. Those regulations (Article 20, section 7 of the Act of 16 October 1991) provided that an unemployed graduate was entitled to 33% of his/her prospective average monthly salary. The Act of 6 December 1996 changed the rules of payment of vocational benefits and stated that vocational benefit can be as high as 20% of unemployment benefit (Article 16, item 2). The Act of 20 April 2004 provided stipend to unemployed persons younger than 25 years old who were sent to vocational training. That stipend cannot be higher than 40% of unemployment benefit. The rest of the unemployed going through the vocational training are entitled to the vocational allowance, which cannot be higher than 20% of the unemployment benefit.

316. Unemployed people drawing vocational benefits are entitled to certain social security benefits paid in cash in case of illness and maternity to which the insured employed individuals are entitled (Article 80).

317. The Act of 20 April 2004 empowers any employer to organize public service employment. The law on the promotion of employment also introduced supported-work experiments. Job creation programmes defined by the Act of 16 October 1991 and the Ordinance of the minister of labour and social policy of 17 December 1991 were novelties under Polish social law. They were carried out by the state government. The Act of 20 April 2004 obliges the head of the local employment agency to partially reimburse an employer who employed an unemployed person at a public service employment project for a period not shorter than six months with expenses paid for wages, bonuses, and social security dues (Article 57, section 1).

318. The public service employment such as public works should be organized in particular branches of the national economy such as: environment protection, water economy, forests, communications, highways, construction, and social infrastructure.

There are certain priorities concerning the structure of unemployed people who should be sent to work at public works. Unemployed graduates, workers qualified to perform certain type of jobs, and those who have the best chances to remain working should enjoy the priority of getting jobs under the programme sponsored by the state.

319. Job creation programmes and supported-work experiments are based on the idea of state financial support. The state local employment agency is in a position to issue a loan to any employer who decides to hire unemployed people. Job creation programmes are not creative at all as far as the decision concerning the creation of a number of working places is concerned. However, job creation programmes give an opportunity to imaginative employers to use public money to serve its own purposes. On the side, the private purpose might serve public interest by employing unemployed people.

Chapter 2. Unemployment Benefit

§1. Introductory Note

320. There are two types of financial measures adopted to countervail unemployment. The first is unemployment benefit. This benefit was introduced for the first time at the end of 1989. It has been effective since 1990. At the very beginning, the unemployment benefit was real proof of the democratic changes that took place in Poland. Under the previous political regime, unemployment benefit was not heard of in a socialist country. As was mentioned earlier, very quickly unemployment benefit changed its political character. Instead of a sign of political changes, unemployment benefit became an indicator of economic opportunity for people who were reluctant to be busy but wanted to get some money out of the new market-oriented state economy.

321. Since unemployment benefit is the most important and so far the most extensively used financial tool to combat unemployment in Poland, the current legal regulations are quite detailed as far as legal requirements regarding the right to the unemployment benefits are concerned.

§2. Field of Application

322. The Act of 20 April 2004 regulates who is eligible to qualify for unemployment benefit (Article 71, section 1). It states that only a jobless person looking for a job within Polish territory, who does not have any offers to perform a suitable job, who does not get any offers to start a suitable vocational training, and who cannot be sent to work at a public work site, qualifies, if registered – after seven days – as unemployed at the state local employment agency, for unemployment benefit. An unemployment benefit might be paid only to a person who was employed and earned a minimal salary for at least 365 days during the last eighteen months prior to the day on which the jobless person was registered as unemployed by the state local employment agency or was engaged in any type of professional activity listed in Article 71, section 1, item 2 of the Act of 20 April 2004.

§3. Amount of Benefit

323. The Act of 20 April 2004 specifies the amount of unemployment benefit (Article 72, sections 1, 2, and 3). The amount of unemployment benefit does not depend any longer on the duration of unemployment. Initially, the law provided that during the first three months of unemployment, unemployment benefit could not exceed 70% of the estimated average salary an unemployed person could draw if employed. After three months of an unemployment, the benefit dropped to 50% of the latter-mentioned salary, and after nine months the benefit dropped further to 40%. Unemployment benefit could not be lower than 33% and not higher than 100% of the above-mentioned salary. The right to draw unemployment benefit stopped after twelve months (Article 21, section 2).

First, the Act of 14 December 1994 and later, the Act of 6 December 1996 changed those conditions. Those regulations provided for payment of unemployment benefit in lump sums on a monthly basis. As already mentioned, only some categories of unemployed people were treated in a different way as far as calculation of unemployment benefit was concerned. Those categories included employees made redundant by employers (unemployment benefit equals 75% of their previous wages). If those employees lived in areas considered by the state government as areas with a high risk of unemployment, they were entitled to draw 160% unemployment benefit. For some categories of unemployed people (those with seniority of twenty-five years – females, or thirty years – males), the right to draw unemployment benefit was extended to eighteen months.

The Act of 20 April 2004 decided to introduce only one basic unemployment benefit – PLN 504.20 = EUR 126 (Article 72, section 1). Its level may be reduced to 80% or extended to 120% to those unemployed with the employment records shorter than five years (80% of the basic unemployment benefit) or longer than twenty years (120% of the basic unemployment benefit). The periods during which an unemployment benefits may be drawn depends on the following condition: the level of unemployment: lower or higher than 125% of average unemployment on the national scale. If level of unemployment on a given territory does not exceed 125% of the average national unemployment, an unemployment benefit is paid for six months. If the level of unemployment on particular territory exceeds 125% of average unemployment, an unemployment benefit is paid for twelve months. The right to draw unemployment benefit for a period of twelve months is also vested to unemployed who are over 50 years of age and who were employed at least for twenty years. The unemployment benefit is paid for eighteen months to two categories of the unemployed:

- those who reside on the territory on which unemployment rate exceeds the national unemployment average at least two times if they were employed in the past at least for twenty years;
- they must support at least one child not older than 15 years old and an unemployed spouse not entitled to unemployment benefit.

§4. Conditions

324. The Act of 20 April 2004 sets up legal requirements under which the right to draw unemployment benefit may be maintained. The law states under what conditions an unemployed person loses his/her right to draw unemployment benefit out of the labour fund. Those conditions include:

- unjust refusal of a job offer or vocational training as well as an offer to participate in one of the manpower programmes set up to countervail an unemployment;

- termination of an employment contract by an unemployed person within six months before registration at the state employment agency. The only exception is made for those unemployed people who agreed to terminate an employment contract for the reasons of bankruptcy of employer or redundancy;
- summary dismissal for disciplinary reasons within six months prior to the date of registration as unemployed;
- compensation for termination of employment contract without due notice;
- financial compensation listed in Article 75, section 1, item 4.

In such a case, an employment benefit may be drawn after the waiting period of 90–180 days depending on the reason that an unemployment benefit is nullified.

§5. Financial Arrangements

325. Unemployment benefit is paid, and financial loans are granted out of the labour fund. The labour fund is run by the minister of labour and social policy. The labour fund income comes from social dues paid by employers, employees working abroad, donation from the central state budget, bank interest, and profits paid out of commercial and industries ventures in which the state administrative organs engage while using financial funds deposited in the account owned by the labour fund (Article 106). During the period of 1 January until 31 December 2005, employers are obliged to contribute in dues to the labour fund of 2.45% of the basic amount used by the State Social Security Agency to count social security dues paid by the insured to the old-age pension and invalidity fund. During the last three months: June, July and August 2005, the basic amount to count social security dues cannot be lower than PLN 1,449.27 (EUR 362). During that period, each employer is obliged to contribute to the labour fund in social dues PLN 35.51 (EUR 8.75).

326. The list of ventures that can be financed by the labour fund contains forty-seven items (Article 108, section 1). Generally, all legal and administrative measures set up by the state employment agencies to countervail unemployment and promote full employment policy might be financed out of the money deposited in the bank account held by the labour fund.

327. The major problem of the current social policy is that still the great amount of expenses paid out of the labour fund is used to finance unemployment benefit. The division of funds paid out of the state labour fund serves as a clear indicator of the preferences of the state social policy and measures adopted by the state to fight unemployment.

§6. Miscellaneous Measures

328. The Act of 20 April 2004 regulates the legal and administrative measures adopted in order to countervail unemployment among individual farmers and young people. The law provides specific measures that could be used in order to help jobless people to find employment in different geographic areas of the country as well as abroad.

329. People who are covered by the social security regulations issued to guarantee benefits to individual farmers are eligible for benefits paid out of the labour fund upon being laid off from work under condition they are not eligible for unemployment benefit under the Act of 20 April 2004. Chapter 12 of the Act of 20 April 2004 enables those people to apply for funds paid out of the labour fund, which allows them to maintain payment of social security dues to the farmers' social security fund. They are also eligible for vocational benefit as well as benefits paid in cases of industrial injury, payment of which depends upon the condition that they are injured while learning a new craft.

330. Voluntary Labour Detachments (Ochotnicze Hufce Pracy) are defined by the Act of 20 April 2004 as the institutions of labour market. They are organized by the state for the purpose of fighting social exclusion and unemployment, especially among youth. The Act of 20 April 2004 does not extend the scope of power of voluntary labour detachments. It repeats what was stated long ago by legal regulations: that one of the tasks of voluntary labour detachments is to create an environment sympathetic to the needs of young people: to learn a new trade and to get a job according to their vocational qualifications.

331. Voluntary Labour Detachments as an administrative framework to fulfil the goals of full and productive employment among the younger community have a limited value. Voluntary Labour Detachments may be used to train young people in simple crafts, but they do not guarantee jobs to those who have completed quasi-military training. Voluntary Labour Detachments, which right now are considered by the Act of 20 April 2004 as a part of the state enterprise, are in a shape similar to that of any organization run by the state.

332. A displaced person who due to economic conditions gets a job in a different part of the country may turn to the local authorities for financial help. The Act of 20 April 2004 entitles them to apply for financial support to cover travel expenses, lodging in case of necessity to move to another part of the country with the purpose of getting a job or attending vocational training. Those financial aids are called by the Act of 20 April 2004 'the labour market instruments' (Chapter 11). They are available to both the unemployed and the prospective employers.

333. Without doubt, the most attractive legal form to combat an unemployment from an economic point of view is the administrative opportunity to create opportunities for employment abroad. Poles have always been eager to work abroad. The most important reason is because of the favourable currency exchange rate under which a Western currency could be changed to the Polish zloty. That was attractive due to the huge black market and the enormous difference between the official exchange rate and the free market. Because the currency exchange rate between Western currency and the Polish zloty has more or less stabilized, and because prices of goods on the national market have gone up rapidly, salaries earned abroad have become less attractive to many Poles. Nevertheless, a huge number of people are still looking for an opportunity to enter into the labour markets of highly industrialized countries of Western Europe and the United States. The Act of 20 April 2004 provides (Chapter 16) that employment abroad can be carried out by the base of administrative license given to a particular business entity acting as an employment agency sending people to work abroad. A candidate for a job abroad enters into a civil type of contract with an employment agency with international connections. This particular contract states: the duration of employment outside Poland, the legal obligations of the parties entering into the contract that serves as a legal basis for a contract of employment signed abroad with a foreign employer, and reimbursement of expenses covered by the employment agency negotiating terms and conditions of employment on behalf of Polish workers with foreign employers.

334. The law provides that a period of employment performed abroad is treated by the social security regulation on an equal basis with the periods of employment within the Polish territory as far as social security benefits are concerned. The only condition for treatment of the period of employment abroad on the same basis with the period of employment in Poland is payment by or on behalf of Polish employee working abroad in social dues to the labour fund 9.75% of the average national monthly wages (Article 86, section 3).

335. The Act of 20 April 2004 entitles Polish employers to employ foreign workers on Polish soil under the condition that they receive a work permit from branch employment agencies. This administrative requirement was introduced to protect local labour markets.

§7. Conclusion

336. The early legal and administrative experience of combating unemployment in Poland is quite extensive. During past ten years, several major legal acts were introduced. None of them worked properly, though. At the very beginning of the new political era, the majority of the population expressed the attitude that unemployment is the price society must pay during the transition period from central planning to a market economy.

337. As a matter of principle of both economic and social policy, society was willing to pay such a price. Initially, unemployment benefit was treated with amusement as a legal tool of which anyone, even people who had never worked in their entire life, could take advantage. And people who never worked – for example, a housewife – took advantage of the new benefit. They registered themselves as willing to work and looking for a job even though prior to the day of registration they had never expressed any type of willingness to work. The majority of them lack any professional qualifications or vocational skills at all.

338. It is a well-known feature that Polish society on the whole is impatient. Since the market economy was introduced and unemployment benefits were paid, society expected changes for better in the general standard of living. Some people eventually got richer. The majority of population, though, have become poorer. Thus, unemployment has become a real issue. It has affected the life of a growing number of Polish families. It has intruded into the former pattern of living characterized by a relative level of stability.

339. The state government has found itself in a difficult position. A huge amount of money was spent on combating unemployment, but the number of unemployed people has still grown. As the result of this discovery, the state government made a change in the conditions under which unemployment benefits could be paid out of the labour fund to unemployed people.

340. The Act of 20 April 2004 established new legal conditions of the payment of unemployment benefit. The law provides that unemployment benefit is paid only to those jobless people who have worked for at least 365 days during the last eighteen months. Thus, people without former work records cannot register as unemployed if they decide to enter the labour market and find themselves in a difficult situation due to lack of job openings.

341. This rule is a harsh one. It can open a vicious circle. No unemployment benefit without a prior job record; no job due to the high unemployment rate. Obviously in the next legal regulations on unemployment benefit, the state government must cope with a new problem.

342. It is worth noting that the new state government not only solves social problems, but it also creates them. The high turnover of government officials elected to deal with social policy issues, as well as frequent changes in legal regulations in the area of unemployment benefit, justifies the question of whether or not the state government is ready to tackle the problem of unemployment and to create an economic environment sympathetic to the idea of full and productive employment.

343. Almost half a century of a socialist regime made certain changes in the behaviour of society *en masse*. An average member of the society grows dependent on the state government. The present social policy is based on an idea of aggressiveness. After a certain period of time, people change their attitudes towards the state government. They will grow accustomed to the idea that their personal prosperity depends upon their individual activity. As a result of those changes, they will try more vigorously to place themselves on the labour market.

344. The most severe wave of criticism of the new legal regulations is based on the assumption that the law on the promotion of employment and institutions of labour market is short on making the state government, local authorities, and social partners employ legal and administrative measures designed to countervail unemployment. Of all the legal and administrative measures described in this monograph, only unemployment benefit and to a certain extent licenses to export workers abroad are utilized by the state employment agencies. It proves that the state government and its employment agencies are not sufficiently prepared to cope with the question of unemployment. They try to use the easiest way of paying off those who cannot remain employed. In order to save money, the state tries to cut expenses by introducing new legal requirements that make life more difficult for those people who are willing to work but who face difficulties while trying to enter the labour market. In the short run, such a policy cannot be carried out for longer than six, twelve or eighteen months. The law established an eighteen-month ceiling on duration for which unemployment benefit may be drawn.

345. Thus, real social and economic problems emerge when people who are drawing unemployment benefits are not put back to work by the employment agencies. The Act of 20 April 2004 was introduced as the Statute on Promotion of Employment and Labour Market Institutions. Legal and administrative tools to lead a battle against unemployment are there. The law provides a legal framework to set up different social programmes, such as: labour exchange, vocational training, public service employment, the supported-work experiments and job creation programmes. The problem is that none of those programmes are utilized to an extent that they can countervail growing unemployment. Instead of preventing unemployment, the state employment agencies still mostly focus their activities on paying unemployment benefit to jobless workers. The policy of the present government limits itself to the policy of coping with unemployment issue, not fighting it.

346. In conclusion, one can say that the state government does not do its best to fight unemployment. The state employment agencies are sufficiently equipped to lead a battle against unemployment. Legal and administrative measures are defined by the Act of 20 April 2004. The very problem of 2005 is how to use those legal and administrative measures to successfully fight against excessive unemployment and then to keep under control jobless people whose number exceeds international standards set up to describe the state of full employment within national borders. Presently, Poland is neither a country that enjoys a full employment policy nor a country that copes successfully with unemployment.

Part VIII. Pensions and Invalidity Benefits

Chapter 1. Pensions for Wage Earners

§1. Old-Age Pension

347. There are two systems of old-age pension: the old one based on the principles established by the Act of 14 December 1982 applies to employees born prior to 1 January 1949; the new one based on the Act of 17 December 1998 (*Journal of Laws of 1998*, No. 162, item 1118 as amended) applies to those categories of insured employees: those who were born after 31 December 1948 on the condition they did decide before 31 December 1999 to join the new-age pension scheme and to those born after 31 December 1968. In order to present the current old-age pension scheme, it is necessary to present the system applicable to those insured employees who were born prior to 1 January 1949 as well as the new system applicable to those insured born after 31 December 1968. Insured employees born between 1 January 1949 and 31 December 1968 enjoyed having the choice of staying with the old system or joining the new one.

I. Beneficiaries

A. *Territorial Field of Application*

348. For entitlement to old-age pensions, the law (the Act of 14 December 1982, *Journal of Laws*, No. 40, item 267 as amended) applies to any worker who works or worked on the Polish territory. This statutory act has been amended many times. Among the most important amendments are: the Act of 17 October 1991 (*Journal of Laws*, No. 104, item 450 as amended), and the Act of 28 June 1996 (*Journal of Laws*, No. 100, item 461). Because after the Second World War the borders of Poland changed considerably, the law takes into account any employment relationship on Polish territory between the Great Wars. An official administrative Polish border between the World Wars in Europe is taken as a legal indicator according to which any person employed within either the previous or present Polish border is eligible for an old-age benefit.

349. As an exception to the rule, a Polish citizen's employment outside Polish territory is taken into account by the State Social Security Agency, which calculates the length of career for the purpose of making a decision concerning an old-age pension in any official Polish institutions established abroad. Also, the members of family of Polish citizens employed at an official Polish institution can count on the positive consideration of years spent abroad if during those years they were employed by any official Polish institution.

350. Another exception to the rule of work performed on national territory is employment abroad in international organizations or foreign institutions. This exception is regulated by the ordinance issued on 9 March 1984 by the Council of Ministers (*Journal of Laws*, No. 17, item 81 as amended). There are two different conditions that determine whether the years spent working abroad by a Polish worker should be taken into account by the State Social Security Agency calculating the old-age pension. If employed after 9 May 1945, Polish workers abroad should be directed to international or foreign employers by Polish authorities, or their conditions of employment must be negotiated with foreign employers by the proper Polish authorities. This condition does not apply to Polish workers employed abroad before 9 May 1945.

The other condition applies to Polish workers employed abroad under treaties negotiated by Polish authorities with their foreign counterparts. The most important legal condition is that Polish workers employed abroad contribute to the Polish social security fund in social security dues.

The Act of 17 December 1998 states that periods of employment of Polish citizens outside Poland are taken into account in case when insured individuals applying for old-age pensions reside in Poland.

B. Personal Field of Application

351. Employment within the Polish territory, as well as employment at Polish institutions abroad, is taken into account regardless of the citizenship of the applicant for an old-age pension. An individual who is not a Polish citizen may accept employment legally within the Polish territory or at an official Polish institution representing the Polish interest outside Poland on the condition that such an employee has a work permit.

352. An exception to the above-mentioned rule applies to those individuals who were employed abroad by foreign employers if they reemigrated to Poland after 22 July 1994. This exception deals mostly with former Polish citizens who during the Second World War were forced to accept Soviet citizenship and returned to Poland after liberation. The State Social Security Agency was under a legal obligation to take into account the years that Poles working in Russia spent in the former Soviet Union.

II. Conditions

353. The old-age pension for wage earners born prior to 1 January 1949 is calculated on the basis of three elements:

- the age of applicant;
- the working career;

– the wages earned.

This group of wage earners is entitled to receive an old-age pension regulated by the Act of 14 December 1982 managed by the State Social Security Agency.

The old-age pension of insured born between 1949 and 1969 had the choice between an old-age pension to which the insured born before 1 January 1949 had and the mixed system: an old-age pension partially paid according to the old and new regulations. The Act of 17 December 1998 stated the deadline for this group to make a decision: 31 December 1999. Those insured who did opt for the partially new system of old-age pension before that date are covered entirely by the old old-age pension scheme if they met the conditions established by the Act of 14 December 1982 before 31 December 2006. However, an amount of their old-age pension is calculated according to legal rules introduced by the Act of 17 December 1998. If they decided to join the new old-age pension scheme, the Social Security Agency was obliged to transfer part of their social security dues (7.3%) to the open social security fund chosen by prospective beneficiaries. If they did not openly declare a preference, they decided to join any open social security fund where social security dues are managed by the State Social Security Agency.

A. The Age and the Working Career of an Applicant for an Old-Age Pension

354. Since 1 January 2013 until 1 October 2017 the normal age of an application for an old-age pension was in principle 67 years old. However, new-age limit was introduced gradually Before 1 January 2013, the normal age of an applicant for an old-age pension was 60 years old for a female and 65 years old for a male worker. For some occupations there are shorter careers. For example, males employed as coal miners may retire at the age of 55. Before 1 January 1986, they could retire after they turned 50 on the condition they were employed at the mine for at least twenty-five years. Out of those twenty-five years, at least fifteen working years should be spent under the earth. More favourable conditions concerning the age of applicant are also applied to seamen, fishermen and flying crew members.

355. The Act of 11 May 2012 amending the act of Pensions from Health Insurance Fund and certain acts (*Journal of Laws of 2012*, item 637), in force from 1 January 2013 introduced the age of 67 as common retirement age for all insured (women and men) born after 31 December 1948. The increase of the pension age was regulated to be a gradual process. The retirement age for women born until 31 December 1952 is not changed – 60 years old. However, the retirement age of women born after 1 January 1953 is extended every quarter in every calendar year by a month. The aforementioned mechanism of retirement age extension of working women caused that the retirement age of women born between 30 July 1973 and 30 September 1973 comes to 66 years and 11 months. While the retirement age of women born after 30 September 1973 comes to at least 67 years.

Identical mechanism of retirement age extension was applied against men. Considering the five-year difference in retirement limit of women (60 years old) and men (65 years old), the period when the extension of retirement age is applied was reduced by five years. The monthly extension period was maintained and occurs automatically every quarter of every calendar year. Men born from 1 January 1949 to 31 March 1949 acquire retirement benefits when reaching 65 years and 5 months. Men born between 1 July 1953 and 30 September 1953 retire when reaching the age of 66 and 11 months. The retirement age for men born 30 September 1953 is at least 67 years old.

The retirement age of 67 was introduced also for teachers and the officials of the judicial authority (judges and prosecutors) i.e., the insured being subject to separate social security regulations.

As of 1 October 2017 the previous retirement age – 60 years for women and 65 years for men – was restored. There are several exceptions to this principle which consist in lowering the general basic retirement age by five years that is 55 for women and 60 years for men. They apply to persons who perform onerous work or are employed in harmful conditions.

356. The Act of 14 December 1982 allowed the shortening by five years of the age of the applicant for an old-age pension (females to age 55, males to age 60), as long as an applicant was employed for twenty years (female) or twenty-five years (male) and was declared unable to continue work. Disability should be listed in either the first or the second category.

A female worker with the thirty years of seniority was entitled to an earlier old-age pension if she turned 55. Regardless of age, a female worker with a length of service listed by the Act of 14 December 1982 could retire at the age of 55 if she took personal care of a disabled child under 18. (The Ordinance of the Council of Ministers of 15 May 1989, *Journal of Laws*, No. 28, item 149).

Any redundant worker who has reached the age limit even for early retirement was allowed to draw an old-age pension regardless of the numbers of years he/she has spent at work.

There were separate statutory regulations concerning earlier retirement for disabled workers whose disability was caused by military service, active resistance or an industrial injury. The past tense was used because the Act of 17 December 1998 declared invalid all previous legal regulations concerning early retirement. Instead, temporary legal regulations were introduced, which were enforced until 31 December 2006. Total displacement of legal regulations concerning privileges of certain categories of insured employees to retire at earlier age caused political unrest, which was organized by all trade unions functioning in the coal mine industry and which led to the recent act of Polish Parliament of 27 July 2005 to reintroduce the early retirement regulations for workers employed in the mines. Other groups of formerly privileged categories of employees, such as railroad workers, teachers, and nurses already made some political statements defending their professional interests in the field of early retirement.

357. According to the Act of 11 May 2012 lower retirement age is maintained by insured born before 1 January 1949 and performing work in special conditions or character that are listed in implementing rules issued by the government.

The insured that did not reach the retirement age are entitled to partial pension. The essential terms of acquiring partial retirement pension, defined in the Act of 11 May 2012 enclose: insurance period, that is, paying contributions, at least thirty-five years for women and forty for men and the age of at least 62 (women) and at least 65 (men). The amount of partial pension is 50% of the pension that the insured is entitled to when reaching the age of 67. Partial pension is not subject to an increase in the level of the lowest pension. When acquiring by the entitled insured the age of 67 and – in case of performing work by pensioner receiving partial pension – after ceasing the employment, on application by the insured, the partial pension is changed to the full pension that the insured when reaching the age of 67 is entitled to.

358. The last statement brings us to the second legal condition for an old-age pension: the working career. Under the Act of 14 December 1982, the normal period of the working career is twenty years for female workers and twenty-five years for male workers. The concept of employment, which is the legal basis for calculating the working career, is strictly regulated. It includes only those periods of employment based on an employment relationship during which an employee either earned wages or drew social security benefits. Unpaid periods of employment cannot be taken into account while calculating the working career of an applicant for an old-age pension.

359. The Act of 11 May 2012 introduces uniform minimal twenty-five year insurance periods for women and men – contributory and non-contributory period – being the second apart from the retirement age condition to acquire pension benefits. The extension of insurance period for women occurs in five annual stages. Contributory and non-contributory period of twenty years is in force since 31 December 2013. From 1 January to 31 December 2014, this period is extended to twenty-one years, Further extension of contributory and non-contributory period by a year (twenty-two, twenty-three, and twenty-four years) occurs every two years: since 1 January 2016 (twenty-two years), 1 January 2018 (twenty-three years), 1 January 2020 (twenty-four years). Uniform twenty-five year insurance period for women is in force as of 1 January 2021.

360. Different requirements concerning age limit for males and females as one of the main conditions for earning legal rights to old-age pension benefits do not create major legal problems in the compulsory social security scheme. A five-year difference between males and females in favour of the latter is considered as one of the privileges enjoyed by female employees – a privilege that does not contradict the principle of equal treatment of employees regardless of gender.

At one point, a lower age limit for female employees created a legal problem in the case of employment of civil servants and university teachers. The statutory regulation on civil servants (the Act of 16 September 1982, *Journal of Laws*, No. 31, item 214) empowered an employer – the state agency – to terminate an employment relationship with civil servants on the date of his/her retirement age. Due to the five-year difference between male and female employees employed by the various state agencies, the state was in the position to terminate an employment relationship with a female employee five years earlier than with her male counterpart. The Supreme Court, in its judgment of 14 May 1996 (III ARN 93/95, OSNAPiUS, 1996, No. 23, item 352), declared the provision of the Act of 16 September 1982 valid since it does not oblige an employer to terminate an employment relationship upon a female civil servant's reaching the retirement age.

Another conclusion was reached by the Constitutional Tribunal in its decision of 24 September 1991 (Kw 5/91) concerning legality of gender differences in cases of retirement of university professors and other staff members employed to teach at institutions of higher learning. The previous statutory regulation on the institutions of higher education of 12 September 1990 (*Journal of Laws*, 1990, No. 65, item 385) had introduced a compulsory retirement age for male associate professors of 70 years of age, while female associate professors were automatically transferred into retirement at the age of 65. The Constitutional Tribunal declared this differentiation discriminatory. As a result of this judgment, an amendment of 24 July 1992 (*Journal of Laws*, No. 63, item 314) to the statutory regulation on the institution of higher education was introduced, which abolished the difference in compulsory retirement age for both sexes. Since then, the compulsory retirement age for professors and associate professors is 70 years of age.

Taking into account the above remarks, the difference in the retirement age between male and female employees plays an important part only when related to the question of the right to work. If the age difference does not create any automatic legal consequence in the employment relationship, a lower age limit for female employees is being considered to be in accordance with the principle of equal treatment and the principle of non-discrimination based on gender.

361. The Act of 17 October 1991 lists periods that are declared as the periods ending before the act was enforced (15 November 1991) during which social security dues were paid as well as periods during which there was no legal duty to contribute to the social security fund in social security dues. Those periods include periods during which any type of professional activity under employment contract or the civil law type of contract was performed.

There are other periods that are considered by the Act of 17 October 1991 as periods that must be taken into account by the State Social Security Agency during the process of accumulating the number of years for the purpose of the pensioner's career, despite the fact that there was no contribution to the social security fund in social security dues. There are those periods during which a person applying for an old-age pension benefit was either fighting in various wars, studying, or taking care of dependent members of the family.

362. Only the proven periods either for which social security dues were paid or periods during which there was no duty to contribute to the social security fund may be taken into account by the State Social Security Agency. An individual applying for the old-age pension must be able to show that he/she either worked in insured employment for the whole of his/her career, or that he/she has been in the same condition.

363. The burden of proof of eligibility relies upon an applicant. He/she must either show documents stating that social security dues were contributed, or present any other possible affidavits that support an application. An employer is under a legal duty to cooperate with an applicant during the process of preparing an application. This means that an employer must do their best to help a worker applying for an old-age pension to collect the necessary documents that prove his/her pension career and wages earned. Under the Act of 17 December 1998, the age stated by the Social Security Law (60 for females and 65 for males) is the only condition to get an old-age pension. Insured employees born between 1949 and 1968 are entitled to early retirement according to above-presented conditions if they did not join before 31 December 1999 one of new social security funds and meet necessary requirements stated by the above-mentioned social security regulations for those who would prefer to take early retirement before 31 December 2006.

364. The Bridging Retirement Act, enforced on 19 December 2008 (*Journal of Laws of 2008*, No. 237*, item 1656), regulated the conditions and the acquiring of such retirement rights by certain employees carrying out work in exceptional natural environments (e.g., work carried out underground, underwater, or in the air). This also includes work carried out that is determined by technological processes (e.g., in hot or cold microclimates). Employees who also have a right to bridge retirement are those whose work is of a specific nature, including work where there is an exceptional level of responsibility or a high level of demand for physical and psychological agility.

Employees entitled to such bridging of retirement must fulfil the conditions outlined in Article 4 of the Act, passed on the 19 December 2008. Such employees must have been born after the 31 December 1948, have been employed in exceptional conditions, or have carried out work of a particular nature for at least fifteen years. Further, such employees must have made insurance premium payments to the retirement fund for at least twenty years (women) or twenty-five years (men) and that the work carried out in exceptional conditions or the work of an exceptional nature was done before 1 January 1999 or after 31 December 2008. Also, such employees must have had their work agreements terminated.

The level of retirement benefits for such workers depends on the amount of capital collected on a special Bridging Retirement Fund from premiums paid to the individual retirement account of the employee. The right to bridging retirement benefits ceases the day prior to when normal retirement entitlements are granted, for example, when the general retirement age is reached (60 years of age for women and 65 years of age for men). Bridging retirement benefits are paid out to those employees who are entitled to early retirement benefits rather than having to reach the generally applicable retirement age.

365. The act of 16 November 2016 on the amendment of the act on old-age pensions and invalidity benefits paid from the Social Security Fund governs two issues: (1) it reverses the process of increase and equalization of the retirement age of men and women initiated by the act of 11 May 2012; (2) it introduces transitional provisions governing the pension rights of persons who in the period from 1 January 2013 until 31 December 2015, under the conditions laid down in the act of 11 May 2012, reached the retirement age applicable until 1 January 2013 (60 years for women and 65 years for men), however, because of the extension of that age, did not become entitled to the pension benefits, as well as persons who, as from the date of entry into force of the act of 16 November 2016, will be removed from the pension system.

The amendments introduced by the act of 11 May 2012 on the amendment of provisions governing the pension schemes of professional soldiers and their families, police officers, officers of the Internal Security Agency, the Foreign Intelligence Agency, the Military Counterintelligence Service, the Military Intelligence Service, the Central Anti-Corruption Bureau, the Border Guard, the Government Protection Bureau, the State Fire Service, the Prison Service and the families of these public officers, do not fall within the scope of amendments introduced by the act of 16 November 2016.

366. The most important change I have already mentioned, is restoration of the retirement age applicable until 31 December 2012, which was 60 years for women and 65 years for men. The act of 16 November 2016 introduced a general principle which was the very essence of the presented amendment – a legal norm establishing the retirement age at 60 years for women and 65 years for men. In connection with the above, the new act of 16 November 2016 repeals the provisions laying down the terms and conditions for obtainment of pension entitlement at the age of 67. Moreover, the legal provisions which refer to the provisions defining the retirement age at 67 years are amended.

367. The act of 16 November 2016 removed the partial pension concept. Because of the restoration of the previous, lower retirement age, different for men and women, the partial pension payable upon reaching the retirement age which was at least 62 years for women and at least 65 years for men and the varied insurance period, has become irrelevant. The legislature is aware that after the new act enters into force, there will still be persons covered by the general and mandatory social insurance system who obtained their entitlement to the partial pension until the date on which such pension is converted into the full pension. For that reason the regulations governing determination of the basis for partial pensions for the entitled persons remained in force.

368. The act of 16 November 2016 amended several other acts laying down the terms and conditions for the grant to particular categories of the insured of the right to benefits from a pension provision system and not from a pension insurance. The changes consist in replacement of the retirement age extended by the act of 11 May 2012 to 67 years, by a lower and gender-based retirement age of at least 60 years for women and 65 years for men. According to the current authorities, the differentiation in the general retirement age of men and women does not cause discrimination of women but – as ruled by the Constitutional Tribunal in its judgment of 15 July 2010 in K 63/07 – is a 'compensatory privilege' of women. In the mentioned judgment the Constitutional Tribunal held that there exist differences which result from specific social and family roles of women. It applies in particular to women who fulfil several functions – not only maternity and childcare functions but also those involving professional work and family duties. For that reason, there still exist, although to a smaller extent than in the past, certain social differences as regards position of women performing several social roles in the traditional family model. Therefore, the differentiation of the retirement age of the insured consisting in granting the working women of the entitlement to the pension benefits can be justified by the principle of social justice laid down in Article 2 of the Constitution.

369. According to ZUS, as a result of lowering the retirement age to 60 years for women and 65 for men, there will be almost 1.2 million less skilled employees on the labour market. The Polish state authorities do not have an idea how to use the well experienced persons and encourage them to stay on the labour market.

370. The act of 16 November 2016 made amendments to the provisions on the farmers' insurance schemes. The previous basic earlier retirement age of 60 years for women and 65 years for men was restored, subject to the achievement of at least 25 years of insurance period. Farmers who achieved at least 30 years of insurance period and ceased their agricultural activity, retain their entitlement to retire after they have reached the age of 55 (women) or 60 years (men).

371. Certain changes were made as regards entitlement of public prosecutors and judges to cease professional activity and to retire, equivalent to the retirement of persons covered by the general social insurance system. A principle was restored according to which judges and public prosecutors retire after they have reached the age of 65 years. The above-mentioned basic retirement age applies both to men and women employed in the judiciary. After a person employed as a judge or public prosecutor reaches the age of 55 (women) or 60 years (men), such person may retire if his or her seniority of service in the justice system is 25 (women) or 30 years (men). The retirement age of judges of the Supreme Court, both men and women, was established at 65 years.

372. The act of 16 November 2016 includes extensive transitional provisions. They govern:

(a) a legal situation of the insured persons who have previously obtained their pension entitlement under the act of 11 May 2012 previously in force in a period from 1 January 2013 until 31 December 2015. The situation of these pensioners is not changed. Following the entry into force of the act of 16 November 2016, they receive pension benefits to which they became entitled in the period when the increased retirement age applied. It should only be emphasized that obtainment of an entitlement to an old-age pension or retirement by a judge or a public prosecutor means that a person concerned has met all the conditions necessary for the obtainment of such benefit and not a grant and payment of such benefit (a judgment of the Supreme Court of 13 January 2015, I UK 174/14). The grant of an entitlement to a pension, which consists in establishing the right to receive the pension by an insured person, is subject to a prior application by the person concerned. For that reason the persons who met the conditions to obtain pension in accordance with the provisions applicable before 1 January 2013, become entitled to pension as of 1 January 2016. A decision establishing the entitlement to a pension is issued by competent social insurance institutions upon request of the interested parties;

(b) persons who, at the date of entry into force of the act of 16 November 2016, have their right to invalidity benefit established under a decision of a pension authority for a period until they reach their retirement age, the right to pre-retirement benefit, a bridging allowance or teachers' compensation benefit, will retain their right until they reach the retirement age specified in the amended pension laws – 60 years for women and 65 years for men. The above principle does not apply to invalidity benefit entitlement which ends or expires before a person reaches the retirement age. If a person reaches the age of 60 (woman) or 65 (man) before the date of entry into force of the act of 16 November 2016, the above-mentioned entitlement applies until the effective date of the new act. Identical rules apply to women who benefit from periodic funded pension. A person may benefit from it until reaching the age of 65 years, and if on the date of entry into force of the act of 16 November 2016 such person has already reached the age – until such date of entry into force. This is because the funded pension is a periodic benefit;

(c) because of lowering the retirement age, the partial pensions and partial farmers' pensions have lost their raison d'être. However, persons who, on the date of entry into force of the act of 16 November 2016, already have their right to the partial pension established, will retain the above right until the time when the partial pension is changed into the full pension governed by the provisions of the act of 17 December 1998 on the old-age pensions and invalidity benefits paid from the Social Insurance Fund. The change is made at the request of the insured. In the case of an insured who is an employee, a precondition for retaining the above entitlement is terminating of an employment relationship. It must be noted that because of the age limit set out in the previously applicable regulations which entitled to obtainment of a partial pension – 62 years for women and 65 years for men –, all persons receiving pension on the date of entry into force of the act of 16 November 2016 will be of the age to be entitled to the full pension. On the other hand, the act of 16 November 2016 regulates differently the entitlement to the farmers' partial pension. According to the provisions of the act of 20 December 1990 on the social insurance of farmers, the partial pension is, ex officio, converted into the full pension after the entitled person has reached the statutory common retirement age. The partial pension and the partial farmers' pension is subject to indexation in accordance with the rules laid down in the act of 17 December 1998 on the old-age pensions and invalidity benefits paid from the Social Insurance Fund and the act of 20 December 1990 on the social insurance of farmers;

(d) prosecutors, military prosecutors and judges of general courts who reach the age of 65 before the date of entry into force of the act of 16 November 2016 may – within six months from the effective date of the above act – apply for extension of their period of employment. The application should be accompanied by a medical certificate confirming the ability to perform official duties.

373. Restoration of the retirement age applicable until 31 December 2012 required regulation of the special protection of sustainability of employment of employees who have not more than four years left to reach the retirement age. The special protection of sustainability of employment of the pre-retirement workers guaranteed by Article 39 of the Labour Code of 26 June 1974 prohibits the employer to terminate a contract of employment with an employee who has not more than four years left to reach the retirement age, if his period of employment provides for his entitlement to pension rights upon reaching this age. The mentioned provision does not apply if the employee obtains an invalidity benefit on the basis of his total inability to work. Employees who, on the date of entry into force of the act of 16 November 2016, are covered by the special protection of sustainability of employment under Article 39 of the Labour Code as well as persons who would be subject to such protection if they were employed on that date, enjoy the special protection of sustainability of employment until they reach the retirement age, which is 60 years for women and 65 years for men, for not less than four years.

374. The Polish state authorities have assumed that the lowering of the retirement age will have a positive impact on the national labour market. It will alleviate the entry on the market of secondary school graduates in the next years and will cause a reduction of unemployment among young persons. According to the political and state authorities, the effects of lowering the basic retirement age will not be significant for the state budget. In the next year the increase of expenses of the Social Insurance Fund for the retirement pensions will cover ca. 120 thousand persons. Increase in the payment of pension benefits will result from the increase in the number of the insured who will reach the lowered retirement age and will obtain their pension entitlement upon entry into force of the act of 16 November 2016. According to the official forecast of revenues and expenditures for the social benefits paid from the Social Insurance Fund, in 2017–2019, they will amount to PLN 6.9 billion (EUR 1.7 billion) in each successive calendar year during the next three years. The lowering of the retirement age will result in reduction of expenditures for the benefits paid from the insurance system payable until the retirement age: invalidity allowance in respect of incapacity for work, pre-retirement benefits, bridging allowances, partial pensions, farmers' partial pensions, teachers' compensatory benefits and unemployment benefits. The state authorities believe that the balance of other consequences which increase or decrease the expenditures and income of the public finance sector connected with lowering the retirement age and other funds created from the general social insurance system should not exceed PLN 10 billion (ca. EUR 2.4 billion). The state authorities have planned to undertake actions aimed at increasing the revenue of the Social Insurance Fund. Such actions are not intended to increase an interest rate of a pension insurance contribution but to eliminate such irregularities on the labour market as:

(a) concealing of undeclared remuneration paid to the employees in order to avoid payment of mandatory taxes and social insurance contributions;
(b) taking advantage of civil law contracts and self-employment rather than entering into contracts of employment in order to exclude or limit the obligation to pay social insurance contributions;
(c) grey economy employment;
(d) overlapping of pension benefits under two or more pension insurance titles.

The revenues of the pension fund should be increased by the increase of the minimum remuneration to PLN 2,000 (ca. EUR 479) monthly and of an hourly rate for work under civil law contracts to PLN 13 (more than EUR 3), to such extent that the expenditures for the pension benefits payable as a result of lowering the retirement age and extension of the period of receiving of pensions will be covered from the state budget grant.

375. In December 2015 an average payment of pension from the Social Insurance Institution was PLN 2,116.45 (EUR 506), which accounted for 62.1% of the average remuneration for work reduced by the mandatory insurance contribution paid by the insured. The pension of women was PLN 1,784.07 (EUR 427) which accounted for 52.3% of the average remuneration and 69% of the average remuneration of men which amounted to PLN 2,601.04 (EUR 622), that is 76.3% of the average remuneration.

376. The radical changes made in the Polish pension insurance system during the last five years give rise to a question regarding a relationship between the changes in the pension system based on the provisions adopted in the 1990s and the current political situation in Poland. According to specialists, priority should be given to establishment and maintenance of the established retirement age as a starting point for setting out the conditions for obtainment of pension entitlement by the insured persons. Experience over the last five years shows that the direction of the pension system is dependent on political decisions and therefore the main condition for obtainment of pension rights – the age of the insured – is often changed. Policymakers ignore the fundamental idea of a mature pension system according to which frequent changes of regulations defining the age of the insured who become entitled to the pension benefits prevent implementation of a long-term pension system. The politicians forget that no pension system can produce favourable changes in a short term. The shortcomings of the general, mandatory pension system could be completed by the government programmes promoting the additional forms of saving. However, Poles are not interested in the second or third pillar of the pension security. The low level of participation in those pillars is explained by the lack of clarity of regulations and insufficient promotion of the idea of voluntary forms of saving. The participation in the individual forms of saving should be encouraged by state guarantees of high growth rates of insurance contributions into the individual pension schemes, ensuring security of funds collected in the OFE and development of the state preventive supervision to combat unfair competition among entrepreneurs and consisting in reduction of the costs of employment.

B. *The Wages Earned*

377. The Act of 14 December 1982 stated that the calculation basis for the old-age pension is based on wages earned during the period of the last few years before retirement. There is no direct relationship between wages earned and the level of old-age pension paid out of the social security fund. It is also due to the 250% limit put on the financial basis, which serves as a platform to calculate the amount of the old-age pension. For example, while a worker whose monthly wages are as high as PLN 2,500 = EUR 595.24 pays PLN 1,125 = EUR 267.86 in social security dues and earns PLN 1,137.30 = EUR 270.79 in an old-age pension, exactly the same amount of monies in the form of an old-age pension is paid to a worker who earns twice as much (PLN 5,000 = EUR 1,190.48) and on whose behalf a double contribution is made by his/her employer in social security dues (PLN 2,250 = EUR 595.24).

378. The wages taken into account are not the wages from the entire working career of an applicant. The Act of 17 December 1991 gradually extends the number of years taken into account by the State Social Security Agency during the process of calculation of an old-age pension. For the first year the act was introduced (1992), an applicant was free to choose any of three consecutive years out of the past twelve years as the period from which wages should be taken into account for the purpose of establishing the amount of the old-age pension. The social security agency was obliged to take into account wages earned by an applicant during the chosen eight consecutive years out of the last seventeen years. Since 1 January 1999, the amount of the old-age pension is calculated on a financial basis – wages earned during ten consecutive years chosen by an applicant out of the last twenty years before retirement.

379. Old-age pension calculation is based on the following formula: 24% of the wages earned during the periods taken into account plus 1.3% of the basis for each year taken into account as the year during which social security contributions were paid. Periods during which social security dues were not contributed are calculated on a less favourable basis: 0.7% of the basis for each year not treated by the social security agency as equal to which contributions should be paid.

380. All old-age pensions are adjusted in accordance with the consumer price index prevailing between the time those social security benefits are paid and the previous year. The Act of 25 October 1996 (*Journal of Laws*, No. 136, item 636) announces that the state government is obliged to adjust an old-age pension if the consumer price index grew by at least 10% within the year. In such a case, the act declares an obligatory adjustment of old-age pensions twice a year: on 1 March and on 1 September. If the consumer price index went up less than 10% during a one-year period, an adjustment is made once a year on 1 June.

381. For all workers entitled to the old-age pension, a minimum pension is guaranteed. The Act of 17 October 1991 declares that the minimum amount of the old-age pension cannot be lower than 35% of the wage earned during the process of the last valorization (adjustment).

382. The Act of 11 May 2012 guarantees minimum pension for persons in retirement age who acquired pension rights in 2013 or 2014 in the amount of 20% of pension calculated pursuant to Article 53 and in the amount of 80% of pension pursuant to Article 26 of pension act of 17 December 1998.

383. The maximum amount of an old-age pension cannot exceed 100% of the financial base (wages earned) on which account the amount of the old-age pension benefit was calculated.

Entirely new regulations in the method of calculation of old-age pensions were introduced by the Act of 17 December 1998. According to the new formula for calculation of old-pension benefits, the amount of the retirement pension is obtained by applying the total contributions in social security dues to old-age pension funds and the age (after age 60 for females and after age 65 for males) in which the particular beneficiary decides to retire. Calculation for individual old-age pension are based on total amount of social security dues and average life expectancy. The amount of the capital collected by the beneficiary on his/her individual account run by the social security agency (state or private) and the date in which the given beneficiary decides to retire after reaching the normal retirement age directly affects an amount of the individual old-age pension. Higher contributions to the individual retirement capital in social security dues and postponement of decision to retire guarantee the more favourable individual retirement pension.

§2. Survivor's Pension

I. Beneficiaries

384. A survivor's pension is paid to the members of the family of a deceased worker who at the time of his/her death was entitled either to the old-age pension or invalidity benefit (Article 65, section 1 of the Act of 17 December 1998). The survivor's pension is paid also to an individual not employed at the time of his/her death if such person was eligible either for an old-age pension or invalidity benefit.

385. The following categories of immediate family members are entitled to survivor's pensions:

- natural and adopted children of the deceased worker and the children of his/her spouse;
- minor grandchildren accepted into custody by the deceased worker;
- spouses;
- parents.

386. The essential condition is related to the age of surviving family members. Children are entitled to draw the survivor's pension until they reach the age of 16, or – if they continue their education – 25 years. If a 25-year-old person is about to complete their education, the survivor's pension is extended until the end of the academic year. Regardless of age, children are eligible for a survivor's benefit on the condition that they became disabled before they turn 16 or 25 years of age.

387. A widow is entitled to a survivor's pension if she is at least 50 years old or disabled or takes care of at least one child, grandchild, brother, or sister of her deceased husband eligible for a survivor's pension. The right to the survivor's pension is earned by a widow who turns 50 within five years starting either from the day of the death of her husband or from the day she stopped looking after one of the above-mentioned members of her family entitled to the survivor's pension.

388. A divorced widow, or a widow who during the time of the death of her husband did not maintain a common household with the deceased husband, is entitled to a survivor's benefit only if she can produce a court order that entitles her to demand alimony from the deceased person.

389. A widow who does not qualify for a survivor's pension may be awarded a temporary survivor's pension for a maximum of one year on condition that she is in need.

II. Calculation

390. The calculation of survivor's pension is derived from old-age pension. The survivor's pension for one eligible member of his/her family runs as high as 85% of the old-age pension. If two members of the family are eligible for the survivor's pension, that pension reaches 90% of the old-age pension. In the case when three or more members of the family are eligible for survivor's pension, that pension reaches 95% of an old-age pension. The very same calculation is applied when the deceased person was drawing an invalidity benefit.

391. All members of the family of the deceased worker or pensioner are entitled to share a single survivor's pension. This pension is paid as the common pension. This means that eligible members of the family should divide that pension between themselves. The survivor's pension is divided between eligible family members only upon the request of interested parties, or in the case when different eligible minor members are put under the custody of different persons.

§3. Invalidity Benefits

I. Beneficiaries

392. The Act of 17 December 1998 does not use the term 'invalidity'. Insured individuals who are unable to perform a work due to biological failure are called 'incapable' to work. The Act of 17 December 1998 introduced two elements that play an important role while making decision concerning incapability to work: a biological one and an economic one. The new concept of incapacity to work due to the biological failure does not stop social security lawyers and insured people from calling those benefits 'invalidity' benefits.

Invalidity benefit is paid to any employed person who is declared an invalid or who is totally or partially unable to continue working. The Act of 17 December 1998 stresses two major factors in the process of determining invalidity. Number one is the biological discrepancy of the worker's body. Number two is the worker's lost work potential. Those two factors are analysed by a physician employed by the State Social Security Agency.

393. The length of employment period, which is as a necessary requirement for entitlement to invalidity benefit, is related to the age of the disabled worker. A worker who has lost the ability to work before he/she turned 20 should have a minimum of one-year working experience. An employment period of two years is required if the disability occurred between the ages of 20 and 22. Three years of work experience is needed in the case of disability of a worker who is between 22 and 25 years old. Consequently, four years of work experience is required when a disability has occurred between age of 25 and 30. Finally, five years of work experience is demanded by the social security law when the disabled worker is over 30 of age. There is an additional legal requirement concerning periods of five years of work experience. It should occur during the period of the last ten years before an application for invalidity benefit was submitted. If an applicant is not employed any longer, the period of five years should have occurred during the last ten years preceding the moment in which disability occurred.

394. A third factor is introduced with the purpose of connecting disability to work with an employment relationship. The Act of 17 December 1998 provides that an invalidity benefit is paid to a disabled worker whose disability has occurred either during an employment period or that occurred not longer than eighteen months from the day on which an employment relationship has ended.

II. Conditions

395. Depending on the type of disability, the Act of 17 December 1998 introduces three different types of invalidity benefits: permanent, temporary or educational.

396. Permanent invalidity benefit is paid to a worker whose disability to work is constant and has no chance of recovery.

397. Temporary invalidity benefit is paid during the period in which a worker is unable to work. That period is estimated by a physician. A person drawing temporary invalidity benefit is obliged to report for a medical check-up at the end of that period.

398. Educational invalidity benefit is paid to a worker unable to carry out his/her current work but who is generally able to continue with another type of work. Educational invalidity benefit is paid for a six-month period with the ultimate purpose of giving disabled worker a chance to get new professional qualifications. That period may be extended for an additional thirty months. A person who was awarded an educational invalidity benefit is directed to the director of the district employment agency. All arrangements concerning vocational training of disabled person are both the legal and administrative responsibility of the state employment agency.

III. Calculation

399. Permanent invalidity benefit is calculated in a similar way to old-age pension. Twenty-four per cent of the basic income of the wage earner plus 1.3% for each year in which a contribution in social security dues was paid to the social security fund plus 0.7% for each year treated by the Social Security Law as non-contributory. In addition, 0.7% for each year of those non-contributory years may be taken into account by the social security agency, which can fill the gap between the contributory years and that required by the Social Security Law limit of twenty-five years between the day of claiming invalidity benefit and the day on which an applicant turns 60 years old.

400. Educational invalidity benefits are calculated at 75% of the amount of permanent invalidity benefits. If the worker has lost his/her ability to work due to a work accident or occupational disease, the vocational invalidity benefit is equal to 100% of previous wages.

401. All social security benefits described above are adjusted to the cost of living in the same way that old-age pensions are adjusted.

§4. Common Conditions

I. Application

402. Pension rights can be claimed only when an application is made by the prospective beneficiary. The application for an old-age pension should be made by an employee. When an employer employs a worker about to retire, the employer must, at least two months prior to the day this worker is eligible to draw retirement benefit, help the employee to apply to collect necessary information and prepare a motion. If the length of employment must be proved by the testimony of individuals witnessing the period of employment in question, an application must be submitted at least six months in advance.

403. If the State Social Security Agency has replied negatively to the application or has granted inadequate benefit, the eligible person may take legal action in the court adjudicating social security cases by demanding payment of earned benefits.

II. Accumulation Rules

404. The Polish Social Security Laws provide strict rules against the accumulation of pension benefits with other benefits. An individual entitled to draw an old-age pension and invalidity benefit must make a decision about which of those two benefits he/she wants to draw from the social security fund. An individual entitled to two social security benefits may draw a more favourable benefit or the benefit chosen by an eligible person.

405. An exception is made for benefits paid to victims of military actions, those who served the military in combat, and those workers who were injured because of a work accident. Social Security Laws call for special provisions that allow the accumulation of those benefits and benefits paid out of pension schemes.

406. The right to draw social security benefit is suspended when a beneficiary earns a salary exceeding 130% of the monthly basis for the calculation of an old-age pension.

Chapter 2. Pensions for the Self-Employed

§1. Old-Age Pensions

407. Because in Poland a compulsory social security scheme covers entire groups of the working population, the self-employed do not enjoy a separate social security scheme. The Act of 17 December 1998 states that old-age pensions drawn by the self-employed are regulated by the provisions of the common Social Security Law.

§2. Survivor's Pension

408. The Act of 17 December 1998 does not set any separate regulations concerning the survivor's pension for members of family of a deceased self-employed person covered by the social security scheme. Therefore, conditions for application for the survivor's pension set up by the legal regulations cover in the same grounds both categories of insured people: the self-employed and the wage earners.

§3. Invalidity Benefits

409. Until 31 August 1997, the self-employed were entitled to invalidity benefits if they were classified as invalids of the first or second category. Since 1 September 1997, that legal obstacle has been abolished and the self-employed were treated in the same way as wage earners. The self-employed were eligible, depending on the level of their disability, to continue their professional activities with either permanent or temporary invalidity benefits. They were also eligible for educational invalidity benefits. The Act of 17 December 1998 does not bring any changes in the legal rule introduced by legislation enforced between 1 September 1997 and 1 January 1998.

Chapter 3. Guaranteed Income for Elderly

410. Those individuals who – out of extraordinary circumstances – have not earned their right to social security benefit paid out of the compulsory scheme, are too old to accept an offer of employment, or who are unable to work are entitled to submit an application for appropriate social security benefits. A precondition of successful application is proof of a lack of the necessary means for survival. An application must be submitted to the president of the State Social Security Agency. After a favourable review, a positive decision may be issued to grant one of the social security benefits regulated by the Act of 17 December 1998.

411. The most important condition for entitlement to regular social security benefits in special cases is the lack of sufficient means of existence. This means that the test applies to each applicant individually. The rules concerning the calculation of the means of existence are general. Lack of other sources of income or income per capita in family of an applicant lower than minimum amount drawn in old-age pensions or invalidity benefits are used by the Act of 12 March 2004 on Social Assistance (*Journal of Laws of 2004*, No. 64, item 593 as amended) when they are:

- in need;
- homeless;
- unemployed;
- handicapped;
- severely ill;
- do not possess the necessary funds to support themselves.

Polish citizens, citizens of the European Union countries who were received residence permit in Poland, are entitled to the cash benefits out of social assistance when they are: in need; homeless; unemployed; handicapped; severely ill; and when they do not possess the necessary funds to support themselves. The social minimum established by the Act of 12 March 2004 on Social Assistance runs as high as PLN 461 (EUR 115) for single beneficiary and PLN 316 (EUR 79). Out of social assistance, a permanent or temporary social assistance may be paid to people who are unable to work due to the old age or incapacity. Social assistance allowances are granted to cover the difference between the above-mentioned social minimum and their income. They cannot be higher then PLN 418 (EUR 104) for a single person. They cannot be lower than PLN 30 (EUR 7.25). Social assistance allowances are managed by the local administration. Permanent allowance paid out of social assistance is established are rather low. They are as high as 20% of the average monthly wages used as the basis for the latest adjustments of the lowest old-age pension or invalidity benefit. Permanent allowance actually paid cannot exceed the difference between per capita income within an applicant's family and the lowest monthly old-age pension or invalidity benefit.

412. People who draw social assistance are not covered ex officio by the national social security system. Only those who were forced to resign from employment due to necessity to take personal care of member of their immediate family are covered by the national social security scheme. Local social assistance centres contribute in social security dues for such individuals on the condition that the income in their families does not exceed 150% of minimum income.

413. There is also a possibility of drawing a temporary allowance out of social assistance. A person in need may be awarded a temporary allowance, the amount of which is as high as 28% of the average monthly wage.

414. There is an opportunity to apply for a one-off allowance to cover particular needs such as cost of medical treatment, drugs and the renovation of an apartment.

415. The first condition is related to the economic situation of an applicant and his/her difficulties in supporting themselves due to illness, age, lack of opportunities to find a job, etc. The second condition is related to residence within Polish territory. If granted, the social security benefit paid out of the social security fund is subject to the very same regulations as the old-age pensions or invalidity benefit that is earned in the usual way.

The third condition is related to the activity of the person in need. Neither the State Social Security Agency nor the local community acts ex officio. An application must be made before any social security benefits or social assistance allowances may be paid.

Part IX. The Handicapped Persons

416. In the Act of 27 August 1997 on the employment and rehabilitation of handicapped (*Journal of Laws*, No. 123, item 776 as amended), emphasis was put on the promotion of social integration of all three categories of handicapped.

417. For the purpose of the social integration of handicapped, three categories of handicapped were established: individuals whose level of handicap may be declared as considerable, moderate and light (Article 3, section 1). A person listed as considerably handicapped cannot perform work and function with support of the third person (Article 4, section 1). A person defined as moderately handicapped is eligible to perform work in a special work environment (Article 4, section 2). Such a person may function with the partial support of a third person. A lightly handicapped person may work and function on his/her own however is less able to perform in his/her professional activities in comparison to a non-handicapped individual.

418. Under the Act of 27 August 1997, a national fund for the social rehabilitation of the handicapped was established. All employers employing at least twenty-five workers are obliged to contribute to that fund. Only foreign institutions representing states or international organizations and employers employing at least 6% handicapped people within their work force are free from compulsory contributions to the social rehabilitation fund.

419. Under the Act of 27 August 1997, employers are encouraged to organize job slots for handicapped persons. Those employers who employ handicapped workers enjoy taxation privileges and waivers. They are entitled to reimbursement of the cost of reconstruction of workplaces in order to accommodate the needs of handicapped people.

420. An employer is obliged to rehire within three months a handicapped person who is the victim of a work accident and provide such worker with work in a special environment. If an employer is not able to cope with such a legal obligation, he must contribute to the social rehabilitation fund an amount equal to fifteen times of the average monthly wage for each handicapped person turned down as an applicant for work (Article 14, section 1 in connection with Article 23).

421. Under the Act of 27 August 1997, a handicapped person can receive all kinds of benefits both in kind and in cash useful for his/her rehabilitation: professional and psychological orientation, counselling, guidance, schooling, training, medical rehabilitation, subsidies for placement and special kinds of jobs for the handicapped.

Part X. Minimum Income Benefit

422. There is no special legal regulation on minimum income benefits. The Act of 17 October 1991 sets up standards for minimum old-age pensions, survivor's pensions, and invalidity benefit. As already mentioned in Part VIII of this study, the minimum amount of social security benefit – an old-age pension run as high as 23.4% of the average wage serving as a basis for the latest adjustment of social security benefits. With the exception of temporary invalidity benefits, which may reach 27% amount of the basis used for the calculation of minimum social security benefits, other regular benefits may reach 35% of the financial basis on which social security benefits are calculated.

423. Minimum invalidity benefits and survivor's pensions paid in cases of industrial injury cannot be lower than 120% of the minimum regularly paid social security benefits.

Part XI. Claims and Adjudication

Chapter 1. Introduction

424. Substantive provisions of social security law are worthless without effective procedural regulations that guarantee any person applying for social security benefits that his/her claim will be adjudicated according to procedural justice. Social security benefits are protected against seizure and transfer. That legal principle enlarges the role of the social security courts in the process of adjudication of claims brought by an insured person demanding the payment of social security benefits. Because of the great importance of procedural regulations, I present different models of adjudication of social security benefits that are in effect in the history of Polish social security laws.

425. The Polish model of adjudication of social security cases is not an ideal one. An ideal model of judicial protection in social security cases was formed during the seventeenth session of the International Labour Organization (ILO) in 1933. Conventions No. 35 on Old-Age Insurance (industry, etc.); No. 36 on Old-Age Insurance (agriculture); No. 37 on Invalidity Insurance (industry, etc.); No. 38 on Invalidity Insurance (agriculture); No. 39 on Survivor's Insurance (industry); and No. 40 on Survivor's Insurance (agriculture) guaranteed an insured person and members of his/her family the legal right to appeal an administrative decision taken by an insurance agency in a special type of social security court. The distinctive character of social security matters called for special expertise of judges adjudicating those matters in social security courts. Legal provisions of the respective conventions of ILO required that judges who try social security cases must acquire special knowledge of goals of the national social security scheme and get acquainted with the unique needs of insured people who are covered by various social security schemes.

426. Having professionally qualified judges educated and experienced in social security matters serving in special courts of law was made a vital legal prerequisite in adjudicating social security cases. Eventually laymen chosen from people covered by social security schemes and employers were able to serve in special security courts. Thus, the ILO conventions has as its number one principle the professional quality of judges serving in special courts of law designed by national legislation to adjudicate social security cases. Professional knowledge in legal matters concerning social security was emphasized by international social security legislation.

427. The principle of professional quality gained its priority over the principle of legal control of the adjudication process in social security cases exercised by various interest groups: insured employees and members of their families (beneficiaries) and contributors to the social security scheme in social security dues (employers). Since both employees and employers pose as members of society, their involvement in the adjudication process of social security benefits was treated in legal literature as 'social control' of the judicial process in social security cases. One may try to explain this euphemism in a different way, by putting all the blame on an antiquated political system that was preoccupied, or fascinated even, with the importance of the working class as the most powerful representative of the socialist society in the post-Second World War, the Polish People's Republic. One must bear in mind, however, that under totally different political systems, both in the capitalist Poland between the Great Wars and now in the democratic system, which was reintroduced in the second half of 1989, various representatives of society at large were taking part in the adjudication process of social security cases. One of the most important questions one must ask is this: to what extent did first the capitalist government of Poland, and later the socialist government of thc Polish People's Republic and at the present time the democratic government of the Republic of Poland, comply with a set of legal standards set upon an international social security community in the above-mentioned conventions of the ILO? After all, the Conventions No. 35, 36, 37, 39, and 40 were ratified by the Polish government on 30 August 1948 (*Journal of Laws of 1949*, No. 31, items 223, 225, 227, 231, 233). Convention No. 39 was ratified on 30 November 1948 (*Journal of Laws of 1949*, No. 31, item 229).

428. Thus, one of the different purposes of this presentation is to detect, by analysing the judicial protection systems in social security cases in capitalist, socialist and democratic Poland, whether or not under different political regimes the principle of professionalism in the process of adjudication of social security cases was implemented. If the answer is yes, we must estimate how close was, and as a matter of fact still is, Polish legislation to fulfilling the overwhelming principle of professionalism in the process of adjudication of social security cases.

429. There is no doubt that the adjudication process in social security cases must serve many purposes and play for the favour of many masters. It must take care of legal rights of beneficiaries of a particular social security scheme. It must take into consideration the economic interests of employers – contributors to the fund out of which social security benefits are paid. Last but not least, it must take care of the economic interest of the fund itself. The two last remarks are even more important if one realizes that under the socialist system, employers and the social security fund were run by the same master – the powerful state government.

430. The ILO was, and still is, quite convinced that in social security matters the most important problem is to put a professional judge in charge of the control of administrative decisions made by a social security agency. The Polish government happened to share this point of view. Or, at least it did so on the surface when ratifying all ILO conventions in which the principle of professionalism was expressed. One must bear in mind, though, that the ratification process took place at the beginning of the Cold War period, which in internal relations distinguished itself by strengthening the power of the state government in virtually all areas, including adjudication of social security cases. The idea of so-called social control in the judicial process was just a cover-up for state control. After all, the state was represented by its civil servant (a professional judge), its economic functionaries (representatives of the state-owned enterprises acting as employers), and its major ally (representatives of trade unions) acting as an official representation of the core of the socialist society, which was the working class.

431. Taking for granted what was stated in the conventions adopted by the ILO, that justice in social security cannot be served by people for the benefit of other people but must be delivered by professionals, I examine from structural and procedural angles the role of the judge in adjudicating social security cases.

432. Serving justice in social security matters takes at least two representatives of two different professional communities: legal and medical. As experience in litigating social security cases has taught any lawyer, in the vast majority of cases, legal ruling is overwhelmingly influenced by the professional opinion of physicians. This encyclopaedia does not deal with the role of medical examiner in the process of adjudication of social security cases.

433. In order to present the most comprehensive analysis, one must distinguish three models of judicial protection in social security cases over the hundred years since social insurance was introduced on Polish territory.

Chapter 2. Legal Grounds of the National Model of Judicial Protection in Social Security Cases

434. Legal grounds of past and present national models of judicial protection in social security cases in Poland have a strong foreign origin. In the Polish social security system, judicial protection in social security case was heavily influenced by Austrian and Prussian systems of adjudication of social security matters.

435. The Austrian judicial system, which was adopted in the southern part of Poland, distinguished cases concerning social security benefits and cases in which the scope of social security coverage and social security dues were under judicial consideration. All sorts of decisions concerning social security benefits fell within judicial control of special courts that dealt exclusively with this type of case. Those courts were made part of the common judicial court system. Since social security courts were incorporated into the common structure of judicial organs, it is possible to conclude that as far as the organizational structure was concerned, social security courts did not distinguish themselves any better than criminal or civil courts. From the procedural viewpoint, there was a significant difference, though, between social security courts and other courts that tried criminal or civil types of cases. The social security court only had a one-tiered structure. This means that all court orders rendered in cases concerning decisions made by social security agencies in matters of social security benefits were final and binding upon all parties: the insured person and the social security agency. From this perspective, the judicial system in Austria in social security matters distinguished itself, however unfavourably, from the rest of the judicial structure in which it had its proper place. As an additional argument for the hypothesis of consistency of social security courts with the common court system serving justice on Polish soil, which was then part of Austrian-Hungarian empire, one may point out that in social security courts, cases were tried according to the rule of civil procedure.

436. Decisions concerning the scope of coverage and social security dues were under the judicial scrutiny of administrative courts. Therefore, part of the social security issues concerning the personal scope of application and financing of payment of social security benefits were considered purely administrative matters.

437. From the modern point of view, social security courts taken as administrative tribunals are closer to the idea of special courts expressed in the ILO conventions. Regardless of the political and historical factors, administrative courts were, and still are, considered as a special type of court located outside the organizational structure of the state judicial organs.

438. In the western and northern part of Polish territory, the Prussian judicial system was enforced. A special two-tiered structured social security court adjudicated all social security cases except matters concerning personal scope of coverage and duty to contribute to the social security fund in social security dues.

439. In the eastern part of Polish territory, social security cases were tried by civil courts.

440. As an effect of partition between three superpowers, Austria, Prussia, and Russia, in the field of judicial protection in social security cases, Poland started her march into independence in 1918 as a country influenced by different foreign legislation. Under heavy influence of foreign legal regulations, Poland as an independent country had difficulties in creating her own system of judicial protection in social security cases.

Chapter 3. Heterogeneous National Model of Judicial Protection in Social Security Cases in Poland Between the Great Wars (1918–1939)

441. It is difficult to imagine a greater variety of control of decisions taken by different social security agencies administering various social security schemes that appeared after Poland gained her independence in 1918. Decisions concerning social security matters were under the legal control of various organs called 'courts', 'committees', 'commissions', and 'tribunals'. Those organs were connected with different administrative offices established to oversee either social security administration, or general administration. After analysis of the structure of such organs and their relationships with the administrative organs of social security agencies, one must come to the conclusion that those organs did not fulfil the legal definition of courts of law specializing in social security matters. Regardless of their position in the organizational structure of such organs (inside or outside social security administration), social security committees, tribunals, and commissions did not adjudicate social security cases. Instead, they rendered upon parties (the insured person and the social security agency) orders in controversial social security matters. Those organs were created out of the principle of the solidarity of insured people who were running their social security affairs on the basis of self-management. Either internal or external organs were established to help those people chosen to manage social security matters with legal regulations adopted either on a voluntary basis or provided by the state in order to let them comply with fulfilment of their needs.

442. The Act of March 1933 on social security did not break away from this practice. This particular act created so-called mediation committees that dealt with complaints brought by insured people denied sickness benefit by the director managing the fund out of which social security allowances were paid in case of illness. 'Mediation committee' was organized on a parity basis. It contained six members representing the principle of equality of employees and employers (3 + 3). Those representatives of two major interest groups were chosen by the board of overseers of the social security agency called 'agency council'. The chairman of the 'mediation committee' was appointed by the state administrative organ in charge of social security. The 'mediation committee' proceeded according to regulations established by the minister of labour and public assistance. It is characteristic that even if the 'mediation committee' was partially established as an administrative organ that enabled two of the most interested to voice their opinions in matters concerning sickness allowance of the beneficiaries (employees) and benefactors (employers) and proceed according to administrative regulations, still this organ was regarded as a special type of court of laws. Obviously, the trial, which was conducted by this organ as a procedural requirement of rendering a valid order, did not make a judicial organ out of a partially private, partially public body.

443. As a matter of fact, in the capitalist Poland there did not exist an independent judicial organ eligible to work on the principle of professional quality, social security cases, and to provide judicial protection for those who were denied coverage by particular social security schemes, charged with excessive social security dues, or refused social security benefits. The 'mediation committee' only controlled decisions concerning payment of some type of short-term social security benefit (sickness allowances). It did not even screen decisions concerning the personal scope of coverage and existence of the obligation to contribute to the social security fund in social security dues, or lack of such obligation as far as social security scheme in case of illness was concerned.

444. The act concerning social security courts was passed a few weeks before the outbreak of the Second World War – on 28 July 1939 (*Journal of Laws*, No. 51, item 396). It was never introduced into life due to the political events: first, War World II, and second, changes of the political system. However, since some ideas expressed in the Act of 28 July 1939 were used by the socialist government, I present an outline of this particular piece of legislation, which was quite important in shaping the idea of professionalism in the process of adjudication of social security cases by special social security courts.

445. Social security courts were set up by an Act of Parliament as separate courts of law in charge of all but social security allowances in case of illness. In the last type of case, the legal mandate to adjudicate the above-mentioned 'mediation committees' was extended. However, a party to legal proceedings taking place in front the 'mediation committee' was allowed to appeal the order given by the 'mediation committee' to the social security court. Therefore, the 'mediation committee' served as an intermediary between the social security agency and the social security court.

446. It is hard to explain why matters concerning social security allowances in case of sickness were distinguished from the rest of social security cases. Historical reasons and the concept of self-management on which social security allowances in case of illness were based could serve as at least a partial explanation of the extended legal proceeding concerning legal control over decisions made by the social security agency as far as sickness allowances are concerned. With the exception of adjudication of sickness allowances, the organization of adjudication of social security cases was based on a tiered structure. It contained at a first and the second level social security courts.

447. Social security courts were organized, financed and run totally by the state. Thus, it was considered a 100% public organization. Social security courts fell within administrative control of the minister of justice. As far as professional qualifications were concerned, judges appointed to serve on social security courts had to meet the same legal requirements established by the law that other judges serving on civil, criminal, administrative and labour courts had to fulfil. On the one hand, a social security judge must be a professional of the same standard as other judges serving justice in civil, criminal, administrative and labour matters.

448. On the other hand, the same standard of professionalism did not allow the distinguishing of social security judges as a special category of professional. The matter looked even worse from this perspective if one took into consideration that next to the professional judge laymen representing employees and employers adjudicated social security cases. Only in some social security cases concerning legal issues – such as the right to sickness, death allowances, and family allowances and suspension of payment of those benefits because the right to other social security benefits was earned by the beneficiary – was the power to adjudicate vested into a professional judge only. In other matters, laymen appointed by both ministers – the minister of justice and the minister of labour and social assistance out of the candidates presented by trade unions and employers associations – serve as representatives of two most important pressure groups posing as experts in legal, medical and social matters important in the process of adjudication of social security cases.

449. Totally composed of professional judges was an appellate court called the Social Security Tribunal. The Tribunal served in a legal capacity of the higher court. It reviewed cases brought by 'losing' parties on both legal and factual grounds. It also answered legal questions posed by lower social security courts. Thus the Social Security Tribunal adjudicated on individual social security cases and issued guidelines to be used by lower social security courts. The Social Security Tribunal worked in panels containing either three or – in the most important matters – seven professional judges.

450. One of the most characteristic features of the professionalism in adjudication of social security cases before the Social Security Tribunal was the participation during legal proceedings of a legal representative of the public interest, a sort of public prosecutor. The role of this representative was to take care of the interest of the general public and to prevent the judiciary from any unjustified deviation from the already established line of reasoning while adjudicating similar social security cases.

451. The most characteristic feature of the social security court as a special judicial organ were the legal regulations according to which cases were tried. To show the difference between social security courts and other civil courts, the Act of 28 July 1939 stated that social security courts should not use the Code of Civil Procedure. Taking into account that the social security court dealt with a special type of administrative decision issued in social security matters, one may have expected that the procedure used by the social security court had to mix legal institutions regulated both in the codes of civil and administrative procedure.

452. However after careful examination of legal regulations designed for the usage of the social security court, one must come to the conclusion that a sort of relaxed civil type of procedure was invented for the purpose of conducting social security cases.

453. One of the most important institutions invented for the sole purpose of proceeding in social security cases was the opportunity to bring legal action into a social security court in order to challenge the lack of legal action of the social security agency. This special suit was invented in order to force the State Social Security Agency to react either way (in favour, or in disfavour) in the case when a petition to pay money out of the social security fund was presented. Anyone asking for action by the social security agency was allowed to bring a complaint into the social security court after six months of passiveness on the part of the social security agency.

454. Apart from that invention, the social security proceedings were characterized as far less formal than civil proceedings conducted before the common court. The principle of informality allowed the bringing of an oral claim to any type of court of law, not necessarily just the social security court. Then it was a legal obligation of an improper court to which a claim was presented to register the claim and to transfer it to the proper social security court.

455. Legal proceedings in social security courts were free of charge. However, an attorney's fee was paid by the party that engaged a lawyer. The cost of legal representation, though, was not reimbursed to the winning party by the losing one. That was one of the major reasons why beneficiaries suing against an administrative decision of the State Social Security Agency represented themselves, or were represented by members of their families, trade unions, or various organizations articulating the interests of insured people. From the point of view of professionalism, the lack of legal representation on the part of beneficiaries challenging their benefactor was a major shortcoming of the legal system introduced before the Second World War and was never fully implemented.

456. The idea of judicial protection in social security cases would have been more successful if either the social security agency as a loser, or the state as a protector of losing beneficiaries, would have been bound by legal regulations to reimburse the cost of qualified legal representation.

457. Procedure in the social security court was far less formal than the procedure in any common court. Upon obtaining the agreement of all parties, the social security court, acting as the first-tier adjudication organ, was allowed to try any case in private in judges chambers. The same principle applied to the Social Security Tribunal. If the parties agreed or the matter brought by either party into tribunal consideration was strictly technical, the Social Security Tribunal was allowed to make its decision without a public trial.

458. Taking into account that the average beneficiary was not represented by a lawyer acquainted with social security matters, an exception from the principle of public trial in which, at least in the first instance, representatives of pressure groups took an active part in adjudicating social security cases, a trial taken in the privacy of judge's chambers could contribute to the idea of professionalism in the process of solving legal matters involved in each particular case. This statement is made under the assumption that laymen taking part in a public trial represent different pressure groups. Naturally, stronger voices in these matters are heard from groups that contributed to the social security fund in social security dues. This means that the court structure, based on the principles of professional quality (one professional judge) and social control (two representatives of different categories of the population: contributors and beneficiaries) did not serve the idea of social control. Instead, in average cases, such an organizational structure served the best interest of contributors to the social security fund (employers).

459. Even employers played an important role in adjudicating social security cases. The judicial system of adjudication of individual disputes in labour matters before Second World War was separate from the system of adjudication of social security cases. Labour courts were assimilated within the common system of justice. Only after Second World War in the socialist Poland were those two formerly different types of courts unified. Before a description of the homogenous model of judicial protection in social security, it is necessary to present the state of chaos in judicial matters after Second World War and the beginning of the new political era.

Chapter 4. The Chaotic National Model of Judicial Protection in Social Security Cases During the First Years of Socialist Poland

460. The Second World War and, more importantly, political changes after Second World War, brought disordered conditions to the legal system of adjudication of social security cases. For almost a year after the Victory in Europe was achieved, no one cared to set up legal grounds for the organization of the judicial system in social security matters. By the Decree of 1 March 1946 (*Journal of Laws*, No. 12, item 76), the Act of 28 July 1939 introduced before the Second World War was amended and therefore the system of adjudication of social security cases invented in the capitalist Poland was brought into being for the time being in a different country – the socialist Poland. As one may expect, the system was a dysfunctional and did not work primarily due to the deep distrust of any institution developed in the pre-Second World War capitalist Poland that was scheduled to be implemented in the post-Second World War socialist Poland. One way to express this distrust was a decision made by the minister of labour and social assistance to issue the Ordinance of 19 March 1947 (*Journal of Laws*, No. 34, item 161), in which all matters concerning the organization of 'mediation committees' and the procedure applied in cases adjudicated by those committees. As already stated, the Second World War 'mediation committees' were made a proper forum for screening decisions taken by the social security agency concerning sickness and maternity allowances.

461. The very fact that 'mediation committees' were created, not by the act of the minister of justice but by ordinance of the minister of labour and social assistance, reduced their chance to pose for special organs serving justice in some cases concerning short-term benefits paid out of the social security fund.

462. Representatives of employees and employers sat on 'mediation committees'. They acted under the guidance of chairman, not necessarily a lawyer. Judges were never employed by the 'mediation committees' as chairmen.

463. A 'mediation committee' was not bound by any formal procedure. The Code of Civil Procedure was not even mentioned because it was far too formal. The 'mediation committee' made informality the main principle during proceedings. Only oral arguments were presented. Nothing was required to be presented in a written form. Advocates were allowed to represent either party. As far as legal representation is concerned, that statement was purely theoretical. The majority of beneficiaries claiming sickness and maternity allowances were not acting through qualified representatives. At best, they were represented by trade union officials. The other party – the State Social Security Agency – was always represented by legal counsellors serving only one client. Naturally, the State Social Security Agency was far better represented by professional lawyers. Very often, a lawyer acting for one party was the only person acquainted with the legal matters at stake that were under consideration by amateurish 'mediation committee'.

464. Such unbalanced legal representation and discrepancy of legal knowledge between one party and the rest of the actors taking part in 'mediation' proceedings, the 'mediation committee' included, served the economic interest of the state, which ran both administrative and financial affairs of social security.

465. The state government quickly learned that adopting such a system of adjudication of social security cases did not serve its political and ideological purposes. After all, on the surface, the state government claimed to act as the constitutional representative of the Polish working class. Records of the 'mediation committees' rulings proved the opposite. An average 'mediation committee' tried to make certain that excessive spending was not made from the social security fund, which was a part of the central state budget. Funds deposited in the bank account of the social security fund were considered the state's property and enjoyed special legal protection.

466. At the beginning of the 1950s, official doctrine preached the disappearance of the state in the communist system. Trying to be in keeping with this official ideological doctrine, the minister of labour and social assistance dissolved 'mediation committees'. Instead of 'mediation committees', which were treated as administrative organs run by the central state government, 'appeal social security commissions' were created. Members serving on panels of those commissions were appointed by trade unions. The state did not intrude into procedure. Commissions 'adjudicated' social security cases according to trade unions' guidelines.

467. In 1955, the State Social Security Agency was abolished. Trade unions were put in charge of the administration of short-term social security benefits. By abolishing the state prerogatives in administration and adjudication of short-term social security benefits and transferring those two functions into the scope of power of trade unions the state created a powerful new institution in social security matters, the Central Council of Trade Unions. In the socialist system, total control shifted from one bureaucratic institution (the State Social Security Agency) to the another (the Central Council of Trade Unions). Both institutions were under the heavy influence and political control of the communist party. The shift in power did not contribute to the principle of professionalism in adjudication of social security cases. Decisions concerning short-term social security benefits were moved only from the scope of power of one interest group to another.

468. The state kept its function as far as long-term social security benefits were concerned. Old-age pensions and invalidity benefits were determined by the general organs of the state administration. Administrative decisions in those matters were under the judicial scrutiny of social security courts.

469. Cases concerning industrial injuries were adjudicated by common civil courts. In 1960, the State Social Security Agency was re-created. Claims concerning decisions taken by the social security agency were adjudicated by the Council of Overseers of the very same agency. Again, the central state government took control over all matters concerning social security benefits. To disguise this move towards state control over administration, and at the same time, adjudication of social security cases, a formula for the appointment of the Council of Overseers was created. According to this formula, three-fifths of the members of the Council of Oversees were appointed by trade unions. Two-fifths were nominated by the local administrative offices.

470. Again, the principle of informality and lack of professional qualifications on the part of members of the council favoured the legal representative of the State Social Security Agency. In the adjudication of social security cases, the socialist state

– which at the time ratified conventions of the International Labour Organization listed in Chapter 1 of this article – broke not only the principle of professionalism, but also broke the principle of equality of parties and contradicted the cardinal principle of judicial process: *nemo iudex in causa sua.*

471. To disguise great mistakes made by the state, the Act of February 1962 (*Journal of Laws*, No. 11, item 54) made the Supreme Court the highest judicial organ in the country responsible for judicial control of all organs adjudicating social security cases. The Supreme Court was made responsible for screening court orders in civil, criminal, labour and social security matters regardless of the type of organs: judicial (common type of courts) and special type of courts, quasi-judicial and non-judicial, adjudicating those cases.

472. The Act of 23 January 1969 (*Journal of Laws*, No. 11, item 54), which brought into jurisdiction of social security courts was the second sign that made clear the state was eager to clear legal chaos as far as the organization and adjudication of social security cases was concerned. However, the state government did not want to live up to its promises and provide Polish society with an at least two-tiered structure of special social security courts.

473. Although the Constitution of the Polish People's Republic of 22 July 1952 stated in Article 56 that justice in the People's Poland is served by common courts and special courts, in social security matters, the cases were decided at the first level by various commissions: social and medical.

Chapter 5. The Nearly Homogenous Model of Judicial Control of Social Security Cases in the Later Stage of Development of Socialist Poland

474. The Act of 24 October 1974 on District Labour and Social Security Courts (*Journal of Laws*, No. 39, item 231) created for the first time a semi-homogenous model of judicial control in social security cases. The term 'semi-homogeneous' reflects the linkage between social security courts and labour courts as well as with common civil courts.

475. District labour and social security courts dealt exclusively with labour and social security cases. These courts were not formally treated as separate divisions of the district court. The latter was composed of civil and criminal divisions at that time; however, the president of the district court for labour and social security matters enjoyed a status equal to the deputy president of the district court.

476. The most important feature which, on the one hand, made the district court for labour and social security matters close to the common court system, was the application of the Code of Civil Procedure in all cases tried by both the civil division of the common court and the labour and social security court. However, on the other hand, the Code of Civil Procedure provided for the application of special legal provisions in matters concerning labour and social security cases only. In other matters not regulated by those special provisions included in part three of the Code of Civil Procedure entitled 'proceedings while conducting labour and social security cases', general provisions of the above-mentioned piece of legislation were applied respectively.

477. That made the district court for labour and social security matters a rather peculiar judicial organ. The district court for labour and social security matters was called 'the one which was shaped originally as a special type of court but nevertheless is closely connected with the common civil court structure'.

478. The average district labour and social security court was divided into two separate sections (divisions). One division dealt with labour matters. This division was called the 'labour court'. The other division adjudicated social security cases. Interestingly, the latter division was never called the 'social security court'. It always came under the label of 'the labour court'. The division of the district court for social security matters served as an appellate court for decisions taken by the State Social Security Agency and its Council of Overseer. At the time that the Act of 24 October 1974 was enforced, the most distinguishing feature of the legal procedure in social security cases was its mixed character. The State Social Security Agency proceeded according to administrative regulations (the Code of Administrative Procedure) while the division of the district court for social security matters applied in its proceedings rules of civil procedure (the Code of Civil Procedure).

479. Social security cases were tried by semi-special social security courts implementing judicial control in the second instance only. Since the social security court was a one-tiered, structured judicial organ, only those district social security courts functioned exclusively as appellate courts.

480. The principle of informality during proceedings brought before the district social security court was sustained. Informality as far as procedure was concerned made a peculiar judicial organ out of the district social security court. On the one hand, this court was placed among judicial organs as an appellate court. On the other hand, the district social security court enjoyed the privileges of the first instance court, adjudicating all legal matters together with conducting trials and gathering new evidence, or reviewing evidence collected by the council of overseers of the State Social Security Agency. Anyone who was entitled to bring legal action before the district social security court was allowed to extend his/her critique of the decision made by the State Social Security Agency as he/she wished. The district social security court was not bound by any facts found by the council of overseer. The district social security court was allowed to collect evidence on its own. As a matter of fact, many cases were won in front of the district social security court because the court acted on the professional opinion of either its own medical examiner or independent physician. The district social security court decided social security cases on their merit. This meant that the court usually did not send a social security case back to the State Social Security Agency to correct its mistakes, either legal or medical.

481. Only in exceptional situations, such as cases in which no evidence whatsoever was gathered by the council of overseers that adjudicated in the first instance decisions taken by the State Social Security Agency, was the district social security court entitled to send the case back to the council of overseers with the instruction to collect the necessary evidence.

482. At the later stage of the socialist system, the semi-homogenous model of judicial protection in social security cases was developed. Social security cases were still decided in the first instance by the social type organs established by the State Social Security Agency. In the second instance, though, all cases were screened by the district social security courts. The one-tiered structure of the judicial system in social security cases was considered a great disadvantage to the idea of impartial adjudication of social security cases.

483. Social security courts were not totally independent from the common court system. Those courts were closely connected with labour courts. With minor exceptions, the same regulations concerning civil law procedure were applied by the social security courts while they adjudicated social security cases. Taking these points into consideration, one must conclude this chapter with the following statement: At the later stage of the socialist system, the national model of judicial protection in social security cases, at best, can be described as ‘nearly homogenous’.

Chapter 6. The Nearly Homogenous Model of Judicial Protection in Social Security Cases

484. The idea of special social security courts adjudicating social security matters was nearly achieved during the transition period from a socialist to a democratic society. The Act of 13 July 1990 on the Appellate Courts (*Journal of Laws*, No. 53, item 306) introduced a labour and social security division in each ten appellate courts around the country. The social security division of the appellate court adjudicates social security cases acting as the second instance court.

485. Thus, the two-tiered court structure in social security matters re-emerged almost thirty years after the Social Security Tribunal was dismantled.

In the first instance, social security matters are adjudicated by the social security divisions of common regional and district courts. Article 477[8] of Code of Civil Procedure established as a rule the principle of adjudication of social security cases by the district courts (paragraph 1). Regional courts are competent to adjudicate social security cases in matters concerning sickness and maternity benefits and family allowances as well as one-off compensations caused by industrial accidents and occupational diseases (paragraph 2). The law is ambiguous about the official terminology used to describe courts adjudicating social security matters. The ordinance issued by the Minister of Justice on 17 June 1985 concerning the process of selection of judges and laymen sitting on courts established to adjudicate social security cases (*Journal of Laws*, No. 28, item 124) uses the official term 'social security court' (paragraph 1, section 1). In the very same paragraph, paragraph 1, section 2, the ordinance clarifies what the minister of justice meant by the term 'social security court'. It is stated that this term stands for the social security division of the common district court. Thus, the expectation that special social security courts were created by the ministerial ordinance according to provisions of the conventions of the ILO vanished even before anyone started to examine this possibility.

486. The legal requirements for candidates, judges, and laymen to serve on social security divisions of district courts are stated by the minister of justice. Judges and laymen who must serve in those divisions are nominated by the president of the district court out of candidates selected by the administrative council of the district court. The president and the administrative council of the district court must select candidates who are acquainted with social security regulations, goals of different social security schemes, and needs of insured people covered by the national social security scheme. In addition to these requirements, the candidates must possess some experience in the adjudication of social security cases.

487. In theory, judges assigned to adjudicate social security cases are supposed to be quite experienced with legal, medical, social and economic matters involved in disputes concerning questions regulated by social security law. In practice, however, appointees are picked at random. After all, an appointment to the social security division is considered a promotion to the district court, which is the higher court. It is both prestigious and a better reward in remuneration to any judge who has done his/her term in lower court to get himself/herself nominated to the district court. Since competition to be appointed to either the civil or criminal division of the district court is much tougher, a natural selection process brings those judges who were not appointed to more professionally attractive divisions such as the civil and criminal divisions of the district court to other divisions; the social security division is one of them.

488. There is one promising feature, though. Judges appointed to the social security division of the district court must serve for at least a four-year period. Even more important is the legal provision that adjudication of social security cases cannot be assigned to judges who were not selected to serve for a specified term of four years.

489. That is a kind of important guarantee that those judges who were selected on criteria other than merit will get sufficient on-the-job training while adjudicating social security cases. This statement applied to almost all judges who were selected to serve for the first four-year term, since almost none of them who came from lower courts have had any experience with social security matters, because lower courts did not – and as a matter of fact still do not – adjudicate social security cases. Fortunately, some of the judges selected for the first term to serve on social security divisions of the district courts were involved in the process of litigating labour and social security cases under the previous judicial system created by the Act of 24 October 1974.

490. What makes the previous model of judicial protection in social security cases nearly homogenous is the close association of so-called social security courts with the common court structure both at the district and appellate levels. One major disadvantage of the present judicial system designed to adjudicate social security cases is a requirement that in the second instance, court laymen must be involved in the adjudication of social security cases.

491. In the first instance, court lay judges, as an element of social control over the judiciary executed by a professional judge, have had a long tradition in Polish court systems, both common and special. However, in the second instance, only a panel of professional judges was allowed to control the court's order issued in the first instance. The Act of 13 July 1990 on Appellate Courts has changed this practice. It also introduced laymen serving on the social security branch of the labour and social security division of the appellate court. It is difficult to present legitimate reasons behind this peculiar regulation. It is even harder to explain the involvement of laymen in the social security branch of the appellate court when one learns that no laymen are involved in the adjudication of labour cases. As already stated, those two branches (social security and labour) are structured within the same division of the appellate court. After all, social security and labour cases are adjudicated by the very same division of the appellate court. It is even possible that professional judges employed in the division of labour and social security might be assigned by the president of the division to serve on various panels adjudicating both labour and social security cases. One may suspect that the only reason why laymen are involved in adjudication of social security cases at the appellate level is because of the state government's reluctance to spend more money on hiring additional professional judges for the sole purpose of adjudication of social security cases. Quite recently, lay judges were dropped from the social security divisions of the appellate courts. Panels of three professional judges adjudicate social security cases in the second instance courts.

492. Both district and appellate divisions for social security (and labour matters in the second instance court) must conduct legal proceedings according to regulations in the Code of Civil Procedure. In labour and social security cases, there are some deviations from the standards established in the general provisions of the Code of Civil Procedure.

493. The Code of Civil Procedure introduced the most extensive legal definition of social security matters falling under adjudication of the 'social security court'. According to Article 476, paragraph 2 of the Code of Civil Procedure, the social security matter covers cases related to claims that come out of: social security insurance and family insurance, an old-age pensions and invalidity benefits, and other social benefits and allowances managed by the State Social Security Agency. Any cases falling within the scope of power of the State Social Security Agency, as well as claims concerning injuries caused during a term of military training, service performed during a term of duty in the police force, or as a prison guard, are also considered by the Code of Civil Procedure as 'social security matters'. Social security matters also involve any type of case in which the State Social Security Agency did not act. Any disputes based on legal relationship between the private insurance associations and its members are also considered social security matters.

494. The legal definition of a 'social security matter' relies therefore on two criteria; one positive and one negative. According to the positive criterion, some cases are listed as 'social security matters'. The list is an exclusive one. According to the negative criterion, all cases presented under consideration of the State Social Security Agency are considered as the 'social security matters', regardless of the type of case, only if the agency does not react within the statutory time limitation of two months.

495. Important changes were introduced since 1985 in procedural regulations concerning litigation of social security cases. Since 1 July 1996, parties have been vested with the right to demand further adjudication of social security cases by the Supreme Court if their legal value exceeds PLN 10,000. With an exception of one-off social security benefits, benefits paid in cases of illness and maternity. All other cases concerning social security matters are adjudicated by the Supreme Court.

As far as social security dues are concerned, a limit for adjudication has been set up for cases concerning the financial basis for the calculation of social security dues (Article 393, item 5 of the Code of Civil Procedure). Legal proceedings are much more relaxed than in civil type cases implemented by the social security division of the district court and engage a statutory time limit extended to one month for bringing legal action in any social matter decided by the State Social Security Agency. Taking into consideration that any decision undertaken by the State Social Security Agency is not delivered by registered mail, one must come to the conclusion that the period of time within which a beneficiary may challenge any decision of the State Social Security Agency is treated rather flexibly by the legislator.

496. The only legal requirement stated by the Code of Civil Procedure concerning a legal claim in social security matters is that a claimant must identify the particular social security decision he/she is challenging. The rest is up to the social security division of the district court. The court is empowered to issue a judgment that discharges a claim, send back a challenged decision to the State Social Security Agency for further consideration, or correct a decision made by the agency.

497. In the last case, the 'social security court' decides, instead of the State Social Security Agency, how the particular matter under consideration should be solved.

The court order depends to great extent on opinions presented by medical examiners. Since 1 January 2005, the amendment to the Code of Civil Procedure recognized that important element of the legal procedure in the social security matters. The new provisions Article 477^9, paragraphs 2^1 and 3^1 enforced since 1 January 2005 ban the legal proceedings in the social security courts if any opportunity still exists for the insured individual to challenge an opinion presented by the medical expert. Instead of prolonging lengthy legal battle between medical experts chosen by the social security agency and the social security court, the newly amended Code of Civil Procedure left decisions concerning the state of health of insured persons in hands of medical experts called by the State Social Security Agency. An insured individual claiming any social security benefit out of any social security fund must challenge a medical opinion in matters concerning his/her health state in front of the medical committee established by the State Social Security Agency. One must present strong doubts against that changes brought by the latest regulation into the system of adjudication of social security cases. The latest reform of the Code of Civil Procedure limits the scope of power of social security courts and leaves to doctors appointed by the State Social Security Agency all decisions concerning the state of health of insured claimants. In social security cases, the state of health is the most vital factor during the decision-making process concerning social security benefits.

498. Diachronic analysis of the various national models of judicial protection in social security cases brings us to the conclusion that in Poland, the standard set up by the ILO was never achieved as far as the special type of judicial control over administrative decisions concerning social security cases was concerned.

499. Under various political regimes, different models of judicial protection in social security cases have been applied. Those models ranged from heterogeneous to chaotic to nearly homogenous protection in social security areas.

Selected Bibliography

§1. Sources of Social Security Law

Ustawa o zaopatrzeniu emerytalnym pracowników i ich rodzin (The Act of Employee's and Their Dependant Social Security Scheme) of 14 December 1982, Dziennik Ustaw (*Journal of Laws*, No. 40, item 267) as amended by the law: ustawa o zmianie niektórych przepisów o zaopatrzeniu emerytalnym (The Act Related to the Changes Brought up in the Social Security System) of 24 May 1990, Dziennik Ustaw (*Journal of Laws*, No. 36, item 206).

Ustawa o ubezpieczeniu społecznym osób prowadzących działalność gospodarczą oraz ich rodzin (The Act of the Self-Employed and Their Dependents Social Security Scheme) of 18 December 1976, Dziennik Ustaw z 1989 r. (*Journal of Laws of 1989*, No. 46, item 250).

Ustawa o organizacji i finansowaniu ubezpieczeń społecznych (The Act on Organization and Financing Social Security Schemes) of 25 November 1986, Dziennik Ustaw z 1989 r. (*Journal of Laws of 1989*, No. 25, item 137; *Journal of Laws of 2017*, item 870).

Ustawa o ubezpieczeniu społecznym rolników (The Act on Social Security of Individual Farmers) of 20 December 1990, Dziennik Ustaw z 2016 r. (*Journal of Laws of 2016*, item 277).

Ustawa o zatrudnieniu i przeciwdziałaniu bezrobociu (The Employment and Unemployment Act) of 14 December 1994. Dziennik Ustaw z 1996 (*Journal of Laws of 1996*, No. 47, item 211 as amended).

Ustawa o świadczeniach z tytułu wypadków przy pracy i chorób zawodowych (The Act on Industrial Injury and Occupational Diseases) of 12 June 1975 Dziennik Ustaw z 1983 r. (*Journal of Laws of 1983*, No. 30, item 144).

Kodeks postępowania cywilnego (Code of Civil Procedure) of 17 November 1964, Dziennik Ustaw (*Journal of Laws*, No. 43, item 2; *Journal of Laws of 2016,* items: 1822, 1823, 2860, 1948).

Rozporządzenie Rady Ministrów w sprawie wysokości i podstawy wymiaru składek na ubezpieczenie społeczne, zgłaszania do ubezpieczenia społecznego oraz rozliczania składek i świadczeń z ubezpieczenia społecznego (Decree of Council of Ministers on the Amount and Basis of Social Security Dues) of 29 January 1990, Dziennik Ustaw (*Journal of Laws*, No. 7, item 41) amended by the Decree of 25 February 1997 (*Journal of Laws*, No. 20, item 107).

Ustawa o zasiłkach rodzinnych i pielęgnacyjnych (The Act on Child Allowances) of 1 December 1994, Dziennik Ustaw (*Journal of Laws*, No. 4, item 17). Ustawa o wykorzystaniu wpływów z prywatyzacji części mienia Skarbu Państwa na cele związane z reformą ubezpieczeń społecznych (The Act on Using the Funds from Privatization of the State Funds for the Purpose to Modify the National Social Security System) of 25 June 1997 Dziennik Ustaw z 1997 r. (*Journal of Laws of 1997*, No. 106, item 676 as amended).

Ustawa o funduszach przemysłowych i ich prywatyzacji w związku z reformą ubezpieczeń społecznych (The Act on Industrial Funds and Their Privatization as Related to the Reform of the National Social Security Schemes) of 4 September 1997, Dziennik Ustaw z 1997 r. (*Journal of Laws of 1997*, No. 141, item 945).

Ustawa o organizacji i funkcjonowaniu funduszy emerytalnych (The Act Concerning the Organisation and Functions of the Retirement Funds) of 28 August 1997, Dziennik Ustaw z 1997 r. (*Journal of Laws of 1997*, No. 139, item 934 as amended; *Journal of Laws of 2017*, item 870).

Ustawa o systemie ubezpieczeń społecznych (The Act on the System of Social Security) of 13 October 1998, Dziennik Ustaw z 1998 r. (*Journal of Laws of 1998*, No. 137, item 887 as amended; *Journal of Laws of 2016,* item 963).

Ustawa o świadczeniach pieniężnych z ubezpieczenia społecznego w razie choroby i macierzyństwa (The Act on Allowances from the Social Security Paid in Case of Sickness and Maternity) of 25 June 1999, Dziennik Ustaw z 1999 r. (*Journal of Laws of 2005*, No. 31, item 267 as amended: *Journal of Laws of 2016*, item 372).

Ustawa o ubezpieczeniu społecznym z tytułu wypadków przy pracy i chorób zawodowych (The Act on Coverage by Social Security in Cases of Industrial Injuries and Professional Diseases) of 30 October 2002, Dziennik Ustaw z 2002 r. (*Journal of Laws of 2002*, No. 199, item 1673 as amended; *Journal of Laws of 2015*, item 1242).

Ustawa o świadczeniach rodzinnych (The Act on Family Allowances) of 28 November 2003, Dziennik Ustaw z 2003 (*Journal of Laws of 2003*, No. 228, item 2255 as amended; *Journal of Laws of 2016*, item 1518).

Ustawa o emeryturach i rentach z Funduszu Ubezpieczeń Spodecznych (The Act on Old-Age Pensions and Invalidity Benefits Paid from the Social Security Fund) of 17 December 1998, Dziennik Ustaw z 2004 r. (*Journal of Laws of 2004*, No. 39, item 1353 as amended; *Journal of Laws of 2016*, item 887).

Ustawa o świadczeniach z opieki zdrowotnej finansowanych ze środków publicznych (The Act on Protection of Health Financed from the Public Sources) of 27 August 2004, *Journal of Laws of 2015,* items: 581, 1240, 1269, 1365, 1569, 1692, 1735, 1830, 1844, 1893, 1919, 1991, 1994 and 2016, item 65, 652, 960).

Ustawa o zmianie ustawy o emeryturach i rentach z Funduszu Ubezpieczeń Społecznych oraz o zmianie niektórych innych ustaw (The Act on Amendment of the Act on Old-Age Pensions and Invalidity Benefits Paid from the Social Security Fund) of 16 November 2016, Dziennik Ustaw z 2017 e. (*Journal of Laws of 2017*, item 38).

Selected Bibliography

Ustawa o pracowniczych programach emerytalnych (The Act of Employees Social Security Schemes) of 20 April 2004, Dziennik Ustaw z 2004 r. (*Journal of Laws of 2004*, No. 116, item 1207; *Journal of Laws of 2016*, item1449).

Ustawa o pomocy społecznej (The Act on Social Assistance) of 12 March 2004, Dziennik Ustaw z 2004 (*Journal of Laws of 2004*, No. 64, item 593 as amended; *Journal of Laws of 2016*, item 930).

Ustawa o promocji zatrudnienia i instytucjach rynku pracy (The Act on Promotion of Employment and Institutions of Labour Market) of 20 April 2004, Dziennik Ustaw z 2004 (*Journal of Laws of 2004*, No. 99, item 1001; *Journal of Laws of 2016*, item 645).

Ustawa o indywidualnych kontach emerytalnych (The Act on Private Social Security Schemes) of 20 April 2004, Dziennik Ustaw z 2004 r. (*Journal of Laws of 2004*, No. 116, item 1205; *Journal of Laws of 2016,* item 1776) Rozporządzenie Rady Ministrów w sprawie postępowania w sprawach rozliczania składek, wypłaconych zasiłków z ubezpieczeń chorobowego i wypadkowego, zasiłków rodzinnych, pielęgnacyjnych i wychowawczych oraz kolejności zaliczania wpłat składek na poszczególne fundusze (Decree of Council of Ministers on Proceedings in Matters Concerning Social Security Dues, Social Security Allowances Paid Out of Sickness and Injuries Funds, Family Allowances, Child Allowances) of 1998, Dziennik Ustaw z 1998 r. (*Journal of Laws of 1998*, No. 165, item 1197 as amended).

Ustawa o emeryturach kapitałowych (The Capital Retirement Act), enacted on the 21 November 2008 (*Journal of Laws of 2008*, No. 228, item 1507; *Journal of Laws of 2014*, item 1097).

Ustawa o emeryturach pomostowych (The Bridging Retirement Act), enacted on the 19 December 2008 (*Journal of Laws of 2008*, No. 237*, item 1656; *Journal of Laws of 2017*, item 664).

Ustawa o świadczeniach przedemerytalnych (The Early Pensions Act), enacted on 30 April 2004 (*Journal of Laws of 2013*, item 170).

Ustawa o rencie socjalnej (Social Allowance Act), enacted on 27 June 2003 (*Journal of Laws of 2013*, item 982.

Council of Ministers Regulation Concerning Professional Diseases, passed on the 30 June 2009 (*Journal of Laws of 2009*, No. 105, item 869).

Council of Ministers Regulation Determining the Causes and Circumstances of Industrial Accidents, passed on the 1 July 2009 (*Journal of Laws of 2009*, No. 105, item 870).

The Act on changes of functions of the social security system of 25 March 2011 (*Journal of Laws of 2011*, No. 75, item 398).

The Act on amendments changes to the act of the social security system and other acts of 28 April 2011 (*Journal of Laws of 2011*, No. 138, item 808).

The Act on amendments to changes of the act of old-age pensions and invalidity pensions paid out of the Social Security Fund of 28 July 2011 (*Journal of Laws of 2011*, No. 187, item 1112).

Decree of the President of the Council of Ministers on payments of the cost of overseeing the management activities of old-age pension funds and programmes of 30 May 2011 (*Journal of Laws of 2011*, No. 112, item 655).

Decree of the Council of Ministers on obligation of financial institutions and controlling organs information concerning an individual social security accounts of 28 September 2011 (*Journal of Laws of 2011*, No. 122, item 1327).

Communication of the President of Data Office on the first indication of valorization of social security benefits) of 7 November 2011 (*The Polish Monitor of 2011*, No. 99, item 1006).

Decree of the Council of Ministers on matters and procedure of admittance to the open old-age pension fund of 20 December 2011 (*Journal of Laws of 2011*, No. 284, item 1669).

Decree of the Council of Ministers on the dates and methods of decisions undertaken by the State Social Security Agency and open pension funds concerning an old-age pension paid out of capital funds of 23 December 2011(*Journal of Laws of 2011*, No. 295, item 1745).

Decree of the Council of Ministers on methods and dates in which the State Social Security Agency ought to be informed by the open old-pension fund in matters concerning conclusion of contracts and transfer of funds of 23 December 2011 (*Journal of Laws of 2011*, No. 291, item 1708).

The Act on changing the act of an old-age pensions and invalidity benefits paid out of the State Social security Fund and changes to the other acts of 11 May 2012 (*Journal of Laws of 2012*, item 637).

The Act on changing the other acts in conjunction conjunction with upgrading of the old-age pension age of 23 November 2012 (*Journal of Laws of 2012*, item 1544).

Decree of the Minister of Labour and Social Policy on evidence required to grant an industrial accidents and occupational diseases of 2 April 2012 (*Journal of Laws of 2012*, item 444).

Decree of the Minister of Health on the scope and methods of conveying information concerning an individuals covered by the health insurance, contributors of social security dues and beneficiaries of sickness and industrial accidents benefits, an applicant claiming an old age pensions and benefits as well as an employees on unpaid leaves of 17 December 2012 (*Journal of Laws of 2012*, item 1446).

The Act on changing the Labour Code and other acts of 28 May 2013 (*Journal of Laws of 2013*, item 675).

Information of the Minister of Labour and Social Policy concerning the valorization index of pensions in 2013 of 13 February 2013 (*The Polish Monitor of 2013*, item 78).

Information of the President of the State Social Security Agency concerning minimum levels of pension and some other family benefits of 14 February 2013 (*The Polish Monitor of 2013*, item 95).

Selected Bibliography

Information of the Minister of Labour and Social Policy on the amount of benefits paid in case of an industrial accident an occupational disease of 8 March 2013 (*The Polish Monitor of 2013*, item 164).

Decree of the Council of Ministers concerning valorization index of social security benefits in 2014 of 16 July 2013 (*Journal f Laws of 2013*, item 816).

Ustawa o zmianie niektórych staw w związku z określeniem zasad wypłaty emerytur ze środków zgromadzonych na otwartych funduszach emerytalnych (The Act on Changes of Pacud R., Oczekiwanie prawne na emeryture dożywotnią. II filar (Expectation of Some Previous Acts in Connection with Regulation of Principles of Payment from the Open Pension Funds of 6 December 2013 (*Journal of Laws of 2013*, item 1717).

Ustawa o zmianie ustawy – Kodeks pracy oraz niektórych innych ustaw (The Act on Changes of the Labour Code and Some Other Acts) of 24 July 2015 (*Journal of Laws of 2015*, item 1268).

Ustawa o pomocy państwa w wychowywaniu dzieci (The Act on Assistance of the State in Raising Children) of 11 February 2016 (*Journal of Laws of 2016*, item 195).

Ustawa o zmienie ustawy o emeryturach i rentach z Funduszu Ubezpieczeń Społecznych oraz niektórych innych ustaw (The Act on Changes of the Act on Old Age Pension Benefits and Rehabilitation Benefits as well as Some Other Acts) of 16 November 2016 (*Journal of Laws of 2016,* item 38).

§2. Textbooks

Antonów, K. & Bernicia, M. *Ustawa o emeryturach i rentach z Funduszu UbezpieczeńSpołecznych* (The Act on Old-Age Pensions and Invalidity Benefits Paid from the Social Security Fund), Kraków 2004, 506.

Antonów, K. Sprawy z zakresu ubezpieczeń społecznych (Social Security Cases), Warszawa 2011, 366.

Bezpieczeństwo dzięki różnorodności. Reforma systemu emerytalno-rentowego wPolsce (Security Throughout Differentiation. Old-Age and Invalidity Insurance Reform in Poland), Warszawa 1997.

Bezpieczeństwo dzięki odpowiedzialności. Zielona księga (Security Throughout Responsibility. Green Book), Warsaw 2016.

Emerytury i renty. Wybór przepisów (Old-Age Pension Benefit and Disability Benefit. Sources of Law), Warszawa 1986, 389.

Jędrasik-Jankowska, I. *Prawo do emerytury i renty z ubezpieczenia społecznego* (Right to Old-Age Pension and Invalidity Benefit), Warszawa 1992, 187.

Jędrasik-Jankowska, I. *Świadczenia pieniężne za czas niezdolności do pracy z powodu choroby* (Sickness Benefit), Warszawa 1996, 173.

Jędrasik-Jankowska, I. *Ubezpieczenie emerytalne. Trzy filer* (Retirement Insurance. Three Pillars), Warszawa 2001, 342.

Jędrasik-Jankowska, I. *Ubezpieczenie Społeczne* t.2 *Ubezpieczenie rentowe, ubezpieczenieemerytalne* (Social Security, vol. 2 Invalidity Insurance, Old-Age Insurance), Warszawa 2003, 259.

Jędrasik-Jankowska, I. *Ubezpieczenie społeczne*, t.I *Cześćogólna* (Social Security, vol. 1 General Part), Warszawa 2003, 217.

Jędrasik-Jankowska, I. *Ubezpieczenie wypadkowe i chorobowe* (Insurance in Case of Injury and Sickness), Warszawa 2002, 271.

Jędrasik-Jankowska, I. *Pojecie i Konstrukcje Prawne ubezpieczenia społecznego* (Notion and Construction of Social Security), Warszawa 2009, 488.

Jończyk, J. *Prawo zabezpieczenia społecznego* (Social Welfare Law), Kraków 2006, 381.

Kluszczyńska, Z., et al. *System ubezpieczeńspołecznych. Zagadnienia podstawowe* (Social Security Scheme. Basic Issues), Warszawa 2004, 265.

Kolasiński, K. *Rozpoznawanie spraw z zakresu ubezpieczeńspołecznych* (Adjudication of Social Security Cases), Warszawa 1989, 141.

Liszcz, T. *Ubezpieczenie społeczne i zaopatrzenie społeczne w Polsce* (Social Security in Poland), Kraków 1997, 237.

Lach, E. Zasada równego dostępu do świadczeń opieki zdrowotnej (The Principle of Equal Access to Healthcare), Warszawa 2011, 397.

Martysz, C., S. Nitecki & G. Szpor. *Komentarz do ustawy o pomocy społecznej* (Commentary to the Act of Social Assistance), Gdańsk 2001, 508.

Muszalski, W. *Ubezpieczenie społeczne* (Social Security), Warszawa 2004, 250.

Muszalski, W. *Ubezpieczenia społeczne* (Social Security), Warszawa 1987, 267.

Nowicki K.D., Kapitałowy system emerytalny po zmianach – wybrane zgadnienia prawne (The Capital Retirement System After Changes – Certain Legal Issues), Warszawa 2014, 35.

Pacud R., Oczekiwanie prawne na emeryture dożywotnią. II filar (Expectation of a Pension. Second Pillar), Bydgoszcza-Katowice 2006, 335.

Pacud, R. Stosunki prawne ubezpieczenia emerytalnego, Warszawa 2011 (Legal Aspects of an Old Pension's System), p. 450.

Pension Benefit and Disability Benefit, Warszawa 1985, 312.

Problemy prawa ubezpieczeńspołecznych (Problems of Social Security Law), Kraków 1996, 254.

Przegląd funkcjonowania systemu emerytalnego. Bezpieczeństwo dzięki zrównoważeniu (Review of Application of the Old Age Pensions' System. Security Thanks to Equilibrium), Warszawa 2013, 153.

Sierocka, I. Pracownicze programy emerytalne (An Employees' Retirement Programs), Białystok 2010, 331.

Rozwój ubezpieczeńspołecznych w Polsce (Development of Social Security in Poland), Wrocław 1991, 474.

Selected Bibliography

Szubert, W. *Ubezpieczenie społeczne. Zarys systemu* (Social Security. An Outline), Warsaw 1987, 334.

Ślebzak K. Ochrona emerytalnych praw nabytych (Legal Protection of Acquired an Old Pension Benefits), Warszawa 2009, 349

Świątkowski, A. *Uprawnienia inwalidów wojennych, wojskowych, kombatantów, osób represjonowanych, inwalidów z wypadków przy pracy i chorób zawodowych oraz ich rodzin* (Invalidity Benefits), Warszawa 1997, 202.

Świątkowski, A. *Emerytury i renty pracowników kolejowych i ich rodzin* (Social Security System of Railroad Workers), Warszawa 1987, 215.

Świątkowski, A. *Uprawnienia emerytalne i rentowe pracowników i ich rodzin* (Old-Age Pension and Disability Benefit), Warszawa 1997, 202.

Ubezpieczenia społeczne i zdrowotne (Social Security and Health Insurance), Sopot 1999, 1008.

Uścińska G. Zabezpieczenie społeczne osób korzystających z prawa do przemieszczania się w Unii Europejskiej, Warszawa 2013 (Social Security Schemes and Free Movement of Persons Within European Union) , 502.

Zieliński, T. *Ubezpieczenia społeczne pracowników* (Employees' Social Security Schemes), Warszawa 1992, 236.

§3. Legal Periodicals

Polityka Społeczna (Social Policy), published monthly in Warsaw.

Praca i Zabezpieczenie Społeczne (Labour and Social Security), published monthly in Warsaw.

Studia z Zakresu Prawa Pracy i Polityki Społecznej, (Studies in Labour Law and Social Policy), editor Świątkowski Andrzej, published on yearly basis in Cracow since 1994.

Ubezpieczenia społeczne w procesie zmian. 80 lat ZUS (Social Security in the Process of Changing. 80 Years of ZUS), red. K.W. Froeske, E. Przychodaj, Studia i Monografie IPPiSS, Warszawa 2014.

Ubezpieczenia społeczne. Teoria i praktyka (Social Security. Theory and Practice), ZUS, Warszawa 2016.

Yearbook of Polish Labour Law and Social Policy, The Jagiellonian University Yearbook of Labour Law and Social Policy, editor-in-chief Andrzej Świątkowski, published in Cracow in 1989–1999.

Zabezpieczenie społeczne. Teoria, prawo,praktyka (Social Welfare. Theory, Law and Practice), editor-in-chief Gertruda Uścińska, Warszawa.

Z zagadnień zabezpieczenia społecznego (Issues and Problems of Social Security), editor-in-chief Alina Wypych Żywicka, published quarterly in Gdańsk.

Index

The numbers here refer to paragraph numbers.

Index

Index

Made in the USA
Monee, IL
18 October 2026

66041418R10129